"Behind the raging Christian battle over the state of Israel and its right to the land, Chapman sees another vigorous debate, over how to interpret the Bible. Should the New Testament guide our reading of the Old? Does Jesus fulfill Israel's hope for restoration? Are Gentile followers of Jesus full citizens in the commonwealth of Israel? If Chapman is right, if personal hermeneutics shape global politics, the Bible should come with a warning label!"

—Bruce N. Fisk
Network of Evangelicals for the Middle East

"The church is awash with books about Israel and Christian Zionism written by unreliable and ill-informed nonexperts. Colin Chapman is one of the few international scholars who can address these troubling discussions with authority. He begins with a goldmine of answers for the ten central questions surrounding this religious-political movement. From there he studies the Old Testament prophets' view of the restoration of Israel. As with Chapman's other books on Jerusalem and modern Israel, this volume is grounded in well-reasoned biblical argument and matured wisdom anchored in his long career in the Middle East. Anyone who is drawn to issues of Israel and the Bible needs to have this valuable book close in hand."

—Gary M. Burge
Dean of the Faculty, Calvin Theological Seminary

"An invitation to meaningful and constructive dialogue with Christian Zionists, this book helps move the conversation forward by providing abundant opportunities to engage with biblical passages throughout the Hebrew Scriptures and the New Testament related to Zionism and Israel. Regardless of if one agrees, Chapman's expertise and contextual knowledge provoke critical questions and provide invaluable resources that will help the church bridge divides and move toward a more holistic understanding of the Bible and Israel."

—Mae Elise Cannon
Executive director of Churches for Middle East Peace

"While unrest continues throughout the Middle East and particularly in the land of Israel and Palestine, many Christians continue to debate the meaning of the Scriptures. Some propose that throughout the Old Testament, God unconditionally promised the land to the Jewish people. Others ask: What is the effect of the coming of Christ on our understanding of the promises? Enter Colin Chapman. Chapman grapples with the issues from the perspective that the New Testament is the inspired interpreter of the Old."

—Rob Dalrymple
Author of *These Brothers of Mine: A Biblical Theology of Land*

"Colin Chapman is a man who seeks love and justice. His interpretation of Christian Zionism is the opposite of what I would conclude. It is not about politics but about biblical interpretation. However, it is important that all understand the best versions of the two positions, the Christian Zionist one (that the Jewish people will return to the Land of Israel and there will come to faith in Yeshua; therefore we should support this return) and the non-Zionist position that such prophecies are not to be so interpreted. Colin Chapman gives an important and well-presented case for the opposition. Let the dialogue continue."

—Daniel Juster
Professor, author, and first president of the Union of Messianic Jewish Congregations

"This is an amazing resource and contribution to the discussion of Christian Zionism. With impeccable graciousness, the author makes the case for Christian Zionists better than they can do themselves, by asking a long series of questions from their perspective. He then gently but firmly demolishes their case by responding to each and every one of these questions, with gentleness, empathy, but proper logic and doctrine. He does not avoid or evade any issue, but deals with it with compassion, empathy, and truth. I highly recommend this book for any fair-minded Christian."

—Jonathan Kuttab
Palestinian Christian attorney and author of *Beyond the Two States Solution*

CHRISTIAN ZIONISM
and the RESTORATION OF ISRAEL

CHRISTIAN ZIONISM
and the RESTORATION OF ISRAEL

How Should We Interpret the Scriptures?

COLIN CHAPMAN

CASCADE *Books* • Eugene, Oregon

CHRISTIAN ZIONISM AND THE RESTORATION OF ISRAEL
How Should We Interpret the Scriptures?

Cascade Books
An Imprint of Wipf and Stock Publishers
199 W. 8th Ave., Suite 3
Eugene, OR 97401

www.wipfandstock.com

PAPERBACK ISBN: 978-1-7252-9733-3
HARDCOVER ISBN: 978-1-7252-9734-0
EBOOK ISBN: 978-1-7252-9735-7

Cataloging-in-Publication data:

Names: Chapman, Colin, 1938–, author.

Title: Christian Zionism and the restoration of Israel : how should we interpret the Scriptures? / Colin Chapman.

Description: Eugene, OR : Cascade Books, 2021 | Includes bibliographical references and index.

Identifiers: ISBN 978-1-7252-9733-3 (paperback) | ISBN 978-1-7252-9734-0 (hardcover) | ISBN 978-1-7252-9735-7 (ebook)

Subjects: LCSH: Christian Zionism. | Zionism—Controversial literature. | Jews—Restoration. | Land tenure—Biblical teaching. | Palestine—In the Bible. | Bible. O.T. Ezekiel—Criticism, interpretation, etc. | Bible. O.T. Zechariah—Criticism, interpretation, etc..

Classification: DS150.5 C43 2021 (print) | DS150.5 (ebook)

03/26/21

To my Christian Zionist friends
in the hope that we can continue the dialogue

Contents

Permissions | ix
Acknowlegments | xi

Introduction | 1

PART 1: CHRISTIAN ZIONISM—WHAT ARE THE KEY QUESTIONS? | 7

1   Why do Christians have such different views on these subjects? | 9

2   When Paul expresses his confidence that "all Israel will be saved" (Romans 11:26), is he not speaking about the future of ethnic Israel and their salvation? | 22

3   What about Jesus' prediction concerning the future of Jerusalem (Luke 21:24)? | 30

4   What about Jesus' response to the disciples' question about restoring the kingdom to Israel (Acts 1:1–8)? | 37

5   Why not interpret the Old Testament in its own terms—literally—allowing it to interpret itself instead of importing categories from the New Testament? Isn't there a danger of spiritualizing everything in the Old Testament? | 42

6   If the people and the land are so central to the story of the Old Testament, how can the New Testament offer a re-interpretation of these themes? Part 1. The nation | 53

7   If the people and the land are so central to the story of the Old Testament, how can the New Testament offer a re-interpretation of these themes? Part 2. The land | 67

8   Isn't "Israel" different from "the church"? Doesn't this mean that the church was something new, and that even after Christ, "Israel" still has a distinct identity? | 77

9 What about the millennium? Doesn't a literal millennium assume that Jesus will be reigning from Jerusalem? | 89

10 Isn't there something miraculous about the creation of Israel? Isn't the State of Israel "a miracle of God and a fulfilment of biblical prophecy." | 94

PART 2: THE RESTORATION OF ISRAEL IN EZEKIEL—DOES EZEKIEL HAVE ANYTHING TO SAY ABOUT THE MODERN STATE OF ISRAEL? | 103

1 How would Ezekiel's prophecy have been understood during and immediately after his lifetime? | 105

2 How do New Testament writers understand the fulfillment of Ezekiel's prophecy? | 108

3 Can Ezekiel's prophecy be related to contemporary history? | 120

Conclusion to Part 2 | 124

PART 3: THE VISIONS OF ZECHARIAH—TRAILERS OF THE END TIMES OR HINTS OF THE INCARNATION? | 127

1 Zechariah interpreted as a literal description of the end times | 130

2 Zechariah's message in his own context | 136

3 Zechariah as interpreted in the Gospels and Epistles | 148

4 Zechariah's prophecy as understood in Revelation | 171

Conclusion to Part 3 | 182

Epilogue | 184

Bibliography | 197

Author Index | 203

Subject Index | 205

Scripture Index | 209

Permissions

I would like to express my gratitude to Grove Books Ltd. for permission to use my booklet *Prophecy Fulfilled Today? Does Ezekiel Have Anything to Say about the Modern State of Israel?* (Nottingham, UK: Grove, 2018). This was a shortened and revised version of a chapter "Christian Interpretation of Ezekiel's Prophecies" published in Dutch in Steven Paas (ed.), *Het Israëlisme en de plaats van Christus: Christocentrische interpretatie van Bijbelse profetie* (LIT Verlag, 2017) and in English in Steven Paas (ed.), *Israelism and the Place of Christ: Christocentric Interpretation of Biblical Prophecy* (LIT Verlag, 2018).

I also want to thank Lion Hudson, for permission to use chapter 1.18, "Different Interpretations of the Facts," from my *Whose Promised Land? The Continuing Conflict over Israel-Palestine* (Oxford: Lion-Hudson, 2015 edition).

Acknowlegments

My interest in the interpretation of Ezekiel's prophecy goes back to the early 1980s when I met in Israel with several Christians Zionists who explained their understanding of Ezekiel's prophecy about the restoration of Israel. It was the invitation from Steven Paas to contribute a chapter to his book in 2017 which encouraged me to put pen to paper and write on the subject. An abbreviated version of that chapter was turned into the Grove booklet in 2018.

I am grateful to Fred Martin for challenging me to apply the same approach to Zechariah that I had applied to Ezekiel in my 2018 Grove booklet.

I am grateful to Ian Paul, editor of Grove Books, whose blog about the Ezekiel booklet started a long conversation between several participants who were very critical of my argument. It was this that encouraged me to write the ten chapters of Part 1 dealing with all the basic biblical texts about Christian Zionism.

I want to thank Peter Walker, Philip Jenson, and Fred Martin for reviewing different parts of the book and for their many helpful corrections and suggestions.

Finally, I'm grateful to Robin Parry for his challenging questions and meticulous editing, and to the whole team of Wipf & Stock who must be working under such difficult conditions during the pandemic.

Introduction

From the end of the nineteenth century the leaders of the Zionist movement worked for the return of Jews to their land and the creation of a Jewish homeland in Palestine. This Zionist vision led eventually to the establishment of the State of Israel in 1948.

If this is Zionism, what do we mean by "Christian Zionism"? It is generally understood today to mean Christian support for Zionism and the State of Israel that is based on a particular way of interpreting the Old and New Testaments.

The expression "Christian Zionist" was first used by Theodor Herzl in 1896 to describe a Christian priest in Vienna who supported his Zionist vision; and "Christian Zionism" was first used in 1899.[1] The term began to be used more frequently after the Six Day War in 1967 to describe movements among Christians that turned moral support and advocacy for Israel into political support. But the basic ideas that inspired these movements go back at least to the beginning of the seventeenth century, when more and more Christians in Europe—especially in Protestant churches—were reading the Bible for themselves. As they read the promises and prophecies in the Old Testament about the Jewish people and the land, they began to believe that prophecies of the restoration of Israel and a return to the land would one day be fulfilled literally. This kind of belief is generally described as restorationism, and it can be seen as an early kind of Christian Zionism.[2]

There was a very significant development in the 1830s, when an Irish clergyman called John Nelson Darby, building on the foundations of restorationism, developed a theological system called dispensationalism, in which the whole of history is divided into seven distinct ages or "dispensations."

1. Lewis, *A Short History of Christian Zionism*.

2. For a clear explanation of the relationship between restorationism and Christian Zionism, see Hornstra, "Western Restorationism and Christian Zionism." For a comprehensive history of Christian Zionism see Lewis, *A Short History of Christian Zionism*. For a shorter survey by a Messianic Jewish leader, see Juster, *Passion for Israel*.

1

According to this teaching, the present dispensation in which we live will end with the second coming of Christ, which will usher in the millennium, a literal period of one thousand years in which Christ will rule the world from Jerusalem. This belief is known as pre-millennialism because of its insistence that the second coming of Christ will come *before* the millennium. It was popularized—especially in America—by leading preachers and teachers, and has been adopted by many evangelical Christians all over the world.[3] Dispensationalists have inevitably felt very positive about the Zionist movement and believed that what has been happening in Israel-Palestine is part of God's great plan for the end times and points forward to the second coming of Christ. So dispensationalism, like restorationism, has always had a strongly Christian Zionist flavor.

During the nineteenth century, several Christian leaders in Britain and America—for both theological and political reasons—were calling for the return of Jews to Palestine. It is one of the ironies of history, therefore, that there had been different kinds of *Christian* Zionism long before the modern Zionist movement began in the 1880s.[4] It is also significant that these Christian Zionists helped to prepare the way for the wider acceptance of the Zionist vision in the western world. It is estimated that Christian Zionist beliefs of one kind or another are held today by at least 50 million Christians in the USA[5] and around 50 million more throughout the rest of the world.

There are many varieties of Christian Zionism, and Christian Zionists often differ fiercely among themselves. For example, since the early 1990s some dispensationalists have modified their views and describe themselves as "progressive dispensationalists"[6] while a growing number of Christian

---

3. Stephen Sizer describes dispensationalism as "one of the most influential theological systems within the universal church today. Largely unrecognized and subliminal, it has increasingly shaped the presuppositions of fundamentalist, evangelical, Pentecostal and charismatic thinking concerning Israel and Palestine over the past one hundred and fifty years" ("Dispensationalist Approaches to the Land," 142).

4. For a detailed survey of developments during this period, see Sizer, *Christian Zionism*, 26–103.

5. It is notoriously difficult to obtain accurate estimates. The minimum figure might be the 50 million claimed as supporters by John Hagee, the founder and chairman of Christians United for Israel (CUFI).

https://www.jpost.com/israel-news/50-million-friends-of-zion-celebrate-pastor-john-hagee-571822

https://www.jpost.com/opinion/editorials/editorial-christians-for-israel

6. Craig Blaising, Darrell L. Bock, and Robert L. Saucy are regarded as the first three proponents of this position. See Wikipedia, "Progressive Dispensationalism."

Zionists reject the whole dispensational system altogether.[7] We must therefore beware of the fallacy of guilt by association, in which we assume that the extreme beliefs of *some* Christian Zionists are shared by *all*.

Christian Zionists of different kinds, however, all share the same basic conviction that the Old Testament scriptures give the Jewish people a special right—if not a divine right—to their ancestral land, and that the restoration of Jews to the land in recent history is a fulfillment of what the Bible teaches about the restoration of Israel. They don't question that the Old Testament points forward to the coming of Christ. But they believe that his coming doesn't make any substantial difference to the promises and prophecies about the Jewish nation and the land. Inevitably, therefore, they relate the teaching of the prophets about the restoration of Israel to what has happened in recent history through the Zionist movement.

Is this the only way to understand what the prophets wrote? Is it possible to explain the basic issues in these debates and understand why Christians hold such different views on these subjects? How do those who challenge Christian Zionism argue their case, and can they offer alternative ways of interpreting the Bible?

It may be a relief to many readers to know that we won't be using the terms restorationism and dispensationalism more than is absolutely necessary! There won't be any discussion of "the rapture" or "the great tribulation." We will certainly have to address some of the very literal interpretations of some Christian Zionists—for example about the battle of Armageddon and the rebuilding of the temple. Our main focus, however, is on the basic assumption of *all* Christian Zionists—both restorationists and dispensationalists—that the return of Jews to the land since the 1880s must be interpreted in the light of biblical prophecy.

Part 1. Christian Zionism: What are the key questions? seeks to address ten of the crucial questions to which Christians give different answers. Why, for example, are opinions so divided about the history of the conflict between Israel and the Palestinians? What is the root of the theological differences? How are we to interpret the most important texts—like Romans 11:26 ("all Israel shall be saved"), Luke 21:24 ("until the times of the gentiles are fulfilled"), and Acts 1:6–8 ("Is this the time that you are going to restore the kingdom to Israel?")? Is it right to insist that biblical promises

---

7. David Pawson, for example, speaks of "severing any links with dispensational Zionism" (*Defending Christian Zionism*, 16). Gerald McDermott begins his Introduction to *The New Christian Zionism* with the statement, "Most scholars have assumed that all Christian Zionism is an outgrowth of premillennial dispensationalist theology" (*The New Christian Zionism*, 11–15) and goes on to explain how all the contributors to his volume distance themselves from some traditional dispensationalism.

and prophecies about the nation of Israel and the land must be interpreted literally? How is biblical Israel related to the church? What about the millennium? Isn't there something miraculous about the creation of Israel? And does the creation of the Jewish state have no theological significance?

The second half of the book seeks to challenge the assumptions of Christian Zionism by studying two important Old Testament texts that speak in some detail about the restoration of Israel. Thus *Part 2. The Restoration of Israel in Ezekiel: Does Ezekiel have anything to say about the modern State of Israel?* is a study of the second half of the book of Ezekiel (chapters 33–48), in which the prophet is addressing his people who are in exile in Babylon and presenting a vision of the restoration of the people of Israel to their land. We begin by asking how Ezekiel's contemporaries would have heard his prophecies and seen their immediate fulfilment. We then ask how the disciples of Jesus understood these prophecies in the light of Jesus's life, death, and resurrection. Only after going through these two stages can we ask whether it's appropriate to see some of Ezekiel's prophecies being fulfilled in contemporary history.

Part 3. The Restoration of Israel in Zechariah: Trailers of the end times or hints of the incarnation? adopts the same approach to the study of Zechariah—a book that is full of visions and very much harder to understand than the book of Ezekiel. Jerome, writing in the early fifth century, described the book as "that most obscure book."[8] Martin Luther was very honest about the difficulties in interpreting it, since, in the German edition of his commentary on the book, he stopped at the end of chapter thirteen, admitting "Here in this chapter [14], I give up; because I am not sure what the Prophet is talking about."[9] We need to ask, therefore, whether these strange visions should be understood literally as descriptions of real events in the end times, or whether their apocalyptic language needs to be decoded to find its real meaning. Instead of being descriptions of an actual battle in Jerusalem at the end of the world, could they rather be hints of what was to come in the incarnation, the coming of Jesus the Messiah?

We begin by looking at examples of Christians who interpret the visions of Zechariah very literally. This is followed by an overview of the whole book, focusing on its main themes and trying to understand how these prophecies would have been understood by their original hearers. We then ask how the writers of the Gospels, Epistles, and the book of Revelation seem to have understood Zechariah's visions, noting how they believe

---

8. Jerome, quoted in Baldwin, *Haggai, Zechariah and Malachi*, 59.
9. Strengholt, "Zechariah 14," 246.

particular prophecies have been fulfilled in the coming of Christ, and asking whether some are still to be fulfilled in the future.

The *Epilogue* seeks to draw conclusions from the discussion about the key texts relating to Christian Zionism and the study of the prophecies of Ezekiel and Zechariah. It then asks whether it really matters how we interpret prophecy, and ends with a brief reflection on the teaching of Jesus about being prepared for the end of the world.

Throughout the book I have tried to respond to objections and criticisms received over many years to my *Whose Promised Land?*, which was first published in 1983 and been through four revisions (the latest in 2015), and I have re-worked several sections of the 2015 edition. I have also tried to engage with more recent books like *Christian Perspectives on the Israeli-Palestinian Conflict*, edited by Wesley H. Brown and Peter Penner (2008); *Has Israel Replaced the Church? A Theological Evaluation*, Michael J. Vlach (2010); *The Land Cries Out: Theology of the Land in the Israeli-Palestinian Context*, edited by Salim J. Munayer and Lisa Loden (2012); *Through My Enemy's Eyes: Envisioning Reconciliation in Israel-Palestine*, edited Salim J. Munayer and Lisa Loden (2013); *Defending Christian Zionism*, David Pawson (2013); and *The New Christian Zionism: Fresh Perspectives on Israel and the Land*, edited by Gerald R. McDermott (2015).

PART 1

Christian Zionism

What are the key questions?

Introduction

We begin by asking why there are such fundamental disagreements between Christian Zionists and those who challenge this approach. The answer is that it's partly because of different understandings of the history of the Israeli-Palestinian conflict, and partly because of different assumptions about the interpretation of the Bible.

If so much depends on the way we interpret the Bible, we need to discuss the key texts that are regularly quoted in these debates—like Paul's conviction that "all Israel will be saved" (Rom 11:25), Jesus' saying about Jerusalem being trampled on by the nations "until the times of the gentiles are fulfilled" (Luke 21:24), and his answer to the question "Lord, is this the time when you will restore the kingdom to Israel?" (Acts 1:6–8). These texts are important because most, if not all, Christian Zionists believe that they demonstrate the theological significance of the recent return of Jews to the land and the establishment of the Jewish state.

We then ask one of the most fundamental questions of all: if we want to understand the Old Testament in its own terms, are we not obliged to interpret it literally? Isn't there a danger in spiritualizing everything in the Old Testament? How, for example, do we understand the concept of the nation, the chosen people, in the Old Testament, and the way it is understood in the New Testament? What does it mean that the land was promised to the descendants of Abraham as "an everlasting possession" (NIV), "a possession for all time" (REB)" (Gen 17:8), and is the land an important theme in the

New Testament? We can't escape the fact that questions about the nation and the land are closely related and fundamental in all these debates.

The next question also relates to the way New Testament writers interpret the Old Testament: what is the relationship between biblical Israel and the church? What difference did the coming of Jesus the Messiah make to the disciples' understanding of Israel? Was the new Christian community something completely new or a continuation of Israel? Is there any justification for some Christian Zionists to make a direct connection between God's promise to Abraham and his descendants ("I will bless those who bless you, and the one who curses you I will curse" Gen 12:3) and the present State of Israel?

We then address the controversial question of the millennium, since it is associated in the minds of many Christian Zionists with the return of Jews to the land and the reign of Jesus in Jerusalem after his second coming.

The final question concerns the way we understand the hand of God in the history of Zionism and the State of Israel. Hasn't there been something miraculous about the creation of the Jewish state, and doesn't this suggest that God was behind the whole process because it was part of his plan for the Jewish people and the world?

1

Why do Christians have such different views on these subjects?

The fundamental reason that Christians have differing views on these matters is that there are serious disagreements over *the history* of the conflict and over *the interpretation of the Bible*. It is often hard to decide which of these is more important and takes precedence over the other. For some Christians, biblical interpretation is more important and must inevitably determine the way they understand history. For others, the history is all-important, and the Bible has to be interpreted to fit their understanding of the history. Ideally, however, there should be no tension between our understanding of the history and our interpretation of the Bible.

1. Different interpretations of the history[1]

It may be simplistic to speak of "the facts of history," since any attempt to describe events is likely to include some kind of interpretation. In the context of the Israel-Palestinian conflict, therefore, we need to recognise where there is general agreement about what has actually happened, and at the same time understand the different interpretations that have been given by both sides. So, for example, there can't be much disagreement that Jews were around five per cent of the total population of Palestine in the 1880s when the Zionist movement began. But there is bound to be disagreement about the aims of the early Zionists and the strategies they adopted in order to achieve their goals. Did they, for example have any intention of

---

1. An expanded version of *Whose Promised Land?* 47–53.

integrating with the Arabs? Is it fair to describe Zionism as a settler-colonial movement? There can't be much disagreement about what happened in the different stages of the Six Day War in June 1967. But there is some disagreement about what led up to the war. Was it simply Nasser's bellicose rhetoric, the closure of the Gulf of Aqaba and his request that UN forces should be withdrawn? Or did Israel engage in provocative acts in order to complete the conquest that was unfinished at the time of the armistice in 1948? And how do we understand what happened after that? What were the intentions and policies of successive Israeli governments? Were they ever serious about withdrawing from East Jerusalem and the West Bank? Has the Palestinian leadership ever been serious about making peace with Israel and accepting its existence?

The two narratives can be laid out side by side—the first being more sympathetic to the Jewish/Israeli side, and the second (in italics) more sympathetic to the Palestinian side. This list is not exhaustive, but illustrates the differences between the two narratives.

a) The earlier history

- The Jews say their ancestors first settled in Palestine some time between the twentieth and eighteenth centuries BCE.

- *The Palestinian Arabs say they have been living in Palestine since at least the seventh century CE, and that they are racially mixed since their ancestors include Canaanites, Romans, Greeks, Crusaders, and even Jews.*

- The Jews say that the kingdom that lasted from the tenth century BCE (under David) to the sixth century BCE was the only independent nation state that had ever existed in the land prior to 1948.

- *The Palestinians say that if we accept claims that are based on possession of the land centuries ago, then Mexico would have a right to parts of the USA, the Spaniards could claim Mexico, and the Arabs could claim Spain. The existence of ancient kingdoms cannot lead to a denial of basic rights of freedom and self-determination today.*

- The Jews say that although many of their ancestors were driven out of Palestine by the Romans in 135 CE, groups of Jews remained in several centres in the land, and have continued to live there right up to the present time. There was a regular flow of pilgrims and immigrants from Jewish communities in Europe.

- *The Palestinian Arabs do not deny this—and they add that for 1,300 years there was hardly any friction between these small Jewish communities and their Arab neighbors within Palestine. Indeed, for decades prior to the creation of the State of Israel in 1948 the Jews of the Holy Land regarded themselves as Palestinian Jews.*

b) The Zionist movement

- The Jews say that since 1882 they have constituted a majority in the city of Jerusalem.

- *The Arabs point out that in the whole of Palestine the number of Jews in 1880 was 24,000, which amounted to approximately 5 percent of the total population. In 1900, they were still less than 10 percent.*

- The Jews argue that when they started returning to Palestine from the 1880s onwards, they came in peacefully and acquired land by legal purchase.

- *The Arabs bitterly regret that land was often sold to Jews out of purely selfish motives. They also point out that much of the land was sold by absentee landlords living outside the land, many of whom were not Arabs, and that much of the land now owned by Jews was not acquired by legal purchase, but by expropriation or by war.*

- The Jews say that in settling in Palestine they had the approval of the Turkish government up to 1918, then the League of Nations, and finally of the British government, which was responsible for Palestine under the Mandate from 1920 to 1948.

- *The Arabs point to historical documents that prove beyond doubt that during the First World War the British government made contradictory promises to the Jews and the Arabs. While assuring the Jews that they approved of the idea of a Jewish homeland in Palestine (the Balfour Declaration), they were at the same time secretly promising to help the Arabs to establish their own independent state or states after the collapse of the Turkish empire (the McMahon-Hussein Correspondence). Moreover, although the Balfour Declaration and the League of Nations' Mandate included safeguards to protect the civil and political rights of the non-Jewish population, all the promises made to the Arabs were subsequently broken.*

- After centuries of anti-Semitism and persecution, which led eventually to the killing of six million Jews under the Nazis in Germany, European Jews *had* to find a refuge—and Palestine was the obvious place to choose, because of what the land had meant to them throughout their history, even in their dispersion.

- *The Arabs insist that at first they welcomed the Jewish immigrants, and lived peacefully alongside them for many years. They only began to be more hostile when they realized that many of the immigrants were seeking more land and greater political power. Hostility inevitably led to violence, because the Arabs saw that the Jews would eventually become a majority and take control of the land. The Arabs point out that they were not in any way responsible for the persecution of the Jews in Europe, and ask why they should have to suffer for the crimes of Europe.*

- "We have a right to the land because of all we have invested in it; we have drained the swamps and made the desert 'blossom like a rose.'"

- *"Since when has an argument like this been accepted in a court of law as a valid claim to ownership? Moreover, before the Zionist immigration, the Palestinians had their own rural economy, and this expanded considerably in the first decades of the twentieth century."*

c) Since 1947

- "Israel took the opportunity provided by the 1947 UN Partition Plan to create the State of Israel. The Palestinians could have created a Palestinian state at the same time, but failed to do so and tried to destroy the Jewish state. They therefore permanently forfeited the right to have a Palestinian state."

- *"There were good and understandable reasons for their refusal at the time: they felt that they were not adequately involved in the process; the plan was imposed from outside; and the division of the land was unfair. But the Partition Plan still provides a basis for the Palestinian claim to a Palestinian state at the present time."*

- "In the fighting before and after the establishment of Israel in May 1948, many Arabs were encouraged by their leaders to leave."

- *"This myth—along with many of the other founding myths of Israel— has been exploded by Israeli Jewish historians who have documented the process of ethnic cleansing, based on the concept of 'transfer,' which was intended to leave as few Arabs as possible within the new state."*

- "There was a process of ethnic cleansing of Jews to encourage or force them to leave several Arab countries like Egypt and Iraq."

- *"Israel actually wanted these Jews to leave and to come to Israel, and there is evidence that in Iraq, for example, Jews were responsible for terrorist attacks that encouraged many Jews to leave. Israeli Jewish and Palestinian historians have documented in detail the process of deliberate ethnic cleansing by which 750,000 Palestinians were forced to leave the areas that became part of the State of Israel."*

- "In May 1948 the new state was attacked by the armies of neighboring Arab countries who were determined to prevent the establishment of the state."

- *"In fact, the Palestinians were victims of the rivalries between Arabs states, who were more interested in preventing the establishment of a Palestinian state than in destroying Israel."*

- "Israel has won all the wars it has fought. Should we feel guilty for winning?"

- *"It is not just a matter of winning but of all the injustices that have been committed in the process. And if there is ever to be peace, the victors have to make significant concession and not impose a settlement on the weaker party."*

- "The Arabs have been responsible for starting all the conflicts since 1948—as in 1956 and 1967."

- *"In several of the conflicts it was Israel that provoked the Palestinians in order to give themselves justification for a pre-emptive strike and securing more land. Many Israelis still hold on to the goal of a Greater Israel."*

d) Since 1967

- "Israel felt compelled to build settlements and roads on the West Bank and Gaza for security reasons and to settle new immigrants from Russia. Only Israel knows what it needs to do to ensure its own security. It is vital that Israel continues to control the Jordan Valley and the border with Jordan."

- *"Israel continues to occupy the West Bank, East Jerusalem, and Gaza (which it has blockaded since 2007) in defiance of international law and UN Resolutions. It has been creating facts on the ground in order to make it impossible for any Palestinian state to be created, or to make it as small and as weak as possible. Palestinians find it hard to understand why Israel seems to be the only country in the world that refuses to carry out UN Resolutions and yet is allowed to get away with it."*

- "The Arabs have shown that they are not interested in the peace process, and that most of them would like to destroy the Jewish state."

- *"When the Arabs have at many different stages put out feelers and wanted to make peace, successive Israeli governments have turned a deaf ear. They wanted to maintain the hostility in the hope of eventually gaining more territory."*

- "Many Israeli Jews believe that force is the only language that the Arabs understand."

- *"The only way for Israel to be secure in the long term is to make peace with the Palestinians and the Arabs."*

- "Palestinian leaders say in public that they recognize the State of Israel. But if ever a Palestinian state is created, they will use it as a base from which to drive the Israelis into the sea."

- *"From the very beginning, Zionist leaders like Herzl, Weizmann, and Ben-Gurion said one thing in public and another thing in private. Many Westerners misunderstand the rhetoric of Arab and Muslim leaders: they do not want to drive Israel into the sea and are not calling for the slaughter of Jews in Israel, but for the dismantling of the Zionist state."*

- "Israel took control of the West Bank, East Jerusalem, and Gaza in 1967, and does not see its control of these areas as an 'occupation.'"

- *"The United Nations and the International Court of Justice in the Hague regard it as an occupation. The Geneva Convention does not allow Israel to build settlements on occupied territory or to transfer its own population to these areas."*

- "Israel felt compelled to start building the Security Wall/Fence in 2002 in order to prevent terrorist attacks within Israel."

- *"If Israel had built the wall on the 1967 borders, the Palestinians would have no reason to protest. But in many places the wall encroaches on Palestinian land, and has therefore been seen as a land grab—as a way of creating facts on the ground and reducing the size of any Palestinian entity that might be established. The Palestinians stopped their suicide attacks within Israel for other reasons—not because of the wall. Many thousands of Palestinians cross into Israel every day for work and could easily be launching terrorist attacks if they wanted to."*

e) Religion, identity, and security

- "The Hebrew scriptures describe the early history of the nation. So Jews all over the world have always thought of biblical Palestine as their ancestral homeland, and at Passover each year have continually expressed the hope that they will meet 'next year in Jerusalem.'"

- *"The Arabs insist that Palestine has a special significance for all of the three monotheistic religions—Judaism, Christianity, and Islam—and that most of the world refuses to understand or to recognize the special place that Palestine has for Muslims and Islam. Jews have no right to use their religion to make exclusive claims to sovereignty."*

- "Palestinians, Arabs, and Muslims have in recent years been using Islam in their conflict with Israel, and the Israeli-Palestinian conflict has turned into the Israeli-Islamic conflict. Extremist Islamic groups—like Hamas, Islamic Jihad, and Hizbullah—and countries like Iran are determined to destroy the State of Israel."

- *"If there is fundamentalist Islam, there is also fundamentalist Judaism. If there are extremist among the Palestinians, there are extremists among the Jews, who adopt a thoroughly fundamentalist approach to their scriptures and religion. Perhaps it is Israeli intransigence, the impotence of the Arabs, and the lack of support from the UN and the rest of the world that have driven many Palestinians, Arabs, and Muslims towards radical Islam as the only source of hope in their despair."*

- "Jews have had a strong sense of identity for centuries; but the idea of a distinct Palestinian identity is a comparatively recent invention."

- *"The Arabs living in Palestine have always been aware that they were different from Arabs in other areas and that Palestine was a distinct geographical area. From the 1870s they began to dream of liberation from Turkish rule. Nationalism in Europe and Jewish nationalism (Zionism) stimulated—but did not create—Palestinian nationalism and their sense of a distinct identity as Palestinians."*

- "Jews live with the memories of the Holocaust, and with so many enemies surrounding Israel, have good reason to fear that there could be another Holocaust. If the Arabs, the Muslim world, and the critics of Israel don't understand the significance of the Holocaust and the need for security that Jews feel, they haven't begun to understand the genuine fear that motivates us."

- *"The root of the problem goes back many decades before the Holocaust. The seeds of the conflict were sown even before World War I, since most of the Zionist settlers had no intention of assimilating in the Palestinian context and were determined to establish some kind of Jewish state in a country where they were still a tiny minority. Jews have shamelessly used the Holocaust as a justification for their expansionist goals."*

f) The situation in 2021

- "Israel sees itself as a Jewish state, if not *the* Jewish state. It is the only country in the world where Jews can feel safe and secure."

- *"Israel wants to be the Jewish state and claims to be a democratic state. But it can never be* both *the Jewish state* and *democratic at the same time, since at least 20% of its citizens are not Jewish. Israeli Arabs are inevitably second-class citizens."*

- "Israel feels threatened by its Arab neighbors and by the Islamic Republic of Iran, whose leaders make no secret of their desire to destroy the State of Israel."

- *"While it is true that some Islamists really do want to destroy the State of Israel, the Arab League in 2002 affirmed its willingness to accept the existence of the State of Israel—but within the 1967 borders. Many Arabs want Israel to be the state of all its citizens, a secular democratic state, in which there is complete equality between Jews and Arabs, rather than a Jewish state."*

- "Israel's basic need is security, and the only way for Israelis to feel secure is to annex as much as possible of the West Bank and the Jordan Valley, so that it has complete control of its borders."

- *"Palestinian leaders have repeatedly said that Israel cannot have* both *land* and *peace. It cannot have peace as long as its illegal occupation continues. The only way Israel can feel secure is to make peace with the Palestinians. Any settlement needs to be negotiated by the two sides face to face on the basis of international law, not imposed by one side on the other. Outside observers and even some Israeli politicians use the word 'apartheid' to describe the situation that Israel has created in the occupied territories. The possibility of a two-state solution disappeared many years ago, and Israel has already in effect created one single state, which is an apartheid state."*

- "As long as Gaza is under the control of Hamas, which has sworn to dismantle the Jewish state and repeatedly launches attacks against Israel, Israel feels obliged to maintain its strict control of the borders and to carry out attacks within the Gaza Strip."

- *"Gaza has been described as the largest open-air prison in the world, and Israel as the occupying power is still legally responsible for the well-being of its inhabitants. More than 50 percent of Gazans are descendants of Palestinians who were expelled from their homes in the areas that became Israel in 1948. It is true that Hamas is motivated by its strongly Islamist ideology. But one of its basic demands is that Israel should be compelled to comply with international law and UN resolutions and allow for the return of refugees."*

- "The UN is totally one-sided in its constant condemnation of Israel, and is never as critical of human rights violations in other countries of the region like Saudi Arabia, Syria, Iraq, or Iran."

- *"The reason the UN passes so many resolutions concerning Israel is that Israel has consistently refused to comply with Security Council resolutions. The UN is powerless to force Israel to comply with these resolutions because the USA regularly vetoes any resolutions critical of Israel."*

- "Much criticism of Israel and its policies in recent years, especially in Europe, has been motivated by a resurgent anti-semitism, both in far left and far right circles. There has always been a kind of Islamic anti-semitism."

- *"Israel and its supporters all over the world have shamelessly used this charge of anti-semitism as a way of deflecting all legitimate criticism of Israel and its policies. If most of the criticism of Israel's policies is no different from criticism that has been expressed by many Jews within and outside Israel, it can hardly be dismissed as being anti-semitic."*

2. Different interpretations of the Bible

The second reason why Christians are so divided in their approach to these issues is that they don't agree about how to interpret the Bible, and in particular how to interpret the Old Testament in the light of the New Testament. Generally speaking, there are three different possible starting points:

a) "The creation of Israel should be seen as the fulfillment of biblical promises and prophecies" (restorationism and dispensationalism)

"Restorationism" is the name given to the approach that first became popular among the Puritans in the seventeenth century and that emphasized the conviction that, while prophecies in the Old Testament about a return or restoration of the Jews to the land were fulfilled in the sixth century BCE, they would one day be fulfilled *again* in a return of Jews to Palestine from all over the world. Views of this kind have remained popular in many Christian churches up to the present time.

"Dispensationalism" is the name given to a system of interpretation that built on the foundations of restorationism and was first developed by John Nelson Darby in Britain in the 1840s. It divides the whole of history into a series of seven distinct periods or "dispensations" in which God relates to humankind in different ways. This scheme sees the return of the Jews to the land since 1880 as a sign that we are approaching the second coming of Christ to the world when he will inaugurate "the millennium," a literal period of a thousand years in which he will rule the world from Jerusalem.

While many restorationists do not accept the whole system of dispensationalism, the two views do share the same starting point, which can be summarized as follows:

> Although Jesus as the Messiah is the fulfillment of all the promises and prophecies of the Old Testament, the *promises and prophecies about the land and about biblical Israel remain the same* even after his coming, and *need to be interpreted literally*.

Because of the promise to Abraham, therefore, the *Jewish people have a special, divine right to the land for all times.* And even if the prophecies about a return to the land were fulfilled in a limited way in the return from the exile in Babylon in 538 BCE, they have been *fulfilled once again in recent history* in the return of Jews to the land since the 1880s, the establishment of the State of Israel in 1948, and the capture of East Jerusalem in 1967. These events are signs pointing to the second coming.

b) "The creation of Israel should not be seen as a fulfillment of biblical prophecies and promises; there are other ways to use the Bible to understand the history" (covenant theology)

This view is generally known as "covenant theology," because of its emphasis on the idea of the one covenant that underlies the Old and New Testaments. It differs from both restorationism and dispensationalism because of the way it seeks to interpret the Old Testament through the eyes of Jesus and the writers of the New Testament. It can be summarized in this way:

The promises given to Abraham and all the prophecies in the Old Testament have to be interpreted *in the light of the coming of the kingdom of God in Jesus.* For Christians, therefore, the Old Testament must be read through the spectacles of the New Testament. Because Old Testament promises and prophecies (*including those about the land and about Israel*) have been fulfilled in the coming of the kingdom in Jesus, the return of Jews to the land and the establishment of the State of Israel have taken place under the sovereignty of God, but have *no special theological significance.* They are not to be seen as signs pointing forward to the second coming. *All believers in Jesus inherit all the promises made to Abraham.* They are "a chosen race, a royal priesthood, a holy nation, God's own people" (1 Pet 2:9; cf. Galatians 3:26–29) and enjoy their spiritual inheritance which is "kept in heaven for you" (1 Pet 1:4; cf. Heb 4; 12:18–24).

This approach sees the coming of Jesus as the fulfillment of Old Testament promises and prophecies, and the church as the continuation of Israel (see further Part 1, chapters 2 and 8). Therefore, the church—the people of God, including both Jews and gentiles—develops naturally out of Israel; it does not replace Israel (the teaching of replacement theology) or supersede Israel (supersessionism). Many Christian Zionists today argue that this approach is simply another form of replacement theology. But since covenant theology places a strong emphasis on continuity and fulfilment, there cannot be any suggestion that it sees the church as replacing or superseding Israel. It is therefore misleading for some to suggest that covenant theology and "fulfillment theology" are not essentially different from replacement theology or supersessionism.[2] (See further Part 1, chapter 8.)

c) "Let's get away from the debate about the fulfillment of biblical promises and prophecy and see the general principles about justice and peace that are taught in the Bible."

Many Christians are not familiar with debates of this kind. They instinctively react against both restorationism and dispensationalism and have little interest in covenant theology because they feel that it frames the debate too closely as a response to restorationism and dispensationalism. They, therefore, prefer to emphasize more general themes in the Bible—like justice, equality, and reconciliation. One of the best advocates of this approach is Naim Ateek, a Palestinian Anglican priest who founded the Sabeel Ecumenical Liberation Theology Center in Jerusalem. In his book *A Palestinian Christian Cry for Reconciliation*, he sets out to develop "an inclusive, universal, and non-violent understanding that can lend itself to the achievement of justice, peace, and reconciliation for all the people of Israel-Palestine." He says: "When I read and study the Old Testament it is with an eye towards those narratives that reflect the inclusive and non-violent message of Jesus."[3]

3. Conclusion

If there are such fundamental differences of opinion about the history of the conflict and the interpretation of the Bible, we can only hope that vigorous and sustained debate about all these issues will at least lead to a real meeting of minds. This debate needs to take place in the context of real relationships, where people from both sides—or rather all sides—can meet each other, listen to each other's unique histories and concerns, and develop genuine trust and respect. People can, and do, change their minds. For many people outside Israel-Palestine, visiting the country and seeing the situation on the ground for all the different communities is a really important part of the whole process of thinking through the issues.

2. As Vlach does in *Has the Church Replaced Israel?* 1.
3. Ateek, *A Palestinian Christian Cry for Reconciliation*, 51, 54.

It's very much harder for those who are living in Israel-Palestine to engage in serious dialogue because feelings on both sides are so strong. But this kind of engagement is taking place through organizations like *Musalaha* (the Arabic and Hebrew word for "reconciliation"), which has for thirty years been bringing Palestinian Arabs and Israeli Jews together in order to work towards reconciliation.[4] The book *Through My Enemy's Eyes: Envisioning Reconciliation in Israel-Palestine*, by the Palestinian Salim Munayer and the Israeli Messianic Jew Lisa Loden,[5] is a perfect example of the kind of dialogue that has been taking place between Palestinian Christians and Messianic Jews.

"The hope of life for Israel in the end as Scripture depicts it," writes Darrell Bock in summing up the aspirations of the contributors to *The New Christian Zionism*, "is not only for the land to be a haven of peace for Jews but also for it to be a place of peace and reconciliation that permeates all creation."[6] But if Christians throughout the world really do want to see this kind of "peace and reconciliation" in Israel-Palestine today, there needs to be serious and sustained debate all over the world between Christian Zionists and those who offer a different way of understanding history and using the Bible to interpret this seemingly endless conflict.

4. Musalaha, https://musalaha.org.

5. Munayer and Loden, eds., *Through My Enemy's Eyes*.

6. Bock, "How Should the New Christian Zionism Proceed?" 312.

2

When Paul expresses his confidence that "all Israel will be saved" (Romans 11:26), is he not speaking about the future of ethnic Israel and their salvation?

Towards the end of his discussion of the place of the Jewish people in God's plan for the world in Romans 9–11, Paul expresses his belief about the future of Israel in these words:

> So that you may not claim to be wiser than you are, brothers and sisters, I want you to understand this mystery: a hardening has come upon part of Israel, until the full number of the gentiles has come in. And so all Israel will be saved; as it is written, "Out of Zion will come the Deliverer; he will banish ungodliness from Jacob. And this is my covenant with them when I take away their sins." (Rom 11:25–27)

These verses are often quoted to support the idea that, even after the coming of Jesus, God has never ceased to deal with ethnic Israel in a special way and that they can look forward to some kind of national salvation. Gerald R. McDermott, for example, writes: "We don't know how or when nonmessianic Jewish believers will be joined self-consciously with Israel's Messiah, but we believe that God will bring that about in his perfect way and time."[1] This conversion of Jews to the Messiah is often linked with other ideas about the end of the world: the belief, for example, that the return of Jews to the land and the recovery of Jerusalem have been highly significant events that will eventually lead to the conversion of many (if not all) Jews and the second coming of Christ.

1. McDermott, ed., *The New Christian Zionism*, 333.

1. Two initial observations

First, "Israel" in this verse probably does mean "the Jewish people." In all the other thirteen instances in chapters 9–11 where he uses "Israel," he clearly means "the Jewish people" (9:4, 6, 27, 31; 10:1, 16, 19, 21; 11:1, 2, 7, 11, 25).

Second, Paul has earlier argued that physical descent from Abraham is no guarantee of a right relationship with God: "For not all Israelites truly belong to Israel, and not all Abraham's children are his true descendants" (Rom 9:6–7). "Circumcision indeed is of value if you obey the law; but if you break the law, your circumcision has become uncircumcision. . . . For a person is a not a Jew who is one outwardly, nor is true circumcision something external and physical. Rather, a person is a Jew who is one inwardly; and real circumcision is a matter of the heart—it is spiritual and not literal. Such a person receives praise not from others but from God" (Rom 2:25, 28–29). It would, therefore, be strange if Paul were to be saying in Rom 11:26 that at some stage in the future every single Jew (or even most Jews) will be saved.

2. Paul's main argument in Romans 9–11

a) God has not rejected the people of Israel

The Jews are *still* heirs to all the promises made to their forefathers. Simply by virtue of being the physical descendants of Abraham, the privileges and blessings of the covenant are still theirs:

> I ask, then, has God rejected his people? By no means! I myself am an Israelite, a descendant of Abraham. . . . God has not rejected his people whom he foreknew.
>
> (Rom 11:1–2).

> They are Israelites, and to them belong the adoption, the glory, the covenants, the giving of the law, the worship, and the promises; to them belong the patriarchs, and from them, according to the flesh, comes the Messiah, who is over all. God blessed forever. Amen.
>
> (Rom 9:4–5)

> . . . as regards election they are beloved, for the sake of their ancestors; for the gifts and the calling of God are irrevocable.
>
> (Rom 11:28–29).

b) There are consequences for unbelief

The full blessings of the covenant are now offered in and through Jesus the Messiah. So although Jews are still the people of the covenant, those who do not accept Jesus do not enjoy all the privileges of the covenant. Paul uses several vivid expressions to describe the consequences of the unbelief of the majority of his fellow Jews: "a hardening has come upon part of Israel" (Rom 11:25, cf. 11:7); " their stumbling . . . their defeat" (Rom 11:12–13); "They were broken off because of their unbelief . . . God did not spare the natural branches" (Rom 11:20–21).

We may well ask how Paul could hold together these two ideas, which at first sight seem to be contradictory—that the Jewish people "are beloved," but that some are like branches that are "broken off because of their unbelief." But if Paul was somehow able to hold both these convictions together in tension, Christians today need to do the same, giving equal weight to both convictions at the same time. We should not therefore put all the emphasis, as some Christian Zionists seem to do, on the special relationship that comes from God's covenant with Abraham ("they are beloved"), and downplay the implications of unbelief ("broken off because of their unbelief").

c) Wrong attitudes towards Jewish people need to be challenged and corrected

Paul must have been aware that many Christians had concluded that since the majority of the Jews had failed to accept Jesus as their Messiah, God had totally rejected them as a people, so that they no longer had any role to play in the plan of God for the world. To challenge this idea, he expresses his confident hope about Jewish people being saved as a corrective to these wrong attitudes. He realizes that from now on the church is likely to be a largely *gentile* church, but believes passionately that, in the words of N. T. Wright, there is to be "total equality of Jew and Gentile within the church."[2] He therefore uses every argument he can find to correct any attitudes of pride and superiority in the minds of gentile Christians towards the Jews:

> Now I am speaking to you gentiles, . . . if some of the branches were broken off, and you, a wild olive shoot, were grafted in their place to share the rich root of the olive tree, *do not boast over the branches*. If you do boast, remember that it is not you that support the root, but the root that supports you. You will say, "Branches were broken off so that I might be grafted in."

2. N. T. Wright, *The Climax of the Covenant*, 243.

That is true. They were broken off because of their unbelief, and you stand only through faith. *So do not become proud,* but stand in awe. . . . *So that you may not claim to be wiser than you are,* brothers and sisters, I want you to understand this mystery . . ." (Rom 11:13, 17–20, 25 italics added).

d) "And so all Israel will be saved"

The fact that Paul, himself a Jew, has believed in Jesus as Messiah is part of the evidence that God has not rejected Israel (Rom 11:1). While he doesn't speculate about the number of Jews who will be saved, he has every reason to believe that Jews will continue to come to believe in Jesus and be "grafted back" into the olive tree: "Now if their stumbling means riches for the world, and if their defeat means riches for the gentiles, how much more will their full inclusion (*to pleroma auton*) mean!" (Rom 11:12). He seems at the very least to be looking forward to a larger proportion of the Jewish people coming to faith.

It's worth reflecting on the meaning of the Greek word *pleroma* that is used here, since it may shed light on what Paul means later by "all Israel." The literal meaning is "fullness," and different English translations attempt to spell out what it means in this context: "their full inclusion" (NRSV); "their fullness" (NIV); "full strength" (REB); "the complete number" (TEV). It is also significant that Paul uses the word *pleroma* in relation both *to the Jews* in 11:12 ("how much more will their full inclusion mean," *to pleroma auton*), and in relation *to the gentiles* in 11:25 ("until the full number of the gentiles has come in," *to pleroma ton ethnon*). The REB deliberately uses the same words in both sentences: "how much more will their coming to *full strength* mean!" (11:12); and "until the Gentiles have been admitted in *full strength*" (11:25). The TEV similarly speaks of "*the complete number* of Jews" (11:12) and "*the complete number* of Gentiles" (11:25). If the *pleroma* of the gentiles cannot mean "every single gentile," the *pleroma* of the Jews can hardly mean "every single Jew."

The mystery that Paul seeks to explain is that "a hardening has come upon part of Israel," which will eventually lead to "the full number of the gentiles" coming in, and this in turn will lead to "all Israel" being saved. This is how Owen Palmer Robertson explains the connection in Paul's mind between these three stages—(i) *part of Israel* being hardened, (ii) *the full number of gentiles* coming in, and (iii) *all Israel* being saved:

But into what do the full number of elect Gentiles come? The answer is unavoidable. Believing Gentiles come *into Israel!* Is that not exactly the point made by Paul earlier in this chapter? Gentiles have become additional branches, joined to the single stock that is none other than Israel. As a consequence, the believing Gentile community has become a "fellow sharer" (*synkoinonos*) in the rich root of the olive three that is Israel (Rom. 11:17). In other words they have become "Israelites."[3]

Paul seems therefore to be speaking here about *what Israel has now become and will be from now on*—namely, Israel renewed and transformed in the Messiah, the people of God, including both Jews and gentiles. He sees the church as the *continuation* of Israel, not as the *replacement* for Israel, something that is different from Israel, or taking the place of Israel (See further Part 1, chapter 8). The church does not *supersede* Israel. "All Israel" is made up of the *pleroma* of the Jews coming together with the *pleroma* of the gentiles.

It also needs to be pointed out that in speaking about all Israel being saved, Paul has nothing whatsoever to say about the land or about a national restoration for the Jewish people. There is therefore no explicit justification for linking Paul's hopes for the salvation of Jews with ideas of a return to the land. (We shall see later—in Part 1, chapter 4—that it is questionable whether the words of Jesus in Acts 1:7–8 support the idea of a future national restoration.)

But what is the significance of the way Paul here uses Old Testament quotations, which speak of the salvation that God promised for his people? If Paul is so insistent elsewhere that Jesus the Messiah *has already come* as deliverer and made a covenant to deal with the sins of his people, why does he quote verses from the prophets which speak about a deliverer who is to come *in the future*? Can he be suggesting that when Jesus comes again, he will bring about a new and special kind of salvation for the Jews? The most convincing answer is to be found in the way Paul links together four different Old Testament texts:

> . . . as it is written, "Out of Zion [Isa 2:3] will come the Deliverer [Isa 59:20–21, using the LXX translation]; he will banish ungodliness from Jacob" [Isa 27:9, using the LXX translation]. "And this is my covenant with them, when I take away their sins" [Jer 31:34]. (Rom 11:26–27)

---

3. Robertson, "The Israel of God in Romans 11," 228.

Many assume that Paul is speaking about some time in the future when God will intervene to bring about the salvation of ethnic Israel.[4] But a more convincing way of understanding these words starts by recognizing that all the three texts from Isaiah come in the context of prophecies about how the renewal of God's covenant *with Israel* will bring blessing *to the nations*. Thus, in Isaiah 2:1–4 we read of gentiles coming to Jerusalem as a result of what will come out of Jerusalem: "In days to come, the mountain of the LORD's house shall be established as the highest of the mountains . . . all the nations shall stream to it. Many peoples shall come and say, 'Come, let us go up to the mountain of the LORD. . . .' For *out of Zion* shall go forth instruction (*torah,* the law, RSV), and the word of the LORD from Jerusalem" (Isa 2:2–3, italics added). Paul no doubt deliberately takes the phrase *"out of Zion"* (*ek sion*) from Isaiah 2:3, avoiding the phrase *"to Zion"* which is found in the second verse from Isaiah which he quotes (Isa 59:20–21). Since he knows the Messiah has already come *out of* Zion, he cannot be thinking that the Messiah has to come *to Zion* as deliverer for a second time.

In reflecting on Isaiah's words about the law going out from Zion in Isaiah 2, Paul thinks of Jesus as the fulfillment or the climax of the law, the *torah*, and sees the spread of the gospel to gentiles as the fulfillment of the words about the law coming out of Zion and reaching the nations. Similarly, in Isaiah 59 we read "those in the west shall fear the name of the LORD, and those in the east, his glory" (Isa 59:19). And in Isaiah 27, the nations will be blessed because "Israel shall blossom and put forth shoots, and fill the whole world with fruit" (Isa 27:6). Assyria and Egypt are given (in Isa 27:12–13) as examples of gentiles receiving blessing by coming to worship the Lord in Jerusalem. The close connection between Israel and the gentile nations, therefore, is clear in all the three verses quoted from Isaiah. The rationale behind Paul's use of these four texts is explained in this way by Christopher R. Bruno:

> Paul cites these texts as fulfilled prophecy—YHWH has returned to Zion, dealt with the sin of his people and renewed the covenant; and he has done so in the person of Jesus Christ. The citation of these passages in Romans 11:26–27 does not look forward to the Parousia of Christ, but rather looks back to the already finished work of Christ. In citing these passages, Paul is intentionally drawing on contexts that refer to the inclusion of Gentiles when the promises to Israel are fulfilled. . . . [T]he Gentiles being grafted into the people of God and Jewish jealousy

---

4. For example, Vlach, *Has the Church Replaced Israel?* 180–81.

that leads to faith in Messiah is the way that "all Israel"—the worldwide people of God—will be saved.[5]

There is one further question that affects the way we interpret "all Israel shall be saved": why does Paul say "*and so (kai houtos)* all Israel shall be saved"? Does it mean "then," "after this," i.e., that Israel will be saved "after the full number of the gentiles has come in"? Or does the word *houtos* have its usual meaning of "in this way," "in this manner" ("this is how all Israel will be saved" TEV)? If he means "in this way," Paul is saying that it is through "part of Israel" experiencing "hardening" and "the full number of the gentiles" coming in and being incorporated into Israel that "all Israel will be saved." N. T. Wright explains how the logic of Paul's argument in Romans 9–11 favours this second interpretation:

> Paul's meaning is not a temporal sequence—first the Gentiles, *then* the Jews. Rather, it is the interpretation of a particular process *as* the salvation of "all Israel." And in this context "all Israel" cannot possibly mean "all Jews." . . . What Paul is saying is this. God's method of saving "all Israel" is to harden ethnic Israel (cp. 9:14ff), i.e., not to judge her at once, so as to create a period of time during which the gentile mission could be undertaken, *during the course of which* it remains God's will that the present "remnant" of believing Jews might be enlarged by the process of "jealousy," and consequent faith. . . . This whole process is God's way of saving his whole people: that is the meaning of *kai houtos pas Israel sothesetai*, all Israel shall be saved.[6]

Paul ends the discussion by expressing his confidence that, through seeing evidence of God's mercy to the gentiles, Jews will continue to turn to God and receive mercy:

> Just as you were once disobedient to God but have now received mercy because of their disobedience, so they have now been disobedient in order that, by the mercy shown to you, they too may now receive mercy. For God has imprisoned all in disobedience so that he may be merciful to all.
> (Rom 11:30–32)

---

5. Bruno, "The Deliverer from Zion," 131–33.

6. N. T. Wright, *The Climax of the Covenant*, 249–50.

3. Conclusion

Paul certainly is thinking about ethnic Israel in Romans 11:26, but is speaking about what Israel has now become through Jesus the Messiah—the people of God including both Jews and gentiles. His message to the largely gentile church in Rome about Christian attitudes towards the Jewish people (in Romans 9–11) can therefore be paraphrased as follows: "Don't assume that since the majority of the Jewish people have until now rejected their Messiah, this will always be the case. The refusal of the Jews to recognize Jesus has meant that the gospel has spread all over the gentile world. So think what kind of a future we can look forward to when the full number of Jewish and gentile believers are brought into the kingdom! Don't forget your own Jewish roots! And don't write off the Jews! The people of God will always include *both* gentiles *and* Jews!"

3

What about Jesus' prediction concerning the future of Jerusalem (Luke 21:24)?

The words of Jesus about Jerusalem being "trampled on by the gentiles, until the times of the gentiles are fulfilled" are usually interpreted by Christian Zionists as a prediction that Jerusalem would be under the control of non-Jews *until* the times of the gentiles were fulfilled; but *after* that time, it would again come under Jewish rule. Since East Jerusalem came under Israeli control in June 1967, it is assumed this event must be the fulfillment of Jesus' prediction. This conviction is linked by many with the belief that Jerusalem will play a significant role in the events leading up to the second coming of Christ, and that the millennium and the new earth described in Revelation will be centered in Jerusalem.

But is this the only way to understand this saying of Jesus? And what about his other sayings about Jerusalem?

1. The context of this saying in Luke's account of Jesus' eschatological discourse

It is important to notice several unique words and phrases in Luke's account (printed here in italics) which are not found in either Mark or Matthew's account of the discourse:

> When you see Jerusalem surrounded by armies, then know that its *desolation* has come near. Then those in Judea must flee to the mountains, and those inside the city must leave it, and those out in the country must not enter it; for these are days of *vengeance*,

as a fulfillment of all that is written. Woe to those who are preg-
nant and to those who are nursing infants in those days! For
there will be *great distress on the earth and wrath against this
people;* they will *fall by the edge of the sword* and be taken away as
captives among all nations; and *Jerusalem will be trampled on by
the gentiles, until the times of the gentiles are fulfilled.* There will
be signs in the sun, moon, and the stars, and on earth distress
among nations confused by the roaring of the sea and the waves.
People will faint from fear and foreboding of what is coming
upon the world, for the powers of the heavens will be shaken.
Then they will see "the Son of Man coming in a cloud" with
power and great glory. Now when these things begin to take
place, stand up and raise your heads, *because your redemption
is drawing near.*
(Luke 21:20–28)

This passage contains several very clear (and presumably deliberate) echoes
of Isaiah's prophecy concerning the fall of Babylon in Isaiah 13.

[Luke 21] . . . its *desolation* has come near [verse 20] . . . days of
vengeance [verse 22] . . . *wrath* against this people. . . . [verse 23]
They will *fall by the edge of the sword."* [24]

[Isaiah 13] " . . . to make the earth a *desolation* [verse 9] . . . I
will *punish* the world . . . [verse 11] . . . *wrath* and fierce *anger*
[verse 9] . . . the *wrath* of the LORD . . . his fierce *anger* [verse
13] . . . whoever is caught will *fall by the sword . . ."* [15]

When Jesus says "These are days of vengeance, as a fulfillment of all
that is written" (Luke 21:22), he is emphasizing what is implied in his use
of the quotation from Isaiah: the fall of Jerusalem is to be seen as an act of
divine judgment on the city and the people. Moreover, these events are to
be seen as the fulfillment of "all that has been written"—presumably all that
has been written about Jerusalem.

"Now when these things begin to take place, stand up and raise your
heads, because your redemption is drawing near" (Luke 21:28). In Luke's
birth narratives, Anna the prophetess speaks about Jesus to all who were
looking forward to "the redemption of Jerusalem" (Luke 2:38). The word
occurs again when the two disciples who are walking with Jesus on the road
to Emmaus express their hopes that he was "the one to redeem Israel" (Luke
24:21). The redemption that Jesus speaks about here, therefore, is not something that will be achieved at the end of the world. "Your redemption" must
be no different from the "redemption of Jerusalem" (Luke 2:38), "the consolation of Israel" (Luke 2:25), and the redemption of Israel (Luke 24:21). In

the words of Gary Burge, "'Redeeming Israel" does not refer to the salvation of souls, but to the restoration of the nation, the cleansing of the land, and a divinely endorsed inheritance of the Holy Land that was deeply woven into the fabric of Israel's religious life."[1]

These expressions contain clear echoes of Isaiah's prophecy about the redemption of Jerusalem: "Awake, awake, put on your strength, O Zion! . . . For thus says the LORD: You were sold for nothing, and you shall be redeemed without money. . . . Break forth together into singing, you ruins of Jerusalem; for the LORD has comforted his people, he has redeemed Jerusalem" (Isa 52:1–9). After the birth of John the Baptist, Zechariah's prophecy expresses the conviction that the process of redemption has been set in motion through the birth of John the Baptist: "Blessed be the Lord God of Israel, for he has looked favorably on his people and redeemed them" (Luke 1:68. See further Part 1, chapter 7). So when Jesus speaks of redemption "drawing near" (Luke 21:28), he is signaling that the redemption of Jerusalem and of Israel will be completed in the near future.

2. ". . . until the times of the gentiles are fulfilled"

The best key to the interpretation of these words is probably to be found in the Old Testament, where several prophets speak of the way God will use foreign nations as instruments of judgment on the people of Israel, and will then in turn judge these foreign nations. Therefore, the "times of the nations (gentiles)" that Jesus is referring to, in the words of John Nolland, are:

> the period for a judgment upon the gentile nations that corresponds to the judgment on Jerusalem: after the *kairos*, "time" of Jerusalem . . . come the *kairoi*, "times" of the nations. . . . The underlying pattern here of judgment upon Jerusalem/Judah/Israel followed by judgment upon the instruments of their judgment may be found in Isaiah 10:12–14; 33; 47; Jeremiah 50–51; Daniel 9:26–27 and compare Ezekiel 38; Habakkuk 1:11—2:3.[2]

The words of Jesus would therefore be consistent with a pattern that we find in many of the prophets, in which "The Day of the Lord is characterized by reversal, as God will turn the tables on the nations and do to them what they have done to Israel."[3] We shall see (in Part 3, chapter 2) that the same idea is found in Zechariah, where God says: "I am extremely angry with the

---

1. Burge, *Jesus and the Land*, 26.
2. Nolland, *Luke 18:35—24:53*, 1002–3.
3. Hill, *Haggai, Zechariah and Malachi*, 267–68.

nations that are at ease; for while I was only a little angry, they made the disaster worse . . . ." As a result, God is going to "strike down the horns of the nations that lifted up their horns against the land of Judah to scatter its people" (Zech 1:15–21).

If this is the background to this saying, Jesus not only sees the coming destruction of Jerusalem as a judgment from God, but also indicates that God's judgment will in due course also fall on the Romans who will trample on the holy city of Jerusalem. He emphasizes that all of this will happen during the lifetime of some of his listeners: "Truly I tell you, this generation will not pass away until all things have taken place" (Luke 21:32, cf. Mark 13:30). The emphasis in Jesus' words, therefore, is on the significance of the coming destruction of Jerusalem rather than on the status of Jerusalem in the more distant future. If there is any hint about the future, it has more to do with *Rome* and the judgment that will eventually fall on the *Romans* than with *Jerusalem* ceasing to be trampled on by the gentiles and once again coming under Jewish rule.

This interpretation is entirely consistent with the way Zechariah's visions about the future of Jerusalem are interpreted in the book of Revelation (see Part 3, chapter 4). It will be pointed out later that John's message of encouragement to Christians who were going to be persecuted by the Roman state, was that Rome and its empire would inevitably come under the judgment of God. In this saying in Luke 21:24, therefore, Jesus seems to be saying, "Jerusalem is going to be trampled on by the Romans; but sooner or later Rome itself will come under God's judgment."

3. Other sayings of Jesus about Jerusalem and its future

Alongside Jesus' saying about Jerusalem being trampled on by the gentiles, it's appropriate to look at two other sayings of Jesus about Jerusalem that are recorded by Luke, and to ask whether they offer any hope for a future restoration under Jewish rule. The first is located by Luke in his account of Jesus' journey towards Jerusalem. After being warned that Herod wants to kill Jesus, he responds that he must continue his ministry of healing as he makes his way to Jerusalem, "because it is impossible for a prophet to be killed outside of Jerusalem" (Luke 13:31–33). He then continues:

> Jerusalem, Jerusalem, the city that kills the prophets and stones those who are sent to it! How often have I desired to gather your children together as a hen gathers her brood under her wings, and you were not willing! See, your house is left to you. And I

tell you, you will not see me until the time comes when you say, "Blessed is the one who comes in the name of the Lord." (Luke 13:34–35; cf. Matt 23:37–38. "Your house is left to you, desolate")

This saying is often interpreted as a prediction that Jerusalem will one day be restored and its people will welcome Jesus joyfully as their king. Although they have rejected prophets in the past and are now rejecting Jesus, when he returns at his second coming, Jewish people in a restored Jerusalem will finally welcome him as God's promised Messiah. Joel Willits, for example, sees in these words a prediction of the restoration of Israel: "Jesus envisages a day when there will be a conversion of heart and mind among the Jerusalemites. Whereas they once opposed and murdered their king, they will in the future rejoice and receive him . . . ."[4]

The main reason for questioning this interpretation is that the main thrust of Jesus' message here is one of judgment, not of restoration. Jesus is speaking not only about the way Jerusalem is rejecting him, but the way it has consistently rejected and killed prophets in the past. He is speaking as if he represents the God who has been rejected by the people of Jerusalem over many generations. It is because of this consistent and repeated rejection that he says "your house is left to you," or, as Matthew says, "your house is left to you, desolate" (Matt 23:38). This is almost certainly a reference to the temple, which is going to be totally destroyed and abandoned by God. Just as Ezekiel had spoken about the Shekinah glory of God leaving the temple when it was captured by the Babylonians and the people taken into exile (Ezek 10:1–19), so now Jesus speaks of the temple being left destroyed and abandoned by God.

The final sentence about the time when people will see Jesus again and say "Blessed is the one who comes in the name of the Lord" is introduced with the words "*And* I tell you . . ." (in Matthew "*For* I tell you . . ." Matt 23:39). These words therefore come as a statement amplifying what Jesus has already said, not as the introduction of a completely new message. There is no "but," which would suggest a contrast or a change of tone, as if Jesus is saying, "The temple is going to be destroyed; *but* in the future everything will be different, because Jerusalem and the temple will be restored." This is why Peter Walker argues that "The solemn context of this saying in Luke . . . suggests that the note of judgement is . . . uppermost here. . . . It is not, therefore, a promise of restoration."[5]

---

4. Willits, "Zionism in the Gospel of Matthew," 130–32.

5. Walker, *Jesus and the Holy City,* 99.

The most convincing interpretation of these words of Jesus about people welcoming him at some time in the future, therefore, is that he is speaking about his second coming, when the people of Jerusalem will recognize who he is; but while some welcome him *joyfully*, it is reasonable to infer that others will do so *reluctantly*. Paul must have understood the different ways in which Jesus will be welcomed when he wrote about the time when "at the name of Jesus every knee should bend . . . and every tongue should confess that Jesus Christ is Lord . . ." (Phil 2:9–11). Unless we adopt a universalist interpretation—that ultimately every human being will acknowledge Jesus as Lord willingly and joyfully—we can only assume that Paul believed that many would have to recognize Jesus unwillingly and reluctantly.

The other important saying about Jerusalem comes at the beginning of the last week of his life as he approaches Jerusalem and looks over the city from the Mount of Olives:

> As he came near and saw the city, he wept over it, saying, "If you, even you, had only recognized on this day the things that make for peace! But now they are hidden from your eyes. Indeed, the days will come upon you when your enemies will set up ramparts around you and surround you, and hem you in on every side. They will crush you to the ground, you and your children within you, and they will not leave within you one stone upon another; because you did not recognize the time of your visitation from God."
>
> (Luke 19:41–44)

Here is another saying that is simply about judgment—without any hint of restoration. The beautiful temple buildings are going to be completely destroyed, and this is going to happen because the people have failed to recognize that the coming of Jesus has been their "visitation from God."

All of these three important sayings of Jesus about Jerusalem recorded in Luke, therefore—the first spoken on his way up to Jerusalem (13:34–35), the second as he wept over Jerusalem (Luke 19:41–44), and the third in the final week when he spoke of the destruction of Jerusalem (Luke 21:5–38)—speak *only* in terms of judgment on Jerusalem. When prophets like Isaiah, Jeremiah, and Ezekiel centuries before had spoken of God's judgment on Jerusalem and its people, they had always gone on to predict restoration. But unlike them, Jesus does not convey any positive message about the restoration of the temple or the city after it has come under God's judgment. There is no suggestion of an exile like the Babylonian exile followed by a return to the land.[6] Instead, in the eschatological discourse, he describes

---

6. As is assumed by Kinzer, "Zionism in Luke-Acts," 153, 158.

cosmic disturbances similar to those associated by Isaiah with the fall of Babylon (verses 25–26), and goes on to say, "Then they will see 'the Son of Man coming in a cloud' with power and great glory . . ." (Luke 21:27).

We shall see in our study of Zechariah (Part 3, chapter 3) that the idea of the coming of the Son of Man is found in a vision of Daniel (Daniel 7:13–14), and that the coming described there is not a coming from heaven to earth, but the coming of the Son of Man into the presence of God to receive "dominion and glory and kingship, that all people, nations, and languages should serve him" (7:14). By associating himself in this context with Daniel's Son of Man, Jesus is making the bold claim that the destruction of temple in Jerusalem will demonstrate that the kingly rule of the Son of Man has finally begun through him.

4. Conclusion

It's hard to see how this saying of Jesus can be interpreted as a prediction that Jerusalem will one day come under Jewish rule. *All* his sayings about Jerusalem speak consistently of judgment—a judgment that is coming because of its refusal to recognize its "visitation from God." It must also be significant that, in the accounts of the eschatological discourse in all three Gospels, Jesus' prediction of the destruction of Jerusalem is not followed immediately by a promise of restoration, but by a declaration about the coming of the Son of Man. Jesus doesn't seem to be interested in Jewish sovereignty over Jerusalem. What he is claiming is that the whole series of events that are about to unfold in Jerusalem—leading up to its destruction—will demonstrate comprehensively that the kingdom of God really has begun to come through him.

4

What about Jesus' response to the disciples' question about restoring the kingdom to Israel (Acts 1:1–8)?

Jesus' reply to the disciples' question about "restoring the kingdom to Israel" is interpreted by most Christian Zionists to mean that Jesus *affirmed* their expectation that Israel would one day regain its sovereignty. McDermott in *The New Christian Zionism* speaks for many when he writes: "Jesus did not challenge their assumption that one day the kingdom would be restored to physical Israel."[1] But is this the only way to interpret the words of Jesus?

1. The context of this exchange

Luke tells us that during the forty days after the resurrection, Jesus "presented himself alive to them [the disciples] by many convincing proofs, appearing to them during forty days and speaking about the kingdom of God" (Acts 1:3). On one of these occasions, he tells them not to leave Jerusalem, since they will very soon be "baptized with the Holy Spirit" (Acts 1:4). This is the context in which the disciples put the question to Jesus: "Lord, is this the time when you will restore the kingdom to Israel?" (Acts 1:6. NRSV. "Lord, is this the time at which you are to restore sovereignty to Israel?" REB).

While Jesus has been speaking about *the kingdom of God* (verse 3), the disciples have been thinking about *the kingdom of Israel* (verse 6), as if the kingdom of Israel is a vital part of the kingdom of God. It's likely that Luke

---

1. McDermott, ed., *The New Christian Zionism*, 53.

wants us to make this connection since he uses the same Greek word for "kingdom," *basileia*, in both sentences. The disciples must have been holding onto their traditional Jewish hopes for the future of the nation of Israel, and therefore looking forward to the establishment of an independent Jewish state, no longer under Roman control. And they must have assumed that since this was a vital part of the establishment of the kingdom of God on earth, the resurrection of Jesus provided a unique opportunity for this next stage in the unfolding of God's plan. And how did Jesus reply?

> [verse 7] It is not for you to know the times or periods that the Father has set by his own authority. [verse 8] But you will receive power when the Holy Spirit comes on you; and you will be my witnesses in Jerusalem, in all Judea and Samaria, and to the ends of the earth.
>
> (Acts 1:7–8)

There are two possible interpretations of this answer, and much depends on the connection of thought between verses 7 and 8. According to the first interpretation, we need to separate verses 7 and 8, since there is no vital connection between them. Jesus was not challenging the disciples' *idea* of a restored Jewish state, but only correcting their ideas about the *time* when it would come into being. Jesus was saying in effect: "A restored, independent Jewish state is certainly part of God's plan for the coming of his kingdom; but it will not come into being now and it is not for you to know when it will be established." Those who accept this interpretation generally go on to claim that we in our day *do know* something about "dates and times," since we have witnessed the establishment of an independent Jewish state in Palestine. Two other contributors to *The New Christian Zionism* express this view:

> Jesus himself affirms that the kingdom (Acts 1:3) includes the restoration of Israel (Acts 1:6–8) but at a future time fixed by the Father—after the gospel mission to the nations. . . . [I]n the text Jesus clearly accepts the premise as he answers their question regarding the timing of the kingdom.[2]
>
> —Craig Blaising

---

2. Blaising, "Biblical Hermeneutics," 91–92.

... there is little evidence to suggest that Acts 1:6–8 should be read as anything but a dominican promise of the ultimate restoration of the kingdom to Israel in the holy city of Jerusalem.[3]

—Mark S. Kinzer

According to the second interpretation, however, verses 7 and 8 need to be taken very closely together, because both of them are answering the disciples' question. Jesus therefore is not only trying to correct the disciples' idea about the *timing* of these events (verse 7); he is also trying to correct the *idea* that was implied in the question (verse 8). Jesus is wanting his disciples to put on one side the idea of the kingdom that they have inherited, and to accept a completely new idea of the kingdom of God. It will not be a kingdom for one ethnic group, Israel, or tied to one piece of land, the land of Israel, but a kingdom that will include everyone from Jerusalem, Judea, Samaria, and the ends of the earth who believes the testimony of the apostles. It's for this reason that John Calvin made this comment about the disciples' question: "There are as many mistakes in this question as there are words."[4]

If we follow this interpretation, Jesus is saying to his disciples, "I want you to put out of your minds once and for all the idea that the establishment of a sovereign Jewish state has any special significance in the establishment of the kingdom of God. I want you to see the kingdom of God in a different light—as a kingdom which is spiritual and therefore has nothing to do with any piece of land; a kingdom that is international and has no connection with any one ethnic group, nation, or state." Walker spells out the implications of this interpretation:

> When he [Luke] records Jesus' answer to the disciples' agitated question in Acts 1, he almost certainly intends us to hear this as meaning, "Your understanding of restoration is wrong; Israel has been restored in my resurrection, and you will be witnesses of this fact from Jerusalem to the ends of the earth. The restored kingdom of Israel is the world coming under the rule of Israel's true king." The throne of David is no longer empty, but in accordance with God's promise it has now been occupied by the risen Jesus (Acts 2:30–31). Israel's kingdom has therefore been restored through the resurrection of her king—the one whom God has made both Lord and Messiah (2:36).[5]

---

3. Kinzer, "Zionism in Luke-Acts," 164.
4. Calvin, *Commentary on the Acts of the Apostles*, 29.
5. Walker, "The Land in the New Testament," 108.

2. A similar exchange with the two disciples on the road to Emmaus

If there are two possible interpretations of Jesus' conversation with the disciples recorded in Act 1:1–8, there can hardly be the same doubt about the interpretation of the conversation between the risen Christ and the two disciples on the road to Emmaus, recorded in Luke 24:13–35. The two disciples do not recognize him at first, and start describing the events of the past week in Jerusalem leading up to his death. When Jesus asks them what they are discussing, they express their extreme disappointment—even disillusionment—over what they have experienced:

> "The things about Jesus of Nazareth, who was a prophet mighty in deed and word before God and all the people, and how our chief priests and leaders handed him over to be condemned to death and crucified him. But *we had hoped that he was the one to redeem Israel.* Yes, and besides all this, it is now the third day since these things took place. Moreover, some women of our group astounded us. They were at the tomb early this morning, and when they did not find his body there, they came back and told us that they had indeed seen a vision of angels who said that he was alive. Some of those who were with us went to the tomb and found it just as the women had said; but they did not see him."
>
> (Luke 24:19–24, italics added)

Jesus, however, does not seem at first sight to show a great deal of sympathy over their hopes for the nation of Israel. Instead, he rebukes them for their dullness and slowness to understand the prophets:

> "Oh how foolish you are, and how slow of heart to believe all that the prophets have declared! Was it not necessary that *the Messiah* should suffer these things and then enter into his glory?" Then beginning with Moses and all the prophets, he interpreted to them the things about *himself* in all the scriptures.
>
> (Luke 24:25–27, italics added)

One of the surprising things about this reply is that Jesus appears to ignore the subject that they are really interested in—the redemption of Israel. He simply speaks of himself as "the Christ" (i.e., the Messiah, God's anointed agent), and goes on to say why it was necessary for him to suffer and die. He then explains everything in the scriptures concerning *himself*—not Israel.

Was Jesus deaf to what the two men were saying? Was he talking at cross-purposes with them? Was he thinking only of himself? The most convincing answer is that he wanted them to understand that *all* that the prophets had said about *Israel* and its redemption had been fulfilled in *himself* as Israel's Messiah. It wasn't that he didn't care about their hopes for the nation. Rather, he was trying to tell them that he *had* accomplished the redemption of Israel—*although not in the way they had expected.* The redemption of Israel *had already* been carried out through his suffering, death, and resurrection. In the words of Rowan Williams, therefore, "the disciples realize that a completely new kind of sense has been made of the whole of *their* story, their life and their environment, by this encounter with the risen Christ."[6]

3. Conclusion

The similarities between these two meetings—on the road to Emmaus and in Jerusalem—are striking because of the way they describe the way the disciples had to change their thinking. The two disciples on the road to Emmaus had thought that "the redemption of Israel" would mean some kind of national and political restoration, but had to revise their understanding of the hopes of Israel. The eleven disciples had believed that restoring the sovereignty of Israel was an important part of the coming of the kingdom of God. But now they had to understand that after the death and resurrection of the Messiah, the land and the people of Israel no longer had the same role in the kingdom of God. From now on all their hopes and expectations were to be centred on Jesus, and they were to take the message about him to every ethnic group in every land.

6. Williams, *Luminaries*, viii.

5

Why not interpret the Old Testament in its own terms—literally—allowing it to interpret itself instead of importing categories from the New Testament? Isn't there a danger of spiritualizing everything in the Old Testament?

This objection is frequently expressed by Christian and Messianic Jewish writers:

> Not one instance exists of a "spiritual" or figurative fulfilment of prophecy. . . . Jerusalem is always Jerusalem, Israel is always Israel, Zion is always Zion. . . . Prophecies may never be spiritualized, but are always literal.[1]
>
> —Cyrus I. Scofield, dispensationalist theologian, 1843–1921

> A literal hermeneutic is decidedly the hermeneutic of choice by the overwhelming majority of Messianic Jews writing on these subjects.[2]
>
> —Lisa Loden, Messianic Jewish writer

> I am unhappy with the overuse of the distinction between "literal/physical" and "spiritual." But for me this means both the "physicality" and the "spirituality" of the land promises are held together. I look for a redeemed Israel back in the land, living

1. Scofield, *Scofield Bible Correspondence Course*, 41–46.
2. Loden, "Messianic Jewish Views of Israel's Rebirth and Survival in the Light of Scripture," 48.

in peace and justice alongside her neighbors. I do not want to separate the heavenly Zion from the physical Jerusalem, but rather to see the spiritual truth of Yeshua's teaching lived out in the physical reality of the Old City today. . . . I see . . . an assumed position—that the land of Israel, the people of Israel, and the kingdom of God, would eventually be restored.[3]

—Richard Harvey, Messianic Jewish writer

The worldview of the Old Testament clearly revolves around the chosen people in the promised land, with a functioning temple and a line of kings descended from David. These were all very tangible things, and their continuity was guaranteed by divine promises. But this worldview was challenged profoundly in the exile, when the people were banished from the land, the temple was destroyed, and the royal line came to an end. In this situation the prophets assured the people of restoration to the land, a restored temple, and leaders who would create a just society (see further Part 2 on Ezekiel). When they did return to the land and came under the control of one foreign power after another, they still held onto Yahweh's promises about all the institutions that upheld their national life in the land (see further Part 3 on Zechariah). They wanted to take Yahweh at his word, and expected a very literal fulfilment of all the promises he had made.

There can't be any doubt that this was also the worldview of the disciples of Jesus, who looked forward to a national restoration of the Jewish people in which they could be free from foreign rule and able to obey the *torah* in the land. W. D. Davies sums up this way of thinking by saying, "They could only dwell securely in the promised land when it was not occupied territory."[4] As we have already seen, these hopes were summed up by the Gospel writers in expressions like "the consolation of Israel" (Luke 2:25), "the redemption of Jerusalem" (Luke 2:18), the redemption of Israel (Luke 24:21), and "the hope of Israel" (Acts 28:20; cf. 23:6; 24:15; 26:6). If we had been able to ask the disciples whether they understood all these promises and prophetic hopes "literally or spiritually," they would no doubt have answered that literal and spiritual fulfillment went together, because there could be no spiritual fulfillment without a literal fulfillment.

The crucial question we need to ask, therefore, is this: is there anything in the Gospels and the rest of the New Testament to suggest that Jesus' disciples continued to hold onto these ideas? Or is there any evidence that they had to revise or develop their ideas about the restoration of Israel and the land any significant way? The following are reasons for believing that the

3. Harvey, "Towards a Messianic Jewish Theology of Reconciliation," 89.
4. Davies, *The Gospel and the Land*, 95.

disciples did *not* hold onto their expectations of a very literal fulfilment of Old Testament promises and prophecies.

1. New Testament writers see Jesus as the real fulfillment of the promise about the line of David

When David first became king, God made a promise concerning his descendants: "Your house and your kingdom shall be made sure forever before me; your throne shall be established forever" (2 Sam 7:16). Taken at its face value, this would seem to be a promise that God would ensure that the royal line of David would continue throughout history; there would always be a descendant of David sitting on a royal throne in Jerusalem. But this inevitably creates a problem for the literalists, since the royal line of David came to an end at the time of the exile in Babylon in 586 BCE. We find in Zechariah that, after the exile, the community in Jerusalem is led by Zerubbabel, who, although he was a direct descendant of David, is seen as governor rather than king (see further Part 3). Some therefore have to postpone the fulfillment of the promise about the continuity of David's royal line until after the second coming of Christ, when Jesus will reign over the world from his throne in the city of Jerusalem during the millennium.

The New Testament, however, points to a different way of understanding the fulfillment of the promise made to David. In Luke's account of the birth of Jesus, Mary is told by an angel that she is to be the mother of a child who will have a very special role in the purposes of God: "Do not be afraid, Mary, for you have found favor with God. And now, you will conceive in your womb and bear a son, and you will name him Jesus. He will be great, and will be called the Son of the Most High, and the Lord God will give to him the throne of his ancestor David. He will reign over the house of Jacob forever, and of his kingdom there will be no end" (Luke 1:30–33). The most natural interpretation of these words is that Luke believed that the coming of Jesus was the fulfillment of the original promise made to David about the continuity of his royal line. It is *Jesus himself* (not his physical descendants) who will reign forever; his kingly rule will never end and be very different from that of Old Testament kings. This fulfillment in Jesus could never have been described as a "literal fulfillment" of the Old Testament promises.

2. New Testament writers see fulfillment as much more than fulfillment of promises and predictions

We shall see (in Part 3, chapter 3) that when New Testament writers use the idea of fulfillment to make a connection between an event in the life of Jesus and something in the Old Testament, they aren't simply thinking in terms of fulfillment of a promise or a prediction. They are drawing attention to patterns that are repeated, and to correspondences that are more than coincidences. So, for example, in order to make a connection between the return of the holy family to the land after seeking refuge in Egypt and Israel's exodus from Egypt, Matthew quotes words from Hosea: "This was to fulfill what had been spoken by the Lord through the prophet, 'Out of Egypt I have called my son'" (Matt 2:15, quoting Hos 11:1). By doing so, he is pointing out how Jesus has gone through some of the same experiences as the Children of Israel. Pictures of the shepherd in Zechariah are not predictions, but are seen by the Gospel writers as being fulfilled in Jesus (Matt 26:31 quoting Zech 13:7; Matt 24:30 and John 19:36–7 quoting Zech 12:10). The Servant Songs in Isaiah (from chapter 42 to 53), in their original context may have been related to the prophet himself, the whole nation of Israel, or the faithful remnant within the nation. But the disciples of Jesus must have understood that he identified himself with this figure of the Suffering Servant (e.g., Mark 10:45; Acts 4:27).

When we say, therefore, that Jesus is the fulfillment of the Old Testament, we are seeing him as the fulfillment not only of the covenant promise made to Abraham and all the promises about the line of David and the temple with its priesthood and sacrificial system, but also of the figures like the prophet promised by Moses (Deut 18:15), Daniel's Son of Man (Dan 7:13–27), and Isaiah's Suffering Servant (Isa 42—53). The risen Jesus interpreted to the two disciples on the road to Emmaus "the things about himself in all the scriptures" (Luke 24:27). And when he met later with all the disciples in the upper room and spoke about "everything written about me in the law of Moses, the Prophets, and the Psalms" (Luke 24:44), he can't have been speaking only about predictions.

3. New Testament writers don't interpret apocalyptic language from the Old Testament literally as if it's straightforward prediction

When Jesus speaks about the destruction of Jerusalem (Mark 13:24–25), he quotes verses from Isaiah (Isa 13:9, 11, 13, 15), which, in their original context, are images of cosmic disturbances coinciding with the coming destruction of Babylon. He uses them, however, not to speak of phenomena at the end of the world, but to describe the coming destruction of Jerusalem. Similarly, Joel's prophecy about God pouring out his Spirit on all flesh contains similar images of cosmic disturbances: "portents in the heaven above and signs on the earth below, blood, and fire, and smoky mist. The sun shall be turned to darkness and the moon to blood . . ." (Acts 2:19–20, quoting Joel 2:30–31). Peter has no difficulty in quoting these words on the Day of Pentecost, declaring that they have been fulfilled in what has happened that day. He must have believed that these vivid pictures of phenomena in the natural world were simply Joel's way of describing a spectacular divine intervention in the future that would have life-changing consequences. It therefore seems very unnatural for Michael Vlach to suggest that Joel's prophecy about the pouring out of the Spirit was fulfilled on the Day of Pentecost, but that the words about cosmic disturbances describe something that will happen literally at the second coming.[5]

This same principle can be applied to the way Jesus refers to the picture, which is found in Ezekiel, Zechariah, and Joel, of water flowing down from Jerusalem to the Dead Sea (see Part 3, chapter 3). This seems to be the only image in the Old Testament to which Jesus could be referring when he says, "Let anyone who is thirsty come to me, and let the one who believes in me drink. As the scripture has said, 'Out of the believer's heart shall flow rivers of living water'" (John 7:37–38). Jesus clearly did not understand this image as a description of a clever irrigation scheme that would channel water from Jerusalem down to the Dead Sea.

4. New Testament writers believe that Old Testament prophecies about the national restoration of Israel have already been fulfilled in the coming of Jesus

The clearest example is to be found in the way that James at a council meeting in Jerusalem quotes a prophecy of national restoration in Amos in order to support the idea that gentile believers should be welcomed into the people of God (Acts 15:1–21). This special council is addressing the new situation that has been created by more and more gentiles accepting the gospel message. There is strong disagreement over their status in the Christian community, since some Jewish believers insist that these gentile converts must be circumcised and told to keep the law of Moses.

---

5. Vlach, *Has the Church Replaced Israel?* 102.

At this meeting, Peter, Paul, and Barnabas describe how gentiles have believed the gospel message, and argue that because these gentiles have so clearly received the gift of the Holy Spirit, they should be welcomed into the church. After some discussion, James, as chairman of the council, gives the ruling that these gentile believers do *not* have to be circumcised or obliged the keep the law of Moses. The only requirement is that they "abstain only from things polluted by idols and from fornication and from whatever has been strangled and from blood." He quotes verses from the final chapter of the book of Amos about the restoration of Israel, arguing that gentiles coming to faith is evidence that these prophetic hopes for the nation have now been fulfilled.

The two verses in Amos which are quoted by James (Amos 9:11–12) cannot be isolated from the rest of the passage (9:11–15), which contains several graphic images describing God's promise to restore the nation of Israel:

> On that day I will raise up the booth of David that is fallen, and repair its breaches, and raise up its ruins, and rebuild it as in the days of old; *in order that* they may possess the remnant of Edom *and all the nations who are called by my name,* says the Lord who does this. . . . [T]he mountains shall drip with sweet wine, and all the hills shall flow with it. I will restore the fortunes of my people Israel, and they shall rebuild the ruined cities and inhabit them. . . . I will plant them upon their land, and they shall never again be plucked up out of the land that I have given them, says the Lord your God.
>
> (Amos 9:11–15, italics added)

When James quotes this passage, he is trying to show that the inclusion of the gentiles in the church is *a* fulfilment—or perhaps *the* fulfilment—of Amos' prophecy about the restoration of Israel and the nations calling on the name of the Lord. He understands this restoration of Israel not as something still in the future, but as something that has *already* taken place in the coming of Christ. The inclusion of the gentiles in the church is seen as a result of the restoration of Israel ("*so that* all other peoples may seek the Lord—even all the gentiles over whom my name has been called." Acts 15:17). This idea of the link between the restoration of Israel and the inclusion of the gentiles is also found in these words of Isaiah: "It is too light a thing that you should be my servant to raise up the tribes of Jacob and to restore the survivors of Israel; I will give you as a light to the nations (*goyim*, gentiles), that my salvation my reach to the end of the earth." (Isa 49:6). For James, therefore, the fact that gentiles have received the Holy Spirit is evidence that the restoration of Israel described by Amos has already been completed.

Some Christian Zionists, however, argue that while the inclusion of gentiles in the early church can be seen as a *partial* and *initial* fulfillment of Amos' prophecy of national restoration, it will be fulfilled once again *in the end times*—but in a literal way. Vlach, for example, writes: "There is an initial application/fulfillment of the Amos 9:11–15 prophecy with believing Gentiles today, but this in no way rules out a future fulfillment with the nation Israel when Jesus returns. . . .[W]hen Jesus comes again, the nation Israel will be saved and restored. . . . The concept of *restoration* . . . includes the ideas of Israel being saved and replanted in their land and given a unique role and mission to the nations."[6] He argues that the issue at the council on Jerusalem was simply "soteriological": can gentiles be saved in the same ways that Jews are saved? But the issue also had to do with the nature of the church: can gentiles be regarded as full and equal members of the church along with Jews? Vlach presumably believes that Amos' prophecy about the restoration of the nation of Israel is being fulfilled literally in contemporary history because Jewish people have now been "replanted in their land."

In our study of Ezekiel (Part 2), however, we shall see how difficult it is to justify this "both/and" approach. If Ezekiel's picture of the valley of dry ones and his prophecy of the nation being restored to the land was fulfilled *initially* in the return from exile in Babylon, and if New Testament writers believed that this same prophecy had been fulfilled *once again* in the resurrection of Jesus and the emergence of the church, it is hard to see how it could *also* be seen as a prophecy about the return of Jews to the land and the creation of a Jewish state. Biblical prophecies can certainly be fulfilled at several levels and at different times. But if prophecies of the restoration of Israel are seen to be fulfilled initially in the return to the land after the exile, and then in the incarnation, a *third* fulfilment of the very same prophecies in the recent return and the establishment of the State of Israel must seem by comparison a strange anti-climax.

5. It is difficult to see how the word "forever" must always be understood literally

The English word "forever" is used to translate the Hebrew *olam*, and is generally understood to mean "for all time." When it is related to something to do with God, it must of course be understood very literally. For example, "O give thanks to the LORD, for . . . his steadfast love endures forever" (Ps

6. Vlach, *Has the Church Replaced Israel?* 99–102, 19.

106:1; cf. Pss 107:1; 118:1; 136:1; 146:10); and "The LORD is king forever and ever" (Ps 10:16; cf. Pss 45:6; 102:12).

But does *olam* mean "for all time" when it occurs, for example, in God's promise of the land to Abraham and his descendants? Christians Zionists emphasise that God promised the land of Canaan to them "as an everlasting possession" (Gen 17:8 NIV; "a perpetual holding" NRSV), and argue that this must be taken at its face value, demonstrating that the Jewish people have a right—a divine right—to the land for all time.

What happens, however, when we put the divine promise concerning the land alongside several other divine promises in the Old Testament that use the word *olam*, and ask if Christians interpret them all in a very literal way? In the following verses, the same Hebrew word *olam* is translated in different English translations by the words "forever," or "perpetual," "everlasting," and "lasting" (italicized here):

- The land: "I will give to you, and to your offspring after you, the land where you are now an alien, all the land of Canaan, for a *perpetual* holding." (Gen 17:8, NRSV; "as an *everlasting* inheritance" NIV)

- The Sabbath: "It is a sign *forever* between me and the people of Israel" (Exod 31:17)

- The festival of Passover: "you shall observe it as a *perpetual* ordinance." (Exod 12:14–17, NRSV; "as a *lasting* ordinance" NIV)

- The festival of Tabernacles: "You shall keep it as a festival to the LORD . . . as a statute *forever* throughout your generations." (Lev 23:41)

- The Day of Atonement: "This shall be a statute to you *forever*." (Lev 16:29)

- The ordination of Aaron and his descendants as priests: "You shall take the anointing oil and pour it on his head and anoint him. Then you shall bring his sons . . . and the priesthood shall be theirs by a *perpetual* ordinance." (Lev 29:7–9; "*lasting* ordinance" NIV)

- The line of king David: "When your days are fulfilled and you lie down with your ancestors, I will raise up your offspring after you . . . and I will establish his kingdom. He shall build a house for my name, and I will establish the throne of his kingdom *forever*." (2 Sam 7:12–13; cf. 1 Kgs 9:5; 1 Chr 28:7; 2 Chr 13:5; Ps 89:4)

- Jerusalem as the place where the name of God dwells: ". . . the house of the LORD, of which the LORD had said, 'In Jerusalem shall be my name *forever*.'" (2 Chr 33:4; cf. 2 Kgs 21:7; Ps 48:8; 132:13–14; 68:16; Jer 17:25)

- The vision of God dwelling in the restored temple in Jerusalem: "While the man was standing beside me, I heard someone speaking to me out of the temple. He said to me: Mortal, this is the place of my throne and the place for the sole of my feet, where I will reside among the people of Israel *forever*." (Ezek 43:7)

While Jews today still recognize their obligation to keep the festivals of Passover, Tabernacles, and the Day of Atonement, Christians don't feel the same obligation. They have no difficulty in seeing the promise to Aaron about his priestly line and the promise to David about his royal line as being fulfilled in Jesus. They don't believe that God still dwells in Jerusalem and its temple, because they see Jesus as the fulfilment of all that the temple symbolized. It is in Jesus that God has come to dwell among us. If the word "forever" (*olam*) is not understood literally by Christians in all these contexts, is there any reason to insist that the promise about the land "as a perpetual holding," "an everlasting possession," must be interpreted literally? Frederic Martin sums up the more convincing, non-literal way of understanding "forever":

> Careful study of the Old and New Testament demonstrate that it is better to understand the Hebrew word *olam* in a less absolute sense than the English words "forever" and "everlasting." The term is better interpreted as describing something that is of "indefinite continuance into the very distant future." Practices that are described in the Old Testament as *olam* may last a long time, but they do not necessarily continue into perpetuity or apply in the future in exactly the same way they did before.[7]

6. Conclusion

The disciples of Jesus, like those who first heard the promises and prophecies of the Old Testament—about the land, the nation, the covenant relationship between God and his people, blessing for all peoples of the world, the royal line of David, the temple and its priesthood—would at first certainly have expected them to be fulfilled in very literal and concrete terms. There is plenty of evidence, however, that their interpretation of the Old Testament

7. Martin, *American Evangelicals and Modern Israel*, 113, quoting A. A. MacRae, in *Theological Word Book of the Old Testament*, edited by R. Laird Harris, Gleason J. Archer, Jr. and Bruce K. Waltke (Chicago: Moody, 1980), 1631.

must have developed and changed as a result of their time with Jesus. New Testament writers do not always interpret Old Testament promises and prophecies in a very literal way.

Does this create problems about the reliability and trustworthiness of God's revelation in the Old Testament? Christian Zionists like Darell Bock argue that what is at stake here is the faithfulness of God:

> Could God have made a promise to Abraham and his seed, with a corporate-national element from the start, and then later exclude the nation that originally received that promise? . . . The veracity and faithfulness of God are at stake when some of them are excluded from the biblical story of blessings promised and fulfilled.[8]

Dan Juster takes a similar approach when he argues that any reinterpretation of Old Testament teaching that is found in the New Testament cannot go beyond what the original writer intended:

> The original intent is the primary meaning of the text. . . . If by reinterpretation we mean additional applications by analogy that are prophetically given by the New Testament writer, I have no objection, but rather believe that this is part of New Testament revelation. If, however, we mean a change of meaning from what the original author intended to be understood by his targeted audience, then I beg to strongly disagree. . . . If the New Testament reinterprets those texts in a way that they were not true to the original intent, then I as a Jew would be duty bound to reject them on the basis of the principle that later revelation must be in accord with earlier revelation (Deuteronomy 18).[9]

But should literal fulfillment with exact correspondence with the meaning of the original author be the only criterion by which to understand the faithfulness of God? None of the examples reviewed in this chapter could remotely be described as literal interpretation in the New Testament or exact correspondence with the meaning of the Old Testament.

The next two chapters address this issue by looking in detail at how promises and prophecies about the nation and the land are interpreted in the New Testament. What we shall find is that the disciples of Jesus started out with hopes of a literal fulfillment but came to understand that these Old Testament promises and prophecies had been fulfilled and embodied *in a person*, Jesus the Messiah. They therefore came to believe that all the

---

8. Bock, "How Should the New Christian Zionism Proceed?" 312.

9. Juster, "A Messianic Jew Looks at the Land Promises," 66, 71.

promises and prophecies *had* been fulfilled—*but in a much fuller and more profound way than they had expected.* Jesus for them was the real, the substantial fulfillment of *all* the hopes of Israel. This was because New Testament writers, in the words of Richard Hays, were seeking to "develop modes of interpretation that recognize the historical sense of the biblical texts but then take their original meaning up into a larger theological framework in which the texts are seen to mean more than their original authors and readers had in mind."[10]

10. Hays, "Response to Robert Wilken," 526.

6

If the people and the land are so central to the story of the Old Testament, how can the New Testament offer a re-interpretation of these themes?

Part 1. The nation

In chapter 5 we have discussed in general terms the approach that insists on a literal interpretation of Old Testament promises and prophecies. In this chapter and the next we look more closely at two particular areas—the people/nation and the land—where this debate is especially significant. We need to take people and land together, since, as John Goldingay writes, "the notion of land is intrinsic to the notion of peoplehood. Any people's identity is rooted in the land. . . . Taking seriously God's commitment regarding the land is involved in taking seriously God's commitment to Israel at all."[1] David Pawson similarly emphasizes the link between "people" and "land": "If the Jews are still 'his people,' then the land must still be theirs. If ethnic Israel is still special, then territorial Israel is as well."[2] And Derek Prince emphasizes that "The central theme of biblical prophecy . . . revolves around the land and the people of Israel."[3]

It is argued by many that ideas about the people of Israel and the land in the Old Testament are so central to the history of Israel that they cannot be changed in any significant way by New Testament writers:

---

1. Goldingay, "The Jews, the Land and the Kingdom," 10.
2. Pawson, *Defending Christian Zionism*, 73.
3. Prince, *The Last Word on the Middle East*, 54.

> The burden of these chapters [in *The New Christian Zionism*] is to show *theologically* that the people of Israel *continue* to be significant for the history of redemption and that the land of Israel, which is at the heart of the covenantal promises, *continues* to be important to God's providential purposes. . . . The people and the land of Israel are central to the story of the Bible. . . . [T]he history of salvation is ongoing: the people of Israel and their land continue to have theological significance . . . .[4]
>
> —Gerald McDermott

> . . . one must understand the meaning of Old Testament prophecies about Israel's future in their own Old Testament context, rather than reinterpreting these prophecies in light of how some New Testament writers apply them to the church.[5]
>
> —Charles L. Feinberg

> The New Testament affirms the expectation of the Tanak of an ethnic, national, territorial Israel in the consummation of the divine plan—a plan that includes both Israel and the nations as well as the individual human beings who populate them.[6]
>
> —Craig Blaising

> What is in question neither for Matthew nor for me is the eternal link between the land and people of Israel in God's eschatological purposes: the people as well as the land have a future.[7]
>
> —Joel Willits

The disciples of Jesus must have grown up with very traditional ideas about the chosen people and the promised land. They would have known what Jeremiah had written: "Thus says the LORD, who gives the sun for light by day and the fixed order of the moon and the stars for light by night, . . . the LORD of hosts is his name: If this fixed order were ever to cease from my presence, says the LORD, then also the offspring of Israel would cease to be a nation before me forever" (Jer 31:35–36). They would have remembered that the promise of the land "as an everlasting possession" was part of the "everlasting covenant" that God made with Abraham (Gen 17:6–8, NIV; cf. Ps 105:7–11). They must also have cherished hopes for the future of Israel which were inspired by the prophets, and longed for the day when they could escape from under the yoke of Rome. There can't be any

---

4. McDermott, ed., *The New Christian Zionism*, 13, 12.

5. Charles Feinberg, *God Remembers*, 199.

6. Blaising, "Biblical Hermeneutics," 81.

7. Willits, "Zionism in the Gospel of Matthew," 139.

doubt that they were expecting the restoration of Israel to be "national and territorial."[8]

But did these ideas change or develop in any way as they listened to Jesus' teaching about the coming of the kingdom of God and as they later reflected on his death and resurrection? If they saw Jesus as the fulfilment of all the hopes of Israel, did they still hold onto their hopes about the nation of Israel living in the land? The following are examples of how gradual changes in the disciples' ideas about the nation are reflected in different books of the New Testament. The first major factor that contributes to these changes is the inclusion of gentiles within the community of Jewish believers. The second is the change in the status of Jews who do not respond to the good news of the kingdom. Both of these factors, coming together, were bound to affect the way the disciples thought about what it meant to belong to the nation of Israel.

1. Matthew's Gospel

Matthew is the most Jewish of all the four Gospels, and records Jesus' insistence that his ministry is limited to the Jewish people: "I was sent only to the lost sheep of the house of Israel" (Matt 15:24). Near the beginning, however, it records the visit of the Magi, non-Jews, who come to offer gifts to the infant Jesus and to "pay him homage" (Matt 2:1–12). The Gospel ends with the commissioning of the disciples to "make disciples of all nations" (Matt 28:19), which of course must mean "all the gentiles."

Before Jesus begins his ministry, John the Baptist warns against the presumption of those who think they are exempt from judgment simply because they are descended from Abraham: "Do not presume to say to yourselves, 'We have Abraham as our ancestor'; for I tell you, God is able from these stones to raise up children to Abraham. Even now the axe is lying at the root of the trees; every tree therefore that does not bear good fruit is cut down and thrown into the fire" (Matt 3:9–10; cf. Luke 3:7–9). A similar warning comes after the healing of the servant of a centurion, a gentile, since Jesus looks forward to the time when "many will come from east and west and will eat with Abraham and Isaac and Jacob in the kingdom of heaven, while the heirs of the kingdom will be thrown into the outer darkness . . ." (Matt 8:11–12).

When Jesus tells the Parable of the Vineyard (Matt 21:33–46), it produces such a strong reaction that the chief priests and Pharisees want to arrest Jesus. This is no doubt because they understand that Jesus has adapted

8. Blaising, "Biblical Hermeneutics," 92 footnote.

Isaiah's song of the vineyard, in which Israel is portrayed as God's vineyard (Isa 5:1–7), and used it against them. When the tenants of the vineyard reject the messengers who are sent to ask for a share of the produce and even kill his son, Jesus asks what the owner will do to the tenants. The response of the religious leaders is that he will "put those wretches to a miserable death, and lease the vineyard to other tenants who will give him the produce at the harvest time." And this is how Jesus interprets this response: "Therefore I tell you, the kingdom of God will be taken away from you and given to a people that produces the fruits of the kingdom" (Matt 21:43). In Luke's version of the parable (Luke 20:9–18), he says, "he will give the vineyard to others."

But who are the "people," the "others," to whom the kingdom of God will be given? Willits argues that "Jesus' judgment is not on ethnic Israel but on the inept and corrupt leadership. It is they whom God will replace in his kingdom, the land of Israel."[9] While this interpretation is certainly convincing, it leaves open the question of who is to replace "the inept and corrupt leadership" of Israel. The answer suggested by Kenneth Bailey in his study of Luke's version of the parable is very clear—and surprising. He begins by pointing out that Jesus is "retelling and giving new shape to the story recorded in Isaiah."[10] One striking difference is that, whereas in Isaiah's parable, the vineyard is to be totally destroyed, in Jesus' adaptation, the vineyard is not to be destroyed, but the vinedressers are to be replaced. Bailey understands that the crowds knew that Jesus "was not criticizing them or the nation as a whole. The parable was directed against 'the scribes and the chief priests,' and they knew it. Something is to be taken from them and given to others." He goes on to suggest who these "others" might be:

> Arland Hultgren rejects the idea that the "others" are the Gentile or the Christian community. He adds, "It is more fitting that the 'others' are a new or renewed leadership other than the Jerusalem leaders. If the parable is authentic, that could consist of the Twelve, Jesus and the Twelve, or at least a new leadership that God shall rise up that accepts the proclamation of Jesus."[11]

This interpretation would explain why the temple leaders were so angry that they wanted to arrest Jesus. But it also suggests that Jesus, as the one who was proclaiming the coming of the kingdom of God, was indirectly making the incredibly bold claim that he and his disciples would be the "others," "a

---

9. Willits, "Zionism in the Gospel of Matthew," 127.

10. Bailey, *Jesus Through Middle Eastern Eyes*, 414.

11. Bailey, *Jesus Through Middle Eastern Eyes*, 421.

people that produces the fruits of the kingdom." They would provide the new leadership that was required for the people of God.

The disciples are assured by Jesus that they will "sit on twelve thrones, judging the twelve tribes of Israel" (Matt 19:28; cf. Luke 20:30). But because Jesus speaks elsewhere about non-Jews being welcomed into the kingdom (e.g., Matt 8:11–12), he can hardly be speaking about the disciples sitting on thrones and judging *only* the Jewish people. Some believe that references like this to the twelve tribes of Israel imply "the restoration of Israel, particularly in Jerusalem."[12] They argue that "Implicit in this eschatological promise is the political *reconstitution* of the twelve-tribe nation state."[13] It is more convincing, however, to see this as a case of "Israel" being enlarged to include non-Jewish, gentile believers.

2. Luke's Gospel

Luke records the prophecy of Zechariah after the birth of John the Baptist, which expresses the conviction that the covenant promises made to Abraham are about to be fulfilled:

> Blessed be the Lord God of Israel,
> for he has looked favorably on his people and redeemed them.
> He has raised up a mighty savior for us in the house of his servant David,
> as he spoke through the mouth of his holy prophets from of old,
> that we would be saved from our enemies and from the hand of all who
>   hate us.
> Thus he has shown the mercy promised to our ancestors,
> and has remembered his holy covenant,
> the oath he swore to our ancestor Abraham,
> to grant us that we, being rescued from the hands of our enemies,
> might serve him without fear, in holiness and righteousness before him
>   all our days.
> And you, child, will be called the prophet of the Most High;
> for you will go before the Lord to prepare his ways,
> to give knowledge of salvation to his people by the forgiveness of their
>   sins.
> By the tender mercy of our God, the dawn from on high will break
>   upon us,
> to give light to those who sit in darkness and in the shadow of death,
> to guide our feet into the way of peace.
>
> (Luke 1:67–79)

12. McDermott, ed., *The New Christian Zionism*, 53.
13. Willits, "Zionism in the Gospel of Matthew," 138.

What is significant here is that Zechariah understands the promise to Abraham in terms of being saved "from our enemies and from the hand of all who hate us," and believes that this promise is about to be fulfilled through Jesus. His enemies in his context at the time would have been the Roman occupiers. He does not, however, describe the *fulfillment* of the promise in terms of deliverance from enemies, but in terms of "knowledge of salvation . . . by the forgiveness of their sins." This for him is going to be the real fulfillment of all that God had promised to Abraham. There is nothing here about the national deliverance of Israel and rescue from its enemies.

Jesus' predictions of his suffering and death, as recorded by Luke (and Mark), interpret them as the fulfillment of a prophecy in Hosea that includes the significant phrase "on the third day":

> See, we are going up to Jerusalem, and everything that is written about the Son of Man by the prophets will be accomplished. For he will be handed over to the gentiles; and he will be mocked and insulted and spat upon. After they have flogged him, they will kill him, and *on the third day he will rise again.*
>
> (Luke 18:31–33; cf. Mark 8:31, italics added)

It is widely accepted that when Jesus speaks of his resurrection as being "on the third day" he is using the words of Hosea 6:1–2, which, in their original context, express the hope of a national restoration—in other words, the resurrection of the people of Israel:

> Come, let us return to the LORD; for it is he who has torn, and he will heal us; he has struck down, and he will bind us up. After two days he will revive us; *on the third day he will raise us up,* that we may live before him.
>
> (Hos 6:1–2, italics added)

These hopes and aspirations for the nation were hardly fulfilled in the centuries following the prophet's lifetime. So, what does Jesus mean when he makes such a deliberate reference to these hopes and says that he will be raised from the dead "on the third day"? The answer suggested by R. T. France is that "Jesus could only apply Hosea's words to himself if he saw himself as in some way the heir to Israel's hopes." He goes on to quote this significant sentence from C.H. Dodd's book *According to the Scriptures*: "The resurrection of Christ *is* the resurrection of Israel of which the prophets spoke."[14] N. T. Wright makes the same point: "Jesus was claiming in some sense to represent Israel in himself . . . he regarded himself as the one who summed up Israel's vocation and destiny in himself. He was the one in and

14. France, "Old Testament Prophecy and the Future of Israel," 68.

through whom the real 'return from exile' would come about, indeed, was already coming about. He was the Messiah."[15]

Walker similarly writes of how Paul, speaking to the Jewish leaders in Rome (Acts 28:17–30), believes that "the hope of Israel" has been fulfilled: "Paul linked this 'hope' with an event that had already occurred, *Jesus'* resurrection. This implies that Jesus' resurrection was the fulfillment of Israel's hope, or at least its first installment. . . . God has not been unfaithful— through raising Jesus from the dead he has fulfilled his promise to Israel."[16]

Jesus is therefore claiming that in some way *he himself* is a representative of the whole people of Israel, and that the promised restoration *of the nation* is going to take place *in and through him*. If Jesus represents the nation, therefore, the resurrection of Jesus has to be seen as the resurrection of the nation of Israel. As soon as this connection is made, it becomes natural to see the resurrection of Jesus as a further fulfillment of Ezekiel's vision of the valley of dry bones.

Ezekiel is told that the vision of the bones coming to life represents the restoration of the nation to their land: "Mortal, these bones are the whole house of Israel. They say, 'Our bones are dried up, and our hope is lost; we are cut off completely.' Therefore prophesy, and say to them, Thus says the LORD God: I am going to open your graves, and bring you up from your graves, O my people; and I will bring you back to the land of Israel" (Ezek 37:11–12). The immediate fulfillment of this prophecy was seen in the return to the land after the Babylonian captivity in 538 BCE. But when Jesus speaks about his death and being raised from death as a fulfillment of what the prophets had written, he must see his own resurrection as a further fulfillment of the prophecy of the nation coming back to life (See further Part 2). This is a more convincing way of understanding Ezekiel's vision than seeing it as being fulfilled in the creation of the State of Israel.

3. The giving of the Spirit and the restoration of Israel

John tells us that when the risen Jesus met the disciples in the upper room after his resurrection, "he breathed on them and said to them, 'Receive the Holy Spirit. If you forgive the sins of any, they are forgiven them; if you retain the sins of any, they are retained'" (John 20:22). There is a clear echo here, firstly, of the creation story ("then the LORD god formed man from the dust of the ground, and breathed into his nostrils the breath of life; and

---

15. N. T. Wright, *Jesus and the Victory of God*, 521.
16. Walker, *Jesus and the Holy City*, 98.

the man became a living being" (Gen 2:7), and secondly, of Ezekiel's vision of the valley of dry bones, when the prophet is told by God:

> "Prophesy to the breath (*ruh*), prophesy, mortal, and say to the breath: Thus says the LORD God: Come from the four winds, O breath, and breathe upon these slain, that they may live. . . . Thus says the LORD God: I am going to open your graves, and bring you up from your graves, O my people; and I will bring you back to the land of Israel. . . . I will put my Spirit (*ruh*) within you, and you shall live, and I will place you on your own soil; then you shall know that I, the LORD, have spoken and will act . . . ."
>
> (Ezek 37:9–14)

John's thinking must be that, just as the Spirit of God was at work in the creation of humankind and in bringing the nation of Israel back to life by restoring them to the land after exile, so Jesus gives the Holy Spirit to his disciples to enable them to become the people of God, the body of Christ in the world, and to proclaim the good news of God's forgiveness of sin.

If the Gospel writers understood correctly that Jesus made this connection between the resurrection of the nation through their return from exile and his own resurrection, it's hard to see how Ezekiel's prophecy should *also* be interpreted so confidently by Christian Zionists as a prediction of the creation of the State of Israel.[17]

4. Rejecting the prophet like Moses

In one of his addresses in Jerusalem after Pentecost, recorded in Acts, Peter gives a stark warning about the consequences of rejecting the claims of Jesus, quoting words from Deuteronomy 18:15–20:

> "Moses said, 'The Lord your God will raise up for you from your own people a prophet like me. You must listen to whatever he tells you. And it will be that everyone who does not listen to that prophet will be utterly rooted out of the people' And all the prophets, as many as have spoken, from Samuel and those after him, also predicted these days."
>
> (Acts 3:22–24)

Peter is being extremely blunt when he uses Moses' words about people being "utterly rooted out of the people" and applies them to his new context. There are serious consequences for those who refuse to recognize

---

17. As suggested for example by McDermott, ed., *The New Christian Zionism*, 332.

Jesus as the prophet raised up by God. He also believes that what is happening in Jerusalem at this time is the fulfillment of the predictions of "all the prophets, as many as have spoken."

5. The good shepherd and the true vine

John records Jesus as saying: "I am the good shepherd. The good shepherd lays down his life for the sheep. . . . I have other sheep that do not belong to this fold. I must bring them also, and they will listen to my voice. So there will be one flock, one shepherd" (John 10:11–16). John must have been familiar with the Old Testament idea of Yahweh as the shepherd of Israel (e.g., in Ezek 34:11–31; Ps 23:1), and he must have understood Jesus to mean that gentiles who believed in Jesus (the "other sheep") would belong as full and equal members of the people of Israel (See further Part 2).

After the raising of Lazarus, when Caiaphas says, "it is better for you to have one man die for the people than to have the whole nation destroyed," John adds a significant comment: "He did not say this on his own, but being high priest that year he prophesied that Jesus was about to die for the nation, and not for the nation only, but to gather into one the dispersed children of God" (John 11:49–52). In this context, "the dispersed children of God" cannot be only Jews of the dispersion, but must include people of all races who will come to believe in Jesus. By saying "gather into one" he must be thinking of gentiles and Jews who, as followers of the Messiah, become "one nation." This is the same idea that we find in Jesus' saying about the "other sheep" which he must bring to be included in the "one flock" (John 10:16).

6. 1 Peter: the church as Israel

When Peter is addressing churches in Asia Minor, which probably include both Jews and gentiles, he uses titles which in the Old Testament are reserved exclusively for the people of Israel to describe both Jewish and gentile believers: "You are a chosen race, a royal priesthood, a holy nation, God's own people, in order that you may proclaim the mighty acts of him who called you out of darkness into his marvelous light. Once you were not a people, but now you are God's people; once you had not received mercy, but now you have received mercy" (1 Pet 2:9–10). In these words, there is a clear and deliberate echo of the words of God to the people at Sinai, which define the identity of the children of Israel: "you will be for me a priestly kingdom and a holy nation" (Exod 19:6). When these titles are applied to gentile believers, they cannot mean anything less than they mean when applied to Israel.

7. Paul: gentiles included in Israel

Writing to gentile believers in his letter to the Ephesians, Paul reminds them that before they believed they were "aliens from the commonwealth of Israel, and strangers to the covenants of promise" (NRSV); "excluded from citizenship in Israel" (NIV); "excluded from the community of Israel" (REB). But he assures them that they have now been "brought near by the blood of Christ. For he is our peace; in his flesh he has made both groups into one and has broken down the dividing wall, that is the hostility between us." He has done this "that he might create in himself one new humanity in place of the two, thus making peace, and might reconcile both groups to God in one body" (". . . to create in himself one new man out of the two" NIV). He can therefore say to these gentile believers: "So then you are no longer strangers and aliens, but you are citizens with the saints and also members of the household of God, built upon the foundation of the apostles and prophets" (Eph 2:11–21). There could hardly be a stronger statement that gentile believers share *all* the rights and privileges of the people of God. Whereas they were earlier "aliens from the commonwealth of Israel," "excluded from citizenship in Israel," they have now become part of the commonwealth of Israel, full citizens in Israel.

If gentiles really are included within the commonwealth of Israel, and if some Messianic Jews and Christians today insist that the Jewish people retain their very special and distinct identity within that commonwealth, gentile believers are inevitably made to feel as if they are second-class citizens alongside Jewish believers, who enjoy a special, first-class status. It seems to them as if, after the original "dividing wall . . . the hostility between us" (Eph 2:14) has been broken down, a new kind of dividing wall separating Jewish and gentile believers has been created within the body of Christ. As Anthony Hoekema writes, it looks like "putting the scaffolding back on a finished building."[18]

Paul makes the same kind of assertion in writing to the Galatians about the status of gentile believers: "As many of you as were baptized into Christ have clothed yourselves with Christ. There is no longer Jew or Greek, there is no longer slave or free, there is no longer male and female; for all of you are one in Christ Jesus. And if you belong to Christ, then you are Abraham's offspring, heirs according to the promise" (Gal 3:27–29). Differences between the sexes (male and female) and between social classes (slave and free) are clearly not obliterated in the body of Christ. But if unity means anything at all, it must mean that men and women, slaves and free

18. Hoekema, *The Bible and the Future*, quoted in Vlach, *Has the Church Replaced Israel?* 133.

men and women have exactly the same status within the body of Christ and that Jewish believers don't have a specially privileged position compared with gentile believers.

It is hard to think that Paul could have believed that gentile believers inherited all the promises *except* the covenant promises about the nation and the land. If they inherited the promises made to Abraham about the covenant relationship ("my covenant between me and you . . . to be God to you and your offspring after you," Gen 17:7), and the blessing for all nations of the world ("in you all the families of the earth shall be blessed," Gen 12:3), how could they not be included in the promises about the nation ("I will make of you a great nation," Gen 12:2; "You shall be the ancestor of a multitude of nations," Gen 17:4) and the land ("I will give to you, and to your offspring after you, the land . . . for a perpetual holding," Gen 17:8)? Could Paul have added this kind of qualification: "You are the heirs of the promise given to Abraham—*except* that part of the promise which refers to the nation and the land, which applies only to the Jews who are the physical descendants of Abraham"?

The allegory of Hagar and Sarah conveys a very unexpected message about the status of unbelieving Jews:

> Now this is an allegory: these women are two covenants. One woman, in fact, is Hagar, from Mount Sinai in Arabia and corresponds to the present Jerusalem, for she is in slavery with her children. But the other woman corresponds to the Jerusalem above, and she is our mother.
>
> (Gal 4:24–26)

What is so surprising—even shocking—about this allegory is that, in Paul's interpretation, unbelieving Jews are compared to the descendants of Hagar, while it is only believers in Jesus the Messiah that are described as descendants of Sarah. As Burge points out, "Paul attaches Judaism *without* Christ to Ishmael and bondage while claiming the lineage of Isaac for the community of Christ."[19]

Writing to the Romans, Paul quotes verses from Hosea that seem to be looking forward to the time when gentiles will be included within the people of God: "As indeed he says in Hosea, 'Those who were not my people I will call "my people," and her who was not beloved I will call "beloved." And in every place where it was said to them "You are not my people," they shall be called children of the living God'" (Rom 9:25–26, quoting Hosea 2:23; 1:10). Vlach, however, is so insistent on making a distinction between Israel and

---

19. Burge, *Jesus and the Land*, 82.

the church, that he offers this alternative explanation: "God's electing purposes for Gentiles is parallel or analogous to God's choosing Israel . . . there
is a divine correspondence between God's calling of Israel and His calling of
Gentiles."[20] But if God calls gentile believers "my people" and "beloved," it is
hard to see how there is nothing more than a "correspondence," a "parallel"
or an "analogy" between his call of Israel and his call of gentiles.

In this context, we can understand why there has been such a controversy about the interpretation of the expression "the Israel of God" in
Galatians 6:16. Having challenged the Jewish Christians who are insisting
that gentile converts should be circumcised, Paul states the principle that
"neither circumcision nor uncircumcision is anything: but a new creation
is everything!" He then goes on to say: "As for those who will follow this
rule—peace be upon them, and mercy, *kai* upon the Israel of God." This
blessing is probably modeled on the traditional Nineteenth Benediction,
which was additional to the Eighteen Benedictions: "Peace and mercy on us
and on all Israel your people."

Everything here depends on whether the Greek *kai* is translated "*and*
the Israel of God," or "*even* the Israel of God." If it is "and" (NRSV, TEV),
Paul is saying "peace be upon them, and mercy, *and* upon the Israel of God."
It is unlikely that Paul is pronouncing a blessing on all Jews—including those
who do not recognize Jesus as Messiah. So it is more likely that he sees "the
Israel of God" as those among the Jewish people who believe in Christ and
who follow the rule that he has laid down. But if we choose the translation
"*even* to the Israel of God" (RSV, NIV, REB), Paul sees "the Israel of God"
as both Jewish and gentile believers who follow this rule. Grammarians call
this use of *kai* "epexegetic," meaning that it introduces the same thing under
a new aspect.[21] In this case, the name "Israel" for Paul is no longer the exclusive possession of the physical descendants of Abraham, Isaac, and Jacob,
but embraces all Jews and gentiles who are disciples of Jesus the Messiah
and follow the same rule. "The Israel of God" would therefore mean the
same as "all Israel" in Romans 11:26, and be contrasted with "Israel after the
flesh" (*kata sarka*, 1 Cor 10:18) (see further Part 1, chapters 2 and 8). This
would therefore be another example of "Israel" being expanded to include
gentile believers. Burge comments that "This is perhaps the apostle's most
stark example of universalizing the new identity of the people of God."[22]

20. Vlach, *Has the Church Replaced Israel?* 103.

21. Lightfoot, *St Paul's Epistle to the Galatians*, 224–25.

22. Burge, *Jesus and the Land*, 84.

8. Revelation

In the book of Revelation, John puts two visions of the people of God in heaven side by side. In the first, he sees 144,000 people made up of 12,000 from each of the twelve tribes of Israel (Rev 7:4–8). In the second, he sees "a multitude that no one could count, from every nation, from all tribes and people and languages, standing before the throne and before the Lamb" (Rev 7:9–12). According to one interpretation, the first vision pictures the full number of Jews who believe in Jesus, while the second pictures the whole church including both Jews and gentiles or only gentiles. The more convincing interpretation, however, is that *both* these visions are describing the *same* reality. In the first, the whole church is seen as the tribes of Israel— with gentile believer incorporated into these twelve tribes. In the second vision, Jewish believers are included with all the other believers "from every nation . . . all tribes and peoples and languages."

9. Conclusion

These New Testament texts taken together show how the inclusion of gentiles within the Christian community and the unbelief of many within Israel must have changed the disciples' understanding of Israel. If Jesus foresees that the good news of the kingdom of God will be welcomed by gentiles, it's hardly surprising that New Testament writers think of gentile believers as being incorporated into Israel and sharing all the privileges of God's covenant with Israel. If they really are seen as equal members along with Jews, it's not surprising that terms that are reserved in the Old Testament for Israel are now applied to the whole church. It is inevitable, therefore, that the concept of Israel in the minds of the disciples of Jesus has to change. From now on "Israel" can no longer simply mean "ethnic Israel," because it includes people of all races who have believed in Israel's Messiah.

When some Christian Zionists insist that Israel in the New Testament always means only ethnic Israel, it looks as if they find it hard to give any meaning to the idea of gentiles being incorporated into Israel. Juster, for example, argues that when Old Testament terminology about Israel is applied to Christians, it is nothing more than a kind of analogy that doesn't in any way change the Old Testament understanding of Israel as the people of God:

> It is true that the New Testament applies terms and promises given to Israel to Christians. . . . Since Christians are now also the seed of Abraham by faith and share in a complementary priesthood, *the promises of God have analogous meaning for*

Christians. The meek shall inherit the earth, and the Bride of Messiah shall rule and reign with him. These new analogous applications are in addition to the promises to Israel, not in replacement, as Romans 9 and 11 make clear with finality. . . . We might see the church as analogous to Israel with analogous promises, but supersession or replacement is impossible for anyone who takes the biblical texts with any degree of straightforward contextual meaning.[23]

According to this way of thinking, using Old Testament terminology for the church is simply an *additional* application that leaves the earlier Old Testament understanding of Israel completely unchanged. But Paul's language about gentile believers being incorporated into the commonwealth of Israel can hardly mean that the church as the body of Christ, including both Jews and gentiles, is merely "analogous to Israel." And since for him gentile believers are incorporated into ethnic Israel, there cannot be any suggestion that the church is "replacing" or "superseding" Israel. If the language of incorporation means anything at all, gentile believers must become equal members along with Jews and share all the privileges of belonging to the people of God.

While noting how the full inclusion of gentile believers inevitably changes the way Israel comes to be understood by New Testament writers, we are at the same time reminded of the uncomfortable truth that membership of the chosen people is not an automatic privilege, and that the status of those who do not believe must inevitably change. Many Christian Zionists, however, seem to find it difficult to live with the kind of tension which Paul was able to accept (see Part 1, chapter 2). While they constantly emphasize that the Jewish people "are beloved," they give little weight to the idea that some are like branches that are "broken off because of their unbelief." Lisa Loden, for example, writes that "The Messianic Jewish reading of Scripture sees God as having ordained Israel to remain intact until the end of history. . . . Israel is the embodiment of God's purposes for the world."[24] But it is hard to understand how this kind of language can be squared with all the texts considered in this chapter, which speak *both* of gentiles becoming members of God's covenant people *and* of the serious consequences of unbelief. If enjoyment of the privileges of the covenant is now mediated through Jesus, there must inevitably be a change in the position of those within Israel who are unable to recognize him as Messiah.

23. Juster, "A Messianic Jew Looks at the Land Promises," 78, 66.
24. Loden, "Where Do We Begin?" 52.

7

If the people and the land are so central to the story of the Old Testament, how can the New Testament offer a re-interpretation of these themes?

Part 2. The land

The land is described by the Old Testament scholar Walter Brueggemann as "a central, if not the central theme of biblical faith."[1] The disciples of Jesus would have known this and understood that the promise of the land was part of the covenant that God had made with Abraham: ". . . his covenant forever . . . the word that he commanded, for a thousand generations . . . as an everlasting covenant" (Ps 105:8–10). They would have grown up with very traditional ideas about the importance of the land alongside their ideas about the nation. In his magisterial study, *The Gospel and the Land*, W. D. Davies illustrates the central place of the land in the thinking of Jews around the time of Jesus by quoting a rabbi who said that anyone who says grace after a meal which does not include thanksgiving for the land "has not fulfilled his duty," because God has said, "The Land of Israel is more precious to Me than everything."[2] Willits is therefore right to speak about "the traditional Jewish hope for territorial restoration."[3]

But did the disciples hold onto these ideas after being with Jesus? What is so surprising is that there is so little about the subject of the land in the whole of the New Testament. One obvious explanation for this silence is that the political context in Palestine at the time required considerable caution,

1. Brueggemann, *The Land*, 3.
2. Davies, *The Gospel and the Land*, 68.
3. Willits, "Zionism in the Gospel of Matthew," 109.

as Burge explains: "In the volatile climate of first-century politics—among a people living under the harsh realities of the Roman military occupation— we should not expect a public religious teacher to speak explicitly about the land and its rightful owners. To exhibit resistance to Rome is to run up against a skilled army which is watching for signs of subversion. To show cooperation with Rome is to run up against fellow Jews for whom such sympathies are intolerable."[4]

But we must also look for other reasons. Christians Zionists explain this silence by arguing that Old Testament ideas about the land were so widely accepted that they could be taken for granted. If Jesus and his disciples believed that promises and prophecies about the land in the Old Testament would one day be fulfilled in a very literal way, there was no need to labor the point and constantly reaffirm these expectations.

The other possible explanation is that there was a substantial change in the thinking of the disciples as a result of their time with Jesus. All their hopes about the land now had to be understood in the context of the coming of the kingdom of God through Jesus. They no longer needed to write about the land, because they no longer looked forward to an independent Jewish state in the land. This approach is often dismissed by Christian Zionists as an argument from silence. But if we can find ideas and terminology related to the land that are taken from the Old Testament and given a new meaning in the New Testament, this would explain why the land ceased to have the same significance for the disciples of Jesus.

Where then is the evidence in the Gospels and the rest of the New Testament to suggest that the disciples' ideas about the land changed or developed as a result of their experience with Jesus? The following are examples of how their thinking about the land must have changed and developed.

1. The Gospels

Davies concludes that the only unmistakable reference to the land in the Gospels comes in the Beatitudes: "Blessed are the meek, for they shall inherit the earth" (Matt 5:5).[5] This is clearly a quotation from the Septuagint version of Psalm 37:11 ("the meek shall inherit the land"). All the six references to "the land" in this psalm must be referring to the promised land (vv. 3, 9, 11, 22, 29, 34).

The Sermon on the Mount is about what it means to live in the kingdom of God. The blessing of inheriting the land/earth that is promised to

---

4. Burge, *Jesus and the Land*, 27–28.

5. Davies, *The Gospel and the Land*, 359–65.

the meek is simply another way of describing the blessings that are promised in the other Beatitudes: "theirs is the kingdom of heaven; . . . they will
be comforted; . . . they will be filled; . . . they will receive mercy; . . . they
will see God; . . . they will be called children of God." What is so significant,
therefore, about Jesus' quotation of this verse from the Psalms about the
land is that he is now interpreting Old Testament ideas about the land in
the context of the coming of the kingdom of God. Davies offers two possible
explanations for the use of this verse in this context:

> There are two possibilities, either to . . . hold that Matt 5:5 refers
> to inheriting, not the earth, but the land of Israel in a trans-
> formed world, in the Messianic Age to Come, or to recognize
> that for Matthew "inheriting the land" is synonymous with
> entering the Kingdom and that this Kingdom transcends all
> geographic dimensions or is spiritualized.[6]

The covenant promise to Abraham had included the promise about
the nation ("I will make of you a great nation," Gen 12:2), and the land ("I
will give to you, and to your offspring after you, the land," Gen 17:8). But for
Jesus it is not only the meek among the Jewish people who inherit the land,
but people all races who live by the values of the kingdom of God.

It must also be significant that the word "inherit" (Greek *kleronomeo*,
which translates the Hebrew *nachala*), the word that is used in the Old Testament for inheriting the land, is used in several places in the New Testament to speak of "inheriting the kingdom" and "inheriting eternal life." In
the Parable of the Sheep and the Goats, for example, the Son of Man will say
to those on his right hand, "Come, you that are blessed by my Father, *inherit the kingdom* prepared for you from the foundation of the world" (Matt
25:34; italics added). This must be no different from the promise that those
who make sacrifices in following Jesus will "*inherit eternal life*" (Matt 19:29;
italics added). Paul similarly uses the expression "inherit the kingdom of
God" in three different contexts (1 Cor 6:9, 10; 15:50; Gal 5:21). It can't
be accidental, therefore, that language used in the Old Testament to speak
about inheriting the land is now being used to speak about a new kind of
inheritance that is offered to disciples of Jesus in every nation.

2. Paul

Paul must have been thinking of the original promise made to Abraham
about his descendants inheriting the land when we wrote: "For the promise

---

6. Davies, *Jesus and the Land*, 362.

that he would inherit the *world* did not come to Abraham or to his descendants through the law but through the righteousness of faith" (Rom 4:13). Bailey has pointed out that in referring to this promise, Paul substitutes "the world" (*kosmos*) for "the land" (*ge*). "For Paul," writes Bailey, "'the children of Abraham' are those Jews and Gentiles who through faith in Christ have been made righteous. The 'land' becomes the 'world' (*kosmos*), which is the inheritance of the righteous."[7] Robertson therefore concludes: "Now . . . in the era of new-covenant fulfilment, the land has expanded to encompass the cosmos."[8]

In Paul's thinking, *all* the divine promises in one way or another find their fulfillment in Christ (2 Cor 1:19). This is why, using terminology that is closely associated with the land, he can say "In Christ we have . . . obtained an inheritance" and speaks of the Holy Spirit as "the pledge of our inheritance" (Eph 1:11, 14). Writing to Jewish and gentile believers in Galatia, he describes all Christians, both Jews and gentiles, as "Abraham's seed" and therefore inheritors of the promise given to Abraham: "In Christ Jesus you are all children of God through faith. As many of you as were baptized into Christ have clothed yourselves with Christ. There is no longer Jew or Greek, there is no longer slave or free, there is no longer male and female; for all of you are one in Christ Jesus. And if you belong to Christ, then you are Abraham's offspring, heirs according to the promise" (Gal 3:26–29). As we have already seen (in Part 1, chapter 6), it is hard to think that Paul could have thought that gentile believers inherit every aspect of the promise made to Abraham *except* the promise about the land.

3. Acts

The book of Acts looks as if it was intended by Luke to be (among other things) a counterpart to the book of Joshua in the Old Testament. Whereas Joshua describes the gradual conquest of the land beginning from Jericho, Acts describes the gradual spread of the Christian church beginning from Jerusalem. The book of Joshua begins with God's command to enter and conquer the land: "go in and take possession of the land the Lord your God is giving you for your own" (Joshua 1:11). The book of Acts begins with the command of the risen Jesus to his disciples to start a different kind of conquest: "you will be my witnesses in Jerusalem, in all Judea and Samaria, and to the ends of the earth" (Acts 1:8).

---

7. Bailey, "St. Paul's Understanding of the Territorial Promise of God of God to Abraham," 63.

8. Robertson, "A New-Covenant Perspective on the Land," 139.

Joshua and the tribes were to possess their allotted inheritance by killing its inhabitants "with the edge of the sword." In Acts, however, Paul speaks of the word of God as the weapon by which Christians are to occupy their inheritance. In his farewell address to leaders in Ephesus, which is similar to Joshua's farewell address to leaders (Josh 23:1–19), he says: "Now I commend you to God and to the message of his grace, a message that is able to build you up and give you an inheritance among all who are sanctified" (Acts 20:32).

The book of Joshua describes the different stages by which the land was conquered—beginning with the capture of Jericho and Ai, then going on with the campaigns in the south and the north. The book of Acts describes how the gospel was first preached in Jerusalem, in Samaria, and then in Caesarea to the first gentile; from Antioch the message was taken by Paul into Asia Minor, then to Greece, and finally to Rome.

Both Joshua and Acts describe the many difficulties that had to be faced and overcome. Thus, the story in Acts of Ananias and Sapphira and their deception over the sale of their land (Acts 5:1–11) parallels the story in Joshua of Achan, whose theft and lying held up the advance of the whole army (Josh 7). In Joshua we find repeated several times in different forms a formula that describes times of peace and consolidation after times of fighting: "and the land had rest from war" (Josh 11:23; see also 14:15; 21:44; 23:1). We find something similar in Acts with sentences like "the church. . . had peace and was built up . . . it increased in numbers" (Acts 9:31). "The word of God continued to spread" (Acts 6:7; see also 2:47; 12:24; 13:49; 19:20).

If Luke was thinking in terms of conquest, he was thinking of the conquest not of the land but of the whole world. The only sword that would be used for this conquest was the sword of the word of God, which would enable those who believed it to possess the inheritance that God had promised them. The gospel of Jesus was not only for the people in the land, but for all nations of the world. "Mission to the world," in the words of N. T. Wright, "seems to have taken the place held, within the Jewish symbolic universe, by the land."[9] This reading of the book of Acts makes more sense than Mark Kinzer's argument that "Luke-Acts displays an orientation to the city of Jerusalem."[10] Jesus leaves the disciples from Jerusalem and the angel tells them that he will return "in the same way as you saw him go into heaven"

9. N. T. Wright, *The New Testament and the People of God*, 367.

10. Kinzer, "Zionism in Luke-Acts," 141; he writes that "Jerusalem possesses a unique status not only because 'the kingdom of Christ' is 'historically anchored' there but even more because that kingdom will achieve its eschatological consummation within its walls" (ibid., 142).

(1:11). But the book of Acts is about how the message about Jesus begins to spread out from Jerusalem "to the ends of the earth" (1:8).[11]

4. Peter

Peter uses the familiar word "inheritance" (*kleronomia*), which is associated in the Old Testament with the land (e.g., Ps 78:52, 54–55), and gives it a new meaning: "Blessed be the God and Father of our Lord Jesus Christ! By his great mercy he has given us a new birth into a living hope through the resurrection of Jesus Christ from the dead, and into an *inheritance* that is imperishable, undefiled, and unfading, kept in heaven for you who are being protected by the power of God through faith for a salvation ready to be revealed in the last time" (1 Pet 1:3–5). We can be sure that Peter has in mind Old Testament ideas about the land, because he goes on to underline the contrast between the inheritance of the land and the inheritance of the Christian believer: the land *could* perish or be defiled, whereas the spiritual inheritance of the believer *cannot* perish or be defiled in any way, because it is kept in heaven for all who believe.

5. Hebrews

The writer of the letter to the Hebrews, who was probably writing to Jewish Christians living *outside* the land of Israel, reflects on the way a whole generation of the Children of Israel were unable to enter the promised land because of their unbelief (Heb 4:1–13). After forty years of wandering in the wilderness, Joshua finally led them into the land, which in Psalm 95:11 is described as God's "rest." The writer then connects this idea of the land being a place of rest with God resting on the Sabbath, the seventh day after the six days of creation, and applies both these ideas to his readers by saying,

11. Kinzer's argument is developed in greater detail in his book *Jerusalem Crucified, Jerusalem Risen: The Resurrected Messiah, the Jewish People, and the Land of Promise,* which focuses on Luke and Acts and puts forward the interpretation of key text like Luke 13:31–35; 21:24; Acts 1:1–8; 3:17–26 that is adopted by most Christian Zionists. He believes that Jesus understood the future destruction of the temple in 70 CE as representing "Jerusalem crucified" and marking the beginning of Israel's "second exile." A future return of Jews to the land, however, would represent "Jerusalem risen." He relates many verses speaking about the redemption or restoration of Israel and Jerusalem to a future redemption. He doesn't discuss Romans 9–11 because he concentrates on Luke-Acts. Consequently, his book doesn't address the tension in Romans 9–11 between Paul's belief that the people of Israel are "loved for the sake of their forefathers" and his understanding that some are like branches that are "broken off because of unbelief."

"We who have believed enter that rest." In speaking about the land in this way, it appears that the writer has little or no interest in the actual land of Israel and that it has no special theological significance for him.

When faith is defined in chapter 11 as "the assurance of things hoped for, the conviction of things not seen" (11:1), Abraham is given as a prime example because he obeyed God's call to emigrate to a land that he had never seen. When he reached the land that God had promised as an inheritance, he was living in tents as a foreigner. But the writer sees him as an example of faith because he saw beyond the land, which he *could see*, to something beyond which he *could not see*—described as "a city that has foundations . . . a homeland . . . a better country, that is a heavenly one (*epouraniou*); . . . a city . . .":

> By faith Abraham obeyed when he was called to set out for a place that he was to receive as an inheritance; and he set out not knowing where he was going. By faith he stayed for a time in the land he had been promised, as in a foreign land, living in tents, as did Isaac and Jacob, who were heirs with him of the same promise. For he looked forward to a city that has foundations, whose architect and builder is God. . . . All of these died in faith without having received the promises, but from a distance they saw and greeted them. They confessed that they were strangers and foreigners on the earth, for people who speak in this way make it clear that they are seeking a homeland. If they had been thinking of the land that they had left behind, they would have had opportunity to return. But as it is, they desire a better country, that is, a heavenly one. Therefore God is not ashamed to be called their God; indeed, he has prepared a city for them. . . . Yet all these, though they were commended for their faith, did not receive what was promised, since God had provided something better so that they would not, apart from us, be made perfect.
>
> (Heb 11:8–10, 13–16, 39–40)

Abraham certainly received part of what God had promised, because he was actually living in the land, and took great pains to purchase a plot of land as a burial site for Sarah (Gen 23). But the writer sees the land as pointing to something more, something which Abraham did *not* receive, but which was very real and "something better." The clear implication is that this "something better" is what has now been given to everyone who believes in Christ.

Towards the end of the letter, when this Jewish writer speaks about Jerusalem, one might have expected that he would show some interest in the holy city of Jerusalem. His Jewish readers living in the Diaspora might even have been in the habit of going up to Jerusalem to celebrate festivals. But the only Zion that he is interested in is "Mount Zion and . . . the city of the living God, the heavenly Jerusalem, and . . . innumerable angels in festal gathering, and . . . the assembly of the firstborn who are enrolled in heaven" (Heb 12:22–23). When Jerusalem is described as "the heavenly Jerusalem," it is the same Greek word *epouranios* that is used in 11:16 to describe "the better country . . . the heavenly one," to which Abraham had looked forward. Gary Burge points out how significant it is that Jerusalem is described in this way for Jewish readers who are probably living outside the land:

> The effect of this on the believer who was located far from Jerusalem must have been astounding. This holy geography was accessible from any province or city. Therefore by relocating the true Jerusalem, Hebrews undercuts any need for literal pilgrimage to Judea. To Christians today who have a limited appreciation for pilgrimage destinations and for whom pilgrimage is not a part of their religious vocabulary or experience, such an adjustment would seem trivial. But for a territorial religion like Judaism it was enormous. No longer is a geographical *place* a destination for religious faithfulness.[12]

It is strange, therefore, for Craig Blaising to suggest that "the future expectation of Hebrews is not inconsistent with the story line from the Tanak regarding a kingdom that God would establish upon the earth."[13] It is hard to think that the writer could see Jerusalem as symbol for the whole people of God past, present, and future, and *at the same time* believe that the actual city of Jerusalem still held profound significance for Jewish believers in Jesus—or would do at some time in the distant future.

6. Conclusion

There is nothing in the New Testament to suggest that the disciples continued to believe that Jewish sovereignty in the land was an important part of the coming of the kingdom of God. So how does their idea of the promised land change? Peter and the letter to the Hebrews seem to *spiritualize* the idea of the land, so that the land becomes a symbol of all that believers inherit when they believe in Jesus the Messiah. On the other hand, Paul seems to *universalize* the land, applying Old Testament ideas about the land

12. Burge, *Jesus and the Land*, 98–99.
13. Blaising, "Biblical Hermeneutics," 86.

of Israel to the whole earth. This is how the Palestinian theologian, Munther Isaac, explains the idea of universalizing the land:

> *The Promised Land is in fact, according to Paul, the promised earth.* . . . As Bailey put it, 'The promise *had to expand*, because the very people of God had expanded." In other words, the inheritance of the land has been expanded or "universalized"; the focus is not on the Promised Land but on the whole earth, inherited by Jews and Gentiles in Christ. . . . *The church inherits the story of Israel, which is a story that includes a promise of land.* . . . The people of God are no longer limited—either by ethnicity or geography. Anyone who believes in Christ is Abraham's seed. The natural conclusion is that this redefined people now receive the earth as an inheritance. . . . Those who are in Christ live out the theology of the land of Israel in new places, and this universalizes the land.[14]

Is it so strange that the ideas of the disciples of Jesus developed and changed? They must have held traditional beliefs that their promised Messiah would either be a conquering warrior or descend from heaven on the clouds, but had to change these beliefs as they followed Jesus. They can't have found it easy to believe that the victorious Messiah could also be Isaiah's Suffering Servant, and that he could only enter into his kingly rule through suffering. If they had to revise their ideas of the Messiah, it's hardly surprising that they had to revise their ideas about the chosen people and the promised land.

It is strange, therefore, for McDermott to claim that "the New Testament authors believed the land *continued* to be God's holy abode."[15] If "the Word was made flesh and dwelt among us" (John 1:14), if Jesus fulfilled everything that the tabernacle and the temple had symbolized (John 2:21), and if the whole worldwide church of Jesus Christ is "a holy temple . . . a dwelling place for God" (Eph 2:21–22; cf. 1 Cor 3:17), it's hard to believe that the land of Israel continues even now to be "God's holy abode." When Jesus said to the Samaritan woman "the hour is coming when you will worship the Father neither on this mountain nor in Jerusalem, . . . when the true worshipers will worship the Father in spirit and truth" (John 4:21–23), he must have been looking forward to the time after his resurrection when people of all races could worship the Father in any place on earth.

This chapter and the previous chapter about the nation have argued that, while the disciples started out with widely accepted Jewish ideas about

---

14. Isaac, *From Land to Lands*, 238, 248–50.

15. McDermott, ed., *The New Christian Zionism*, 22.

the nation and the land, they had to enlarge these ideas as a result of being with Jesus and reflecting on his death and resurrection. Because ideas about nation and land were so closely related, their ideas about the land had to develop and change at the same time as their ideas about the nation changed.

Does this development of their ideas amount to what Blaising calls "change in the entire narrative—the story itself—since the character at issue in the earlier story is *essentially embedded in the narrative*"?[16] Does it involve what David Stern describes as "intellectual sleight of hand aiming at denying, cancelling, and reducing to naught a real promise given to real people in the real world."[17] Is Pawson right to argue that, if we refuse to follow a literal interpretation of the promises, it is the faithfulness and reliability of God that are at stake: "God's moral integrity is at stake, his reliability, his faithfulness. Does he stand by his word? Does he keep his promises? Does he mean what he says and say what he means?"[18]

Our argument has been that the disciples did not "change the narrative," but simply *enlarged* it. There was no "intellectual sleight of hand." They were utterly convinced that God *had* kept his promises—but in a much more wonderful way than they had at first expected. Christians have no difficulty in believing that the promises concerning the covenant relationship between God and his people and about the blessing for all people on earth have been fulfilled in and through Christ. They see themselves included within "the multitude of nations" of which Abraham was the ancestor. They do not, therefore, have to put the promises concerning the nation and the land in a category of their own and apply them only to the Jewish people.

If the disciples of Jesus really did have to enlarge their ideas about the nation and the land in these ways, it is hard to see how they could have continued to believe that the traditional Jewish hopes which they had inherited would have to be fulfilled literally at some time in the distant future. The nation of Israel was enlarged to include all gentile followers of the Messiah. The land was universalized to include the whole earth, and spiritualized to point to the inheritance that every believer of every race enjoys in the Messiah.

16. Blaising, "Biblical Hermeneutics," 80 (author's italics).

17. Stern, *The People of God*, 4–5.

18. Pawson, *Defending Christian Zionism*, 118.

8

Isn't "Israel" different from "the church"? Doesn't this mean that the church was something new, and that even after Christ, "Israel" still has a distinct identity?

How is Israel related to the church? How did the first Jewish and gentile Christians think of the relationship between followers of Christ and the Jewish people? Did they see themselves as a sect within the Jewish community or a completely new community with little connection to the Jewish people? How should we today describe the relationship between the Jewish people and the church? There are four different answers that have generally been given to this basic question:

1. Israel is replaced by or superseded by the church

According to this view, after the coming of Christ and the refusal of many Jews to recognize Jesus as Messiah, biblical Israel ceased to have any significant role in God's plan of salvation, and the church has taken the place of Israel. Paul was aware that this was how many Christians thought, since chapters 9 to 11 of the letter to the Romans was written to challenge this idea (see Part 1, chapter 2). In the second century, Justin Martyr was the first theologian to describe the church as "the new Israel," "the true Israel," "the true spiritual Israel"—with the implication that the Jewish people were "the old Israel" and were no longer as significant in God's scheme as they had been before the coming of Christ.

This view, which is generally known as "replacement theology" or "supersessionism," has sadly been a widely accepted view among Christians during the centuries, and has clearly played a part in creating negative views about Jews and Judaism.[1] While it is hard to find any who openly embrace this position today, many who see the church as the continuation of Israel (the fourth of these views) are often accused of teaching this view by those who maintain that Israel still has a distinct and significant identity (the second view).

2. Israel remains Israel and is distinct from the church; it retains its unique identity, even after the coming of Christ

This is the answer given by many Christians and by many messianic Jews:

> . . . the church is a NT entity; . . . there are good biblical reasons to view the church as beginning in the NT era and not in the OT.[2]
>
> —Michael Vlach

> . . . the great OT covenants . . . were addressed to those who are ethnically, biologically Jewish. . . . When many NT passages speak of Israel or Jews, they refer specifically to those who are ethnically, biologically Jewish, not to the *spiritual* descendants of Abraham—i.e., the church, which is composed of both Jews and Gentiles. . . . The church is something distinctly new in the NT era.[3]
>
> —Joseph S. Feinberg

> Messianic Jews are unanimous in their view that Israel consists of ethnic Jews who have been preserved by God through history to fulfill their destiny in the land of Israel. . . . Ethnic Israel is the embodiment of God's purpose for the world. . . . For the Messianic Jew, Israel *is* the visible witness to the world of God's purposes.[4]
>
> —Lisa Loden

---

1. Vlach, *Has The Church Replaced Israel?* 27–62.

2. Vlach, *Has the Church Replaced Israel?* 207, 209.

3. Joseph Feinberg, "Dispensationalism and Support for the State of Israel," 111. There are some very obvious problems with the idea of someone being "ethnically, biologically Jewish." When non-Jews today convert to Judaism, does that immediately make them "ethnically, biologically Jewish"? How much intermarriage between Jews and non-Jews does there have to be before Jewish ethnic identity becomes minimal and virtually non-existent? Palestinians today recognize their very mixed ancestry, and claim that they have a mixture of Canaanite, Jewish, Roman, Greek, Arab, and even Crusader blood.

4. Loden, "Messianic Jewish Views," 53-54.

> Dispensationalists believe that God has two separate but parallel means of working: one through the church, the other through Israel, the former being a parenthesis to the latter. Thus there is, and always will remain, a distinction "between Israel, the Gentiles and the Church.[5]
>
> —Stephen Sizer, quoting Charles Ryrie

> Israel and the church, Jews and Christians, do exist side by side in the world today, as clearly differentiated entities. . . . It is difficult to avoid the conclusion that God can and does have two peoples on earth at the present time—his church, made up of some Jews and more Gentiles, all of whom believe in Jesus, and his people "Israel," still in an unbelieving state.[6]
>
> —David Pawson

The theological objection to this view is that it misunderstands the ways in which New Testament writers think of the relationship between biblical Israel and the church.

3. Israel and the church can exist side by side since they each have their own distinct covenant with God

This is known as "two covenant theology," since it insists that God has a covenant with the Jewish people through Moses and a covenant with the Christian church through Jesus. While Christians insist that salvation is through Christ alone, Jews can enjoy the same salvation through God's covenant with Israel. In its modern form this approach was first formulated in Germany soon after World War I by the Jewish writer Franz Rosenweig, who summed up his ideas in this way:

> Christianity acknowledges the God of the Jews, not as God but as "the Father of Jesus Christ." Christianity itself cleaves to the "Lord" because it knows that the Father can be reached only through him. . . . We are all wholly agreed as to what Christ and his church mean to the world: no one can reach the Father save through him. No one can reach the Father! But the situation is quite different for one who does not have to reach the Father because he is already with him. And this is true of the people of Israel (though not of individual Jews).[7]

5. Sizer, quoting Charles Ryrie in "Dispensational Approaches to the Land," 144.
6. Pawson, *Defending Christian Zionism*, 64, 70.
7. Franz Rosenweig, quoted in Glatzer, *Franz Rosenweig*, 341.

Many who are concerned about Jewish-Christian relations hold to some form of this belief and find it a helpful basis for mutual respect and dialogue.

4. Israel develops into the church, so that the church is the continuation of Israel—but Israel restored and renewed in the Messiah

This view is based on a reading of the Old Testament, the teaching of Jesus in the Gospels, and the teaching of the rest of the New Testament.

a) In Old Testament times foreigners/gentiles become part of Israel

There are four significant examples of Israelites marrying foreigners. After Joseph carried out the plan that saved Egypt from famine, we are told that "Pharaoh gave Joseph . . . Asenath daughter of Potiphera, priest of On, as his wife" (Gen 41:45). When Moses fled from Pharaoh and settled in Midian, he married Zipporah, the daughter of Jethro, a "priest of Midian" (Exod 2:15–22). In the account of the capture of Jericho, we read that "Rahab the prostitute, with her family and all who belonged to her, Joshua spared. Her family has lived in Israel ever since. For she hid the messengers whom Joshua sent to spy out Jericho" (Josh 6:25). Ruth the Moabitess returned to Bethlehem with her mother-in-law Naomi and married Boaz, thus becoming the great-grandmother of David (Ruth 4:18–22). Matthew's genealogy, which traces the line from Abraham to Jesus, includes the names of both Rahab and Ruth: "Abraham was the father of Isaac . . . and Salmon the father of Boaz by Rahab, and Boaz the father of Obed by Ruth, and Obed the father of Jesse, and Jesse the father of King David" (Matt 1:2–5).

b) The Old Testament prophets look forward to gentiles becoming part of Israel

i. Isaiah 19

Isaiah 19 begins with a vivid description of God's judgement on the nation of Egypt (Isa 19:1–17). The second half of the chapter, however, describes a time when God will bless the nation of Egypt: "The LORD will make himself known to the Egyptians; and the Egyptians will know the LORD on that day . . ." (Isa 19:18–22). In the final verses, Egypt and Assyria are blessed alongside Israel, and are described in words normally reserved only for Israel: "On that day Israel will be the third with Egypt and Assyria, a blessing in the midst of the earth, whom the LORD of hosts has blessed, saying, 'Blessed be Egypt *my people*, and Assyria *the work of my hands*, and Israel *my heritage*'" (Isa 19:24–25, italics added). Israelites would not have had warm feelings towards the nation of Egypt, which had enslaved their ancestors for hundreds of years, or towards the Assyrians, who had taken people from the northern kingdom of Israel into exile. Those who first heard this prophecy would no doubt have been shocked to think that people from these pagan nations would come to acknowledge Yahweh and be seen as his own chosen people.

ii. Isaiah 56

A later chapter of Isaiah looks forward to the time when foreigners will "join themselves to the LORD" and the temple in Jerusalem will be "a house of prayer for all peoples": "And the foreigners who join themselves to the LORD, to minister to him, to love the name of the LORD, and to be his servants . . . and hold fast my covenant—these I will bring to my holy mountain, and make them joyful in my house of prayer; . . . for my house shall be called a house of prayer for all peoples. Thus says the LORD God, who gathers the outcasts of Israel, I will gather others to them besides those already gathered" (Isa 56:6–8). The expectation is that God is not only going to bring exiled Israelites back to the land, but bring gentiles to worship God in the temple alongside the Israelites.

iii. Ezekiel

The second half of Ezekiel describes the restoration of Israel to the land and all the blessings of security and prosperity that will follow. They will be one nation under one king, one flock under one shepherd. There are several chapters describing the vision of the new temple, to which the glory of God returns; and the last two chapters describe how the land of Israel is to be divided up equally among the twelve tribes. It is noteworthy is that foreigners living in the land are included in this vision and are recognized as "citizens of Israel": "So you shall divide this land among you according to the tribes of Israel. You shall allot it as an inheritance for yourselves and for the aliens who reside among you and have begotten children among you. They shall be to you as citizens of Israel; with you they shall be allotted an inheritance among the tribes of Israel" (Ezek 47:21–23) (See further Part 2).

iv. Zechariah

Zechariah includes many verses speaking about God's judgment on the nations that have oppressed Israel in the past. But there are also several verses looking forward to the time when gentiles will be included within the covenant relationship between God and his people: "Many nations shall join themselves to the LORD on that day, and shall be my people; and I will dwell in your midst" (2:11). "Those who are far off shall come and help to build the temple of the LORD" (6:15). "Many peoples and strong nations shall come to seek the LORD of hosts in Jerusalem, and to entreat the favor of the LORD. Thus says the LORD of hosts: In those days ten men from nations of every language shall take hold of a Jew, grasping his garment and saying, 'Let us go with you, for we have heard that God is with you'" (8:22–23). The king who is to come, "humble and riding on a donkey," is going to "command peace to the nations" (9:9–10). And in the final chapter people from many nations are seen coming "year after year to worship the King, the Lord of host, and to keep the festival of booths" (14:16–19) (see further Part 3).

v. Psalm 87

These hopes of the prophets are also expressed in Psalm 87, which begins as a celebration of the glory of Jerusalem: "On the holy mountain stands the city he founded; the LORD loves the gates of Zion more than all the dwellings of Jacob. Glorious things are spoken of you, O city of God." But it continues with the extraordinary vision of Yahweh himself recording people from gentile nations, some of which had oppressed Israel—Rahab (Egypt), Babylon, Philistia, Tyre and Ethiopia—in the birth register of Jerusalem: "This one was born there" (Ps 87:1–7). People from these nations are even described by God as being "among those who know me" (Ps 87:4). This is no celebration of the ethnic purity of Israel, but rather a vision of gentiles being included in Israel.

c) Jesus claims to represent Israel, and sees the disciples as the patriarchs of Israel of the future

i. The shepherd and the scattered flock

We shall see later (Part 3, chapter 3) that Jesus relates to himself words from Zechariah about God striking his shepherd and scattering his sheep: "Then Jesus said to them, 'You will all become deserters because of me this night;

for it is written, "I will strike the shepherd, and the sheep of the flock will be scattered""" (Matt 26:31, quoting Zech 13:7). Jesus sees himself as Yahweh's shepherd, and sees the hand of Yahweh in what he is about to suffer. He also describes his disciples—not the whole Jewish people—as the flock of Israel that is going to be scattered.

ii. Judging the twelve tribes of Israel

When the disciples of Jesus wonder what reward they will have for the sacrifices they have made in following him, Jesus promises them a very surprising role as judges of the twelve tribes of Israel: "Truly I tell you, at the renewal of all things, when the Son of Man is seated on the throne of his glory, you who have followed me will also sit on twelve thrones, judging the twelve tribes of Israel" (Matt 19:28; cf. Luke 20:30). He can hardly be speaking of a role that is limited to the physical descendants of Israel, since he has already spoken of the time when "many will come from east and west and will eat with Abraham and Isaac and Jacob in the kingdom of heaven . . ." (Matt 8:11). He must therefore be speaking about a future in which non-Jews will be welcomed into the kingdom. In this saying of Jesus, we can already see that his understanding of "Israel" is changing, and can no longer include only the Jewish people (see further Part 1, chapter 6).

iii. The true vine

Jesus' description of himself as "the true vine" (John 15:1–11) takes on new meaning when seen against its Old Testament background in which the vine is a symbol for Israel. Referring to the exodus and the conquest of the land, the Psalmist says: "You brought a vine out of Egypt; you drove out the nations and planted it. You cleared the ground for it; it took deep root and filled the land." He goes on to plead with God to come to rescue the people who are in a dire situation: "Turn again, O God of hosts: look down from heaven, and see; have regard for this vine, the stock that your right hand planted. . . . Restore us, O LORD God of hosts; let your face shine, that we may be saved" (Ps 80:8–19). So when Jesus says "I am the true vine, and my Father is the vinegrower" he is claiming to represent Israel; and since his disciples are like the branches of the vine, he sees them as members of the true Israel. Jesus, therefore, says N. T. Wright, "was claiming in some sense to represent Israel in himself . . . he regarded himself as the one who summed up Israel's vocation and destiny in himself."[8]

iv. Jesus' high priestly prayer

The prayer of Jesus recorded in John 17 speaks of a new kind of relationship that brings every single believer into union with Jesus, and thus into union with the Godhead: "I ask not only on behalf of these, but also on behalf of those who will believe in me through their word, that they may all be one. As you, Father, are in me and I am in you, may they also be in us, so that the world may believe that you have sent me" (John 17:20–21). If Jesus, as the true vine, embodies and represents Israel, all who believe in him, both Jews and gentiles, are incorporated into Israel.

d) For the writers of the Epistles and Revelation, the church is not distinct from Israel, but is Israel—but Israel transformed and renewed in the Messiah

Several of the verses discussed earlier (in Part 1, chapter 6) which relate to the nation of Israel are relevant also in this context.

i. Paul

Paul says in Eph 2:11–21 that gentile believers, who had been "aliens from the commonwealth of Israel" (NRSV), "excluded from citizenship in Israel" (NIV), have been "brought near" because Christ who is "our peace . . . has made both groups into one and has broken down the dividing wall" separating Jews and gentiles. He has done this in order to "create in himself one new humanity in place of the two" ("one new man" NIV). If Paul is so insistent that gentile believers are now full members of "the commonwealth of Israel" and this "one new humanity," it is difficult to explain or to justify speaking about "Israel *and* the church" as if they are two quite different and separate entities.[9]

In Romans 9–11, Paul uses the image of the olive tree to represent Israel, and sees gentile believers being grafted into the olive tree of Israel and

8. N.T. Wright, *Jesus and the Victory of God*, 517, 537.

9. This way of thinking is evident in the strapline of the Messianic Jewish organization called "Tikkun International," describing it as "A global messianic family dedicated to the restoration of the Church and Israel."

therefore being incorporated into Israel. We have already seen that when Paul says, "And so all Israel shall be saved" (Rom 11:26), this is understood by many to refer to the future salvation of the Jewish people. But the other possible interpretation is that it refers to the whole church of Jesus Christ, which includes gentile believers who are incorporated into Israel. If biblical Israel grows into the universal church through believers of all nations trusting in Jesus the Messiah of Israel, the church is not a new phenomenon, a new creation, but a reality that develops very naturally out of biblical Israel (see further, Part 1, chapter 2).

In his argument with Jewish teachers who insist that non-Jewish Christians must be circumcised and obey the Mosaic law, Paul makes the bold assertion that "it is we who are the circumcision, who worship in the Spirit of God and boast in Christ Jesus and have no confidence in the flesh" (Phil 3:3). He takes circumcision, a defining mark of being a Jew, and claims it for all, whether Jews or gentiles, who believe in Jesus.

ii. James

James addresses his letter to "the twelve tribes in the Dispersion" (James 1:1). He is addressing Christians, who must include both Jews and gentiles, as if they belong to the twelve tribes of Israel. He uses the word "Dispersion" (*diaspora*), which had regularly been used for Jews dispersed and living outside the land of Israel. Burge explains the significance of this use of the word "Dispersion": "Christianity has here adopted one motif from its Jewish roots and developed it eagerly: as Israel live without a land both in Egypt and in Babylon, so too, Christians are likewise landless."[10]

iii. Peter

Peter addresses his first letter to "the exiles of the Dispersion in Pontus, Galatia, Cappadocia, Asia, and Bithynia" (1 Pet 1:1). Like James, he uses the word "Dispersion" to describe both Jewish and gentile believers who live in these provinces of Asia Minor. Later he speaks of these believers in terms that in the Old Testament are reserved exclusively for Israel: "You are a chosen race, a royal priesthood, a holy nation, God's own people" (1 Pet 2:9–10).

---

10. Burge, *Jesus and the Land*, 96.

iv. Revelation

The two visions of "the servants of our God" in heaven, described in Revelation 7, are relevant to the question of the relationship between Israel and the church. We have already noted (in Part 1, chapter 6) that according to one interpretation the first vision of the 144,000 of the tribes of Israel represents Jewish followers of the Messiah, while the second vision of "a great multitude that no one could count, from every nation, from all tribes and peoples and languages" (Rev 7:9–17) represents the whole body of believers, past, present and future, including both Jews and gentiles. It was argued that it is much more natural to interpret *both* visions as images of the whole church. In this case, the first vision places gentile believers alongside Jewish believers as if they all belong to the twelve tribes of Israel. When the holy city of Jerusalem that comes down out of heaven from God is described as having twelve gates and "on the gates are inscribed the name of the twelve tribes of the Israelites" (Rev 21:12), it is inconceivable that John would have understood that this vision related only to Jewish believers in the Messiah.

5. Conclusion

These biblical texts make a strong case for rejecting both the first view (that the church replaces Israel) and the second view (that the church is distinct from Israel). The third view (that the Jewish people and the church enjoy the benefits of two distinct, but separate covenants) is difficult to reconcile with the New Testament's insistence that everything in the Old Testament points forward to Jesus the Messiah and that salvation is offered only through him.

The fourth view (which sees the church as the continuation of Israel) is well summed up by N. T. Wright in these words:

> Through the Messiah and the preaching which heralds him, Israel is transformed from being an ethnic people into a worldwide family. . . . The Christians regarded themselves as a new family, directly descended from the family of Israel, but now transformed. . . . [T]hey claimed to be the continuation of Israel in a new situation.[11]

Similarly, Isaac uses the word "incorporation" to describe the relationship between Israel and the church:

> Gentile believers do *not* replace Israel in the covenant. This is not replacement theology, but incorporation theology. Gentile

---

11. N. T. Wright, *The Climax of the Covenant*, 240.

believers are incorporated into Israel, and as such become full members. The church does not replace Israel. The church is the continuation of Israel, because those who are in Christ are the seed the Abraham.[12]

Many Messianic Jews and Christian Zionists are so insistent on the need to maintain a clear distinction between Israel and the church that they seem to find it difficult to accept the language of "incorporation." Vlach, for example, writes: "they [gentile believers] do not become Israel; they *share* with Israel. . . . Ephesians 2–3 emphasizes a *sharing with* Israel and not an *incorporation into* Israel. . . . God's electing purposes for Gentiles is parallel or analogous to God's choosing Israel"[13] He argues that when Old Testament terminology related to Israel is applied to the church (as in 1 Pet 2:9–10), this simply means that "The NT could be making analogies. . . . Or the NT could be adding new referents to OT promises, prophecies and covenants, but not at the expense of the original referent."[14] This application simply provides "additional meanings given to OT texts beyond the literal sense";[15] these new meanings are "*compatible* or *complementary* to the hopes of Israel."[16]

This kind of language suggests that some Messianic believers and some Christian Zionists are uncomfortable with the idea of gentile believers sharing all the privileges of belonging to Israel. But if Jesus' image of himself as the vine, Paul's image of gentiles being grafted into the olive tree of Israel, and his understanding of gentiles being included within the commonwealth of Israel as part of "one new humanity" mean anything it all, it is hard to see how Jewish and gentile believers cannot be seen as equal members of the body of Christ. If there is to be "total equality of Jew and Gentile within the church,"[17] gentile believers must be incorporated fully into Israel.

Does this approach amount to a kind of replacement theology which is trying not to be called replacement theology? Doesn't the integration of gentiles into Israel look like an illegitimate attempt to take away the identity of the Jewish people and give it to others? It is only illegitimate if Jesus has no right to claim to be the fulfilment of all the hopes of Israel. If he really is Israel's Messiah who was to bring blessing both to Israel and the gentiles, he has the right to throw open membership of the chosen people to every

---

12. Isaac, *From Land to Lands, from Eden to the Renewed Earth*, 261.

13. Vlach, *Has the Church Replaced Israel?* 153, 103.

14. Vlach, *Has the Church Replaced Israel?* 93.

15. Vlach, *Has the Church Replaced Israel?* 91.

16. Vlach, *Has the Church Replaced Israel?* 205.

17. N. T. Wright, *The Climax of the Covenant*, 243.

human being of every race. Those who accept his invitation are not "replacing" anyone or "taking anyone's place."

9

What about the millennium? Doesn't a literal millennium assume that Jesus will be reigning from Jerusalem?

The word "millennium" is used to refer to the period of one thousand years described in one of John's visions in the book of Revelation (20:1–6). The passage comes towards the end of the book and speaks of how the reign of Christ has severely limited Satan's power, with the result that Christian martyrs are able to share Christ's victory and his reign. The text is as follows, with the references to "the millennium" printed in italics:

> Then I saw an angel coming down from heaven, holding in his hand the key to the bottomless pit and a great chain. He seized the dragon, that ancient serpent, who is the Devil and Satan, and bound him for *a thousand years*, and threw him into the pit, and locked and sealed it over him, so that he would deceive the nations no more, until *the thousand years* were ended. After that he must be let out for a little while. Then I saw thrones, and those seated on them were given authority to judge. I also saw the souls of those who had been beheaded for their testimony to Jesus and for the word of God. They had not worshipped the beast or its image and had not received its mark on their foreheads or their hands. They came to life and reigned with Christ *a thousand years*. (The rest of the dead did not come to life until *the thousand years* were ended.) This is the first resurrection. Blessed and holy are those who share in the first resurrection. Over these the second death has no power, but they will be priests of God and of Christ, and they will reign with him *a thousand years*.

> (Revelation 20:1–6, NRSV)

1. What are the issues?

The debate about the millennium has centered round the following questions:

- Is the millennium as described in Revelation 20 to be understood as a literal period of one thousand years, which has still to come in the future? Or is it to be understood symbolically in the context of John's highly symbolic descriptions in his visions as a way of describing some other reality?

- Does the millennium come *before* or *after* the second coming of Christ? Does the millennium prepare the way for the return of Christ, or does the coming of Christ inaugurate the millennium?

- How many other passages in the Bible (e.g., in the Old Testament prophets) should be related to the millennial rule of Christ?

2. Different views about the millennium

During the first centuries of the Christian era the majority view among theologians seems to have been that John's description of the millennium should be understood literally. Justin Martyr (100–165), for example, wrote: "there will be a resurrection of the dead, and a thousand years in Jerusalem, which will then be built, adorned and enlarged, [as] the prophets Ezekiel and Isaiah and others declare." Irenaeus (130–202) held the same view, and Tertullian (160–225) expected a restoration of Jews to the land: "It will be fitting for the Christian to rejoice, and not to grieve, at the restoration of Israel, if it be true, (as it is), that the whole of our hope is intimately united with the remaining expectation of Israel." Origen (184–254), however, taught that if Jesus was the Messiah, prophecies about the messianic age must have been fulfilled in the coming of Christ. Augustine (354–430) interpreted the millennium as a way of describing a present reality, and this view became the accepted teaching of the churches for many centuries.[1]

Since the eighteenth century three main schools of interpretation have been developed concerning the millennium:

- The *post*millennial position is that the second coming of Christ will take place *after* the millennium. The thousand years represent a period in which Christianity spreads throughout the world. At the end of this period of gradual conversion and transformation for the better,

---

1. McDermott, ed., *The New Christian Zionism*, 54–56.

Christ will come once again to the world. This view became popular in the USA in the eighteenth and nineteenth centuries, but declined in the early twentieth century, partly because the horrors of World War I called into question the idea of gradual improvement in the world. It has, however, emerged again in the North American context.

- The *premillennial* position holds that the second coming of Christ will take place *before* the millennium. The return of Christ to this world will usher in a literal period of a thousand years in which Christ will reign over the world from Jerusalem.

- The *amillennial* interpretation is that the thousand years in the book of Revelation is not to be understood as a literal period of one thousand years, but rather as a symbol describing the period of time in which we now live, following the victory that Christ has won through his death and resurrection. This was John's way of describing what is a present reality—namely the victory of Christ in which all Christian believers (and especially Christian martyrs) can share. Origen and Augustine were the first to articulate this position, which became the dominant view of the churches for many centuries.

3. Problems with the idea of a literal millennium

- Revelation 20:1–6 is the *only* passage in scripture that speaks about "the millennium." This passage must be interpreted in the context of the book, which is full of symbols needing to be interpreted. If all the other numbers in Revelation (like three, seven, and ten) seem to be symbolic, there is no reason why the number one thousand should be understood literally. It would be very questionable to base such an important belief on a single passage in a book that is full of apocalyptic symbols.

- There is no reference here to the return of Christ in his second coming, and nothing that relates the period of a thousand years to the second coming of Jesus.

- There is no suggestion that "the millennium" takes place *on earth*. John sees an angel "coming down from heaven"; but there is no suggestion that the angel is coming down *to earth* or that the binding of Satan and the martyrs sharing in the victory of Christ takes place on earth.

- Those who hold to a literal millennium assume that every believer will be able to share in the millennium. But the main focus in this passage is on the *martyrs* ("those who had been beheaded because of their testimony to Jesus Christ"), and not on the whole church.

For these reasons, it is hard to see how the idea of a literal millennium, based on this one passage in the book of Revelation, could ever become the main hermeneutical key for constructing a complete system of eschatology describing what is to happen at the end times.

4. Conclusion

The assumption underlying this book is that the millennium described in Revelation has nothing whatever to do with the idea of Jesus reigning over the world in a kingdom which is centered in Jerusalem. Rather, it describes "what takes place during the entire history of the church, beginning with the first coming of Christ." This is the amillennial position, which is summed up by the American theologian Anthony A. Hoekema in this way:

> The book of Revelation is full of symbolic numbers. Obviously the number "thousand" which is used here must not be interpreted in a literal sense. Since the number ten signifies completeness, and since a thousand is ten to the third power, we may think of the expression "a thousand years" as standing for a complete period, a very long period of indeterminate length. . . . We may conclude that this thousand-year period extends from Christ's first coming to just before his second coming. . . . That period . . . spans the entire New Testament dispensation, from the time of the first coming of Christ to just the time of Christ's second coming . . . .
>
> We can appreciate the significance of this vision when we remember that in John's time the church was sorely oppressed and frequently persecuted. It would be of great comfort to those believers to know that though many of their fellow Christians had died, some even having been cruelly executed as martyrs, these deceased fellow believers were now actually alive in heaven as far as their souls were concerned—living and reigning with Christ. This living and reigning with Christ, John goes on to say, shall continue throughout the thousand years—that is, throughout the entire gospel era, until Christ shall come again to raise the bodies of these believers from the grave.
>
> There is no indication in these verses that John is describing an earthly millennial reign. The scene . . . is set in heaven. Nothing is said in verses 4–6 about the earth, about Palestine as the center of this reign or about the Jews. The thousand-year

reign of Revelation 20:4 is a reign with Christ in heaven of the souls of believers who have died. This reign is not something to be looked for in the future; it is going on now, and will be until Christ returns.[2]

2. Hoekema, "Amillennialism."

10

Isn't there something miraculous about the creation of Israel? Isn't the State of Israel "a miracle of God and a fulfilment of biblical prophecy."[1]

Several contributors to *The New Christian Zionism* express this view:

> . . . the miraculous appearance of the Israeli state just after the darkest moment in Jewish history is hard to interpret outside of a theological framework.[2]
>
> —Gary A. Anderson

> This writer and many others would see the modern nationalization of Israel as an act of God in keeping with the divine plan. . . . [T]he modern restoration of Israel to national status after so long a dispersion—one lasting almost two thousand years—needs to be understood from the perspective of Scripture (Tanak and New Testament) as an act of God in continuity with the divine plan for (1) an ethnic, national, territorial Israel and (2) the nations of the world.[3]
>
> —Craig Blaising

> The re-emergence of Israel as a nation after almost 2,000 years is truly remarkable. Not only did Israel become a nation recognized by other nations in 1948, but she has survived threats and wars to become a significant national power in the Middle East. This fact has been celebrated by Jews for theological and

1. Brickner, "Don't Pass Over Israel's Jubilee."
2. Gary A. Anderson, quoted by McDermott, ed., *The New Christian Zionism*, 74.
3. Blaising, "Biblical Hermeneutics," 99, 102.

nontheological reasons. However, a significant level of international support has come from Christians convinced that the reemergence of Israel as a nation in the land of promise must be seen as an act of God. . . . Israel's constitution or reconstruction in the land is a divine act.[4]

—Craig Blaising

What are some of the implications of this view? How do those who take this approach make sense of the history of the conflict and all that is happening in Israel-Palestine at the present time? Is this the only way to understand the sovereignty of God in the creation of the State of Israel?

1. Many of those who speak in this way have little to say about the history of the conflict

Some who hold this view see no need to study the history, because the supernatural explanation seems so obvious. If the creation of Israel is so clearly a work of God, is there any need to examine the history and study the whole process that has led to this end? Others are certainly prepared to comment on the history, but spend much more time studying the biblical and theological justification for this approach than commenting on the history.

Ten out of twelve chapters in *The New Christian Zionism: Fresh Perspectives on Israel and the Land* (2016)[5] deal with biblical and theological issues, and only two deal with the present situation in Israel-Palestine. One of these addresses the question of whether Israel has adhered to international law, reaching the surprising conclusion that it has not violated international law. The other is by an Aramaen Christian who is an Israeli citizen and describes the situation of Israeli Arabs in such positive terms that the majority of Israeli Arabs would hardly recognize. One chapter devotes two pages to put forward a defense of Israeli policies in recent years, and other chapters contain statements like these:

Jews did not rob land from poor Arab peasants.[6]

Jews can accurately say that they bought land fairly from Arabs starting in the nineteenth century.[7]

---

4. Blaising, "Biblical Hermeneutics," 98, 102.

5. McDermott, ed., *The New Christian Zionism.*

6. McDermott, ed., *The New Christian Zionism,* 21.

7. Bock, "How Should the New Christian Zionism Proceed?" 326.

... in matters of justice, Israel has a defensible track record.[8]

> I have offered a theological justification for Israel's exceptional case: God has a continuing covenant with Israel that includes land and the promise of return. These combined special claims override even the "natural rights" of the Palestinians to their lands.[9]

One contributor acknowledges the need to "face up to the complexity of the story for those who ended up displaced,"[10] while another stresses that both sides share equal responsibility for creating the conflict: "Jews and Arabs both need to 'share responsibility for the bitterness.'"[11] It is hard to escape the impression that all these contributors are far more interested in biblical interpretation and theology than in history and politics, and that biblical interpretation and theology must trump any judgments about the history.

Mark Kinzer's book *Jerusalem Crucified, Jerusalem Risen*, for example, has a chapter of thirty pages on Zionism, which includes a "theological assessment." He seeks to "provide a set of theological parameters," and addresses "several specific theological questions relating to the status of the Jewish State and its policies."[12] At the same time, he recognizes that "there is ample room for vigorous debate and disagreement concerning the practical details of the Israeli-Palestinian conflict."[13] There is no attempt, however, to investigate or assess the root causes and history of the conflict.

Vlach's book about the relationship between Israel and the church[14] claims to be only "a theological evaluation." He speaks of "the multiple and explicit references to a future for national Israel found in both the OT and the NT."[15] And since he believes that "the concept of *restoration* . . . includes the idea of Israel being saved and replanted in their land and given a unique role and mission to the nations,"[16] he must believe that what has happened in the land in the last 140 years is at least part of the fulfillment of prophecies about the restoration of Israel. He says that "national Israel will be saved

---

8. Bock, "How Should the New Christian Zionism Proceed?" 307.

9. Benne, "Theology and Politics," 245–46.

10. Bock, "How Should the New Christian Zionism Proceed?" 315.

11. McDermott, ed., *The New Christian Zionism*, 326.

12. Kinzer, *Jerusalem Crucified*, 241.

13. Kinzer, *Jerusalem Crucified*, 264.

14. Vlach, *Has the Church Replaced Israel?*

15. Vlach, *Has the Church Replaced Israel?* 104.

16. Vlach, *Has the Church Replaced Israel?* 19.

and restored with a role of service to the nations."[17] But how has the return of Jews to the land given the Jewish people "a unique role and mission to the nations"? Is this "role of service to the nations" being worked out at the present time through the State of Israel or will it only be worked out in the future? Vlach makes no attempt to relate his biblical interpretation and theology to what has happened and continues to happen on the ground.

Pawson has little to say about the nature and history of the conflict, but appeals to what he calls "circumstantial evidence" to support his Christian Zionism—like the increase in rainfall in Palestine "corresponding to the waves of Jewish immigration,"[18] and the fact that four British prime ministers "disappeared from the political scene after letting God's ancient people down," while "three prime ministers who held office for the longest time over the same period were all staunch Zionists."[19]

2. Historians believe they can explain Zionism and the process leading to the creation of Israel without resorting to supernatural explanations

Historians of all kinds—including Israelis and Palestinians—have little difficulty in explaining the whole process, beginning in the 1880s, which led to the creation of the State of Israel and all the different stages of the conflict since then.[20] These, for example, are just some of the factors that, they would say, contributed to the rise of the Zionist movement and subsequent developments in the Israeli-Palestinian conflict.

- Anti-semitism in Europe made many Jews feel that they could never be totally secure and that the only way to escape anti-semitism was to create a homeland in Palestine.

- The growth of nationalisms in Europe encouraged some Jews to feel that, since they were a distinct ethnic group, they could become a nation with a state of their own.

17. Vlach, *Has the Church Replaced Israel?* 205.

18. Pawson, *Defending Christian Zionism*, 94.

19. Pawson, *Defending Christian Zionism*, 115–16.

20. It may be significant that some Jews don't see any need to appeal to the miraculous. The late Rabbi Yeshayahu Leibowitz, for example, an Israeli Zionist rabbi, insisted that Israel was a purely human artifact, and not the fulfillment of biblical prophecy. See his *Judaism, Human Values and the Jewish State*, 214–20.

- There was a strong kind of Christian Zionism in Europe and the USA in the nineteenth century, which pre-dated the Zionist movement itself, and prepared the way for the wider acceptance of Zionism.

- In the Balfour Declaration of 1917, Britain was motivated more by anxiety over the stalemate on the western front in the war with Germany and by its own imperial ambitions than by concern for the Jewish people.

- The conflict developed into a clash of nationalism—Jewish and Palestinian—with two peoples claiming the same piece of land for different reasons.

- At the First Zionist Congress in 1896, under the leadership of Herzl, the Zionists began laying the foundations for eventual statehood, while the Palestinians, with their feudal society, were divided among themselves and found it difficult to respond in a coordinated way to the influx of Jewish settlers.

- Under the leadership of Ben-Gurion, the Zionists began preparing for armed conflict, even before the end of World War II.

- Feelings of guilt over anti-semitism and the Holocaust made many in the West—and especially Christians—sympathetic to the Jewish people and willing to support the creation of Israel.

- The victory of Israeli forces in 1948, 1967, and 1973 can easily be explained in terms of the different levels of motivation, preparation and unity on both sides.

- In the 1980s, the conflict between Israel and the Palestinians was caught up in the Cold War between the USA and its allies, on the one side, and the USSR and its allies, on the other. In recent years it has been caught up in the conflict between the majority Sunni states, supported by the USA, and the Shi'ite state of Iran, supported by Russia.

We have already seen (in Part 1, chapter 1) that there are often at least two different narratives of the history of this conflict. But if this history can be explained in a thoroughly rational and convincing way, most observers see no need to think in terms of miracle. If Christians are convinced by historical explanations, this doesn't mean that they don't believe that God is at work in history. It simply means that they don't need to resort to ideas about divine intervention to explain the process that led to the creation of the State of Israel. They also feel free to make the same kind of judgments that they make about any events in history.

3. However sympathetic we may be with the original vision of Zionism, we need to understand how Zionism actually developed; it didn't have to develop in the way that it did

If we define Zionism in the broadest terms as "a movement for (originally) the re-establishment and (now) the development of a Jewish nation in what is now Israel" (*Oxford English Dictionary*), few would want to question the original vision or to challenge the Jewish sense of attachment to the land and their desire to establish some kind of homeland in Palestine. No one should want to criticize

> the original nineteenth-century American Christian Zionism that sought to restore a long-displaced and tormented people to their ancient homeland as an act of restorative justice and for their ongoing protection from persecution. It looked to a new Zion that would model political and economic justice to a world as well as serve as an ongoing witness of God's faithful fulfilment of his promises.
>
> Blackstone and his earnest adherents, mostly mainline Protestants working with Jewish colleagues in an early mani-festation of interfaith collaboration, offered a vision of spiritual and moral beauty . . . ."[21]

While we today can appreciate the idealism of this vision, however, it is entirely appropriate to ask how much these American Christians knew about the situation in Palestine at the time and how they imagined their vision might be realized in practice. Can anyone seriously claim that the Zionist movement and the State of Israel have been modelling "political and economic justice to the world"? Where in Israel-Palestine today can we see an outworking of this "vision of spiritual and moral beauty"? Are the Palestinian Arabs to blame for not rolling over and allowing the Zionist settlers do exactly what they wanted? Everything depends on how this noble vision has actually been pursued and what it has produced.

Early in the twentieth century there were at least two visions held by committed Zionists. One did *not* strive for Jewish superiority in numbers or political power, but envisaged some kind of genuine co-existence with Palestinian Arabs and a real sharing of land and power with them. The other was convinced that the Jewish community should work to create a state in which Jews were a largely self-sufficient majority with political power. In the struggle between these two visions of Zionism, it was the second that

21. Tooley, "Theology and the Churches," 218.

gradually won the day from the 1920s onwards.[22] There is little point, there-fore, in discussing definitions or visions of Zionism—or trying to develop a Christian view of Zionism—without at the same discussing how it has actually developed in the last 140 years. Discussion of Zionism and Israel as a/the Jewish state also needs to address the actual situation on the ground at the present time rather than situations that might have existed if a different kind of Zionism had evolved.

4. This approach makes it difficult to make moral judgments about the history or to be critical of the State of Israel today

If the creation of Israel is seen as a work of God, the thinking goes, who am I and who are we to make moral judgements about the whole process? In *The New Christian Zionism*, Kinzer acknowledges the need for "a theologi-cal and ethical assessment of a multitude of contingent facts of history."[23] While he and the other authors offer very detailed biblical and theological assessments, they hardly even begin to undertake an ethical assessment of Zionism and the creation of Israel.

But how can one make any serious theological judgment without at the same time asking questions about what the creation of Israel and all its policies since 1948 have meant? Are we not allowed to ask about the appropriateness of Zionist settlers coming from Europe to join the Jewish community in Palestine (which in 1880 numbered less than 5 percent of the total population) and dreaming of establishing a Jewish state when they were such a tiny minority? What right did the British government have in 1917 to issue the Balfour Declaration, which was described by Arthur Koes-tler as "a document in which one nation solemnly promises to a second na-tion the country of a third nation"?[24] Are we not obliged to say something about the process of ethnic cleansing, documented in detail by both Israeli Jewish and Palestinian historians, which forced around 750,000 Palestin-ians to leave their homes between 1948 and 1949 in what became the State of Israel?[25] What about the five million Palestinian refugees all over the Middle East who, under international law, have a right of return? Is it in-appropriate to ask questions about the very concept of Israel as "a Jewish state," or "the Jewish state" when 20 percent of Israeli citizens are Palestinian

22. See Marcus, *Jerusalem 1913*, for an analysis of how this dilemma about the fu-ture of the Zionist movement was evident from around the year 1913.

23. Kinzer, "Zionism in Luke-Acts," 164.

24. Koestler, *Promise and Fulfilment*, 4.

25. Documented for example in Pappé, *The Ethnic Cleansing of Palestine*.

Arabs? Do we overlook the fact that Israel's occupation of the West Bank and East Jerusalem since 1967 is regarded by most of the world as illegal in international law? Would Israel have been able to pursue its policies in recent years without almost total, unquestioning support from the USA?

McDermott, the editor of this volume, writes in his closing chapter: "*That* the emergence of modern Israel is a fulfilment of prophecy seems plain, as we have argued in this book. But *how* all this is working out, and will work out, is a mystery we must not think we can penetrate with any precision."[26] We cannot of course predict how all this will work out in the future. And there is clearly much disagreement about responsibility for way the conflict has developed, and about theological interpretation of the history. But there is no mystery whatsoever about how all this has worked out in practice since 1880, 1948, and 1967, and how it is working out on the ground at the present time. Palestinians in Gaza would remind us that Gaza has been described as "the largest open-air prison in the world," and that the UN said in 2018 that by 2020 the area would be "unlivable." Israeli Arabs could point to statistics showing that their communities receive less proportionately for police, education, medical, and social services than Israeli Jews. Palestinians on the West Bank would speak about the security wall, the road blocks, the settlements, the imprisonment of women and children, the strangling of the economy, and the total control of borders and of water resources. Even Israeli Jewish politicians have been using the word "apartheid" to describe the situation that Israel has created in the occupied territories. There is absolutely no mystery about how all this is working out on the ground at the present time.

5. Conclusion

If we start with the assumption that the recent return of Jews to the land and the creation of the Jewish state must be a realization of the restoration of Israel as described in the Bible, it may seem natural to explain such unexpected developments in terms of the miraculous. But serious study of the history suggests that there are other ways of explaining these events, which allow us—even encourage us—to make moral judgments about all that has happened. It's easy for western theologians in the security of their academic ivory towers to speak about the miraculous and to present theological interpretations of what has been happening in Israel-Palestine. But they don't have to live with the consequences of the events about which they write with such confidence.

26. McDermott, ed., *The New Christian Zionism*, 331.

Those who see the creation of Israel as the fulfillment of biblical promises and prophecies are quick to point out that they do not offer "blind approval of Israel,"[27] and recognize that "this question of justice needs to be
addressed."[28] But they seem remarkably hesitant to comment on the history
and the politics alongside all their biblical and theological reflection. They
major on the predictive element of Old Testament prophecy, but don't seem
to share the passion for justice that we find in those same prophets. If they
recognize that Old Testament prophets predicted the Babylonian exile as
God's judgement on Israel, can they envisage a situation in which God is
obliged to judge the present State of Israel as severely as he judged Judah in
the sixth century BCE? Or do they believing that the State of Israel is secure
for all time, simply because they interpret literally the prophetic promises
that "they shall never again be plucked up out of the land that I have given
them" (Amos 9:15), and that Jerusalem "shall be inhabited, for never again
shall it be doomed to destruction" (Zech 14:11)? It's not unreasonable to
suggest that the more they appeal to scripture to explain the creation of the
State of Israel as the work of God, the more they are asking for this state to
be judged by the moral law contained in these same scriptures.

---

27. McDermott, ed., *The New Christian Zionism*, 102.

28. Bock, "How Should the New Christian Zionism Proceed?" 313.

Part 2

The Restoration of Israel in Ezekiel

Does Ezekiel have anything to say about the modern State of Israel?

Introduction

> The State of Israel is the culmination of 2000 years of Jewish prayer and sacrifice; it is the restoration of an ancient people, a valley of dry bones come back to life in the words of the prophet Ezekiel. It will always be a Jewish state.[29]
>
> —David Friedman, US Ambassador to Israel, 2020

> Ezekiel 37 is the famous "dry bones" passage that repeats the promise of Ezekiel 36 of the people coming back to the land and receiving the Spirit. They will be one nation under one King. This is happening and will continue to happen.[30]
>
> —Dan Juster

> We believe we are actually seeing that come to pass which was prophesied by Ezekiel (ch. 37) viz., the movement amongst the "dry bones" of Israel, bone is uniting with bone. . . . the uniting element being the possibility in the very near future of their being allowed to organise a Jewish State in their own God-given country of Palestine.[31]
>
> —Church Mission to Jews, editorial, 1918

29. Friedman, *The Times of Israel*, July 2020.

30. Juster, "A Messianic Jew Looks at the Land Promises," 75.

31. Editorial of Church Mission to Jews, 1918; quoted in Crombie, "CMJ and the Restoration of Israel."

The first quotation is from an article in the *Jerusalem Post* on 13 July, 2020, written by David Friedman, the US Ambassador to Israel. The second is from Dan Juster, a Messianic Jewish leader, who expresses a common view among Christian Zionists about the creation of Israel. The third quotation is from the editorial of a British Christian mission agency working among Jews, which was published in 1918—just months after the Balfour Declaration of November 1917.

It's very natural for Jewish people to make this connection between Ezekiel's prophecy and contemporary history. It's understandable that a text from Ezekiel, "I will put my breath into you and you shall live again and I will set you upon your own soil" (Ezek 37:14), is inscribed on the archway at the entrance to Yad Vashem, the Holocaust Museum in Jerusalem. But is it legitimate for *Christians* to agree with this way of using the text and therefore to see profound theological significance in the creation of Israel? If Ezekiel was prophesying in the sixth century BCE about his people's return to the land after their exile in Babylon, was he *also*—without knowing it—predicting a return of Jews to the land in the nineteenth and twentieth centuries? Most Christian Zionists don't hesitate to relate Ezekiel's words to both these events, because they see significant parallels between the return of the exiles from Babylon to the land in the sixth century BCE and the return of the Zionist settlers from the 1880s to the present day.

Christians who question this interpretation argue that, before making direct connections between Ezekiel's prophecy and contemporary history, we need to understand Ezekiel's prophecy in its original context, and then through the eyes of Jesus and the writers of the New Testament. Is there any evidence that they related Ezekiel's prophecy about the restoration of Israel to Jesus? Or did they think it was speaking about the end times in a more distant future?

We begin, therefore, by asking how Ezekiel's contemporaries would have heard his prophecies and seen their immediate fulfillment. This is important since, as Vlach insists, it "allows the OT texts to retain their integrity as revelation by paying heed to the original authorial intent of the OT authors."[32]

We then ask how the disciples of Jesus understood these prophecies in the light of Jesus's death and resurrection. Only then are we in a position to ask whether it is appropriate to see some of Ezekiel's prophecies being fulfilled in contemporary history.

---

32. Vlach, *Has the Church Replaced Israel?* 96.

1

How would Ezekiel's prophecy have been understood during and immediately after his lifetime?

Ezekiel was a prophet of the exile, having spent his early years training for the priesthood in Jerusalem. When Jerusalem was captured in 597 BCE, he was taken at the age of twenty-five into exile in Babylon with King Zedekiah. Five years later in 593, at the age of thirty (when he would normally have entered the priesthood), he received his call to be a prophet. Then in 587, ten years after being taken into exile, Jerusalem and the temple were destroyed, and the account of this news reaching Ezekiel in Babylon marks a pivotal point in the whole book (33:21–33).

His first task was to explain to his people that the fall of Jerusalem and the exile were God's judgment for the ways in which they had broken the covenant. God had taken away four of the most fundamental and significant gifts included in the covenant—the land, the city of Jerusalem, the temple, and the monarchy.[1] Having explained the reason for the exile, in the second part of the book (chapters 33–48) Ezekiel gives his people hope for the future. Not only will they be able to return to their land, but they will see that God is going to do something radically new in and through the restoration of the land, the city, the temple, and the monarchy.[2]

How did this glorious vision work out in practice? In 539 Cyrus defeated the Babylonian Empire and issued his proclamation allowing the Jewish exiles to return to their land. The first group of exiles returned with Zerubbabel in 538. A further group returned with Ezra eighty years later in 458. Another group returned with Nehemiah in 445. A total of around

---

1. Christopher Wright, *The Message of Ezekiel*, 227.
2. Christopher Wright, *The Message of Ezekiel*, 271–72.

50,000 exiles therefore returned during the period of around a hundred years. The return of the first group to the land is described in the last verses of 2 Chronicles and the first verses of Ezra:

> In the first year of Cyrus king of Persia, in order to fulfil the word of the LORD spoken by Jeremiah, the LORD moved the heart of Cyrus king of Persia to make a proclamation throughout his realm and to put it in writing: "This is what Cyrus king of Persia says: 'The LORD, the God of heaven, has given me all the kingdoms of the earth and he has appointed me to build a temple for him at Jerusalem in Judah. Anyone of his people among you—may the LORD his God be with him, and let him go up . . . .'"
>
> (2 Chr 36:22–23 and Ezra 1:1–3)

Ezra goes on to give a brief account of how this return worked out in practice:

> Now these are the people of the province who came up from the captivity of the exiles, whom Nebuchadnezzar king of Babylon had taken captive to Babylon (they returned to Jerusalem and Judah, each to his own town) . . . ."
>
> (Ezra 2:1)

The book of Nehemiah describes how Nehemiah received discouraging news about the situation in Jerusalem (Neh 1:3), and then returned to start rebuilding the walls of Jerusalem. This took place in 445.

How then do these accounts of what happened after the return from exile match up to the glorious future predicted by Ezekiel—in particular what he describes about restoration of the land, the city of Jerusalem, the temple and the monarchy? The exiles who returned with Ezra and Nehemiah were not very numerous. They returned "each to his own town" (Ezra 2:1), which must mean that they were returning to the towns and villages that their parents, grandparents, and great-grandparents had left when they were taken into exile. The amount of land that they occupied was only a fraction of the kingdom that had been ruled by David and Solomon. In 520 the prophets Haggai and Zechariah had to work hard to persuade the people to rebuild the temple, and this was eventually completed in 515 (see further Part 3). But it wasn't until around 440 that Nehemiah was able to rebuild the walls of Jerusalem. There was no restoration of the monarchy and no descendant of David sitting on a throne in Jerusalem—only governors like Zerubabel and Nehemiah. There were some signs of spiritual renewal under Ezra and Nehemiah, with a renewed commitment to obey the law.

But was this the glorious future that Ezekiel and the other prophets had described in such vivid pictures? When we look at the history of the people in the land after the return and in the next four centuries, it's hard to see much evidence of the national and spiritual renewal and revival that Ezekiel had envisaged, and the country came under the control of a succession of foreign rulers. It wasn't surprising, therefore, that in the following centuries people began to dream of a time when God would intervene in a miraculous way to fulfil the visions of the prophets. Some of these hopes centered round the figure of a Messiah, who would be either a supernatural figure descending on the clouds or a military figure overcoming oppressive foreign rulers and restoring Israel's independence.

These were the kind of hopes of a better future that were held by many Jews in the first century CE, and summed up by Luke in expressions like "the consolation of Israel" (Luke 2:25), "the redemption of Jerusalem" (Luke 2:38), "the one who was to come" (Luke 7:18), "the one who was going to redeem Israel" (Luke 24:20). People must have thought, "If the visions of Ezekiel and the other prophets have not been fulfilled in the history of the nation until now, surely God has to intervene in a dramatic way to demonstrate his faithfulness to the covenant promises!"

2

How do New Testament writers understand the fulfilment
of Ezekiel's prophecy?

Is there any evidence in the Gospels to suggest that Jesus saw himself as
fulfilling Ezekiel's prophecies? Do Paul and Peter use any images from
Ezekiel to describe what Jesus has achieved? How do the Gospel of John and
Revelation develop Ezekiel's vision of a new temple and life-giving water
flowing from the temple?

We begin by noting seven major themes that are associated with the
restoration to the land in chapters 34 to 48, and especially in 34 to 37, and
see how these themes are taken up in the New Testament. In the column
on the left are the words of Ezekiel, and on the right are texts from several
New Testament writers which contain echoes—sometimes very direct and
sometimes more indirect—of these same themes.

1. The Lord as the shepherd of Israel restoring his people in the land under one shepherd-king

"I myself will search for my sheep and look after them . . . I will rescue them . . . I will bring them out from the nations . . . and I will bring them into their own land." (34:11–13) "I will make them one nation in the land. . . . There will be one king over all of them. . . . My servant David will be king over them and they will all have one shepherd." (37:22, 24) "I will make their people as numerous as sheep. . . . I will establish them and increase their numbers." (36:37; 37:26).	"The Lord God will give him [Jesus] the throne of his father David, and he will reign over the house of Jacob for ever . . . ." (Luke 1:32–33) "I am the good shepherd. . . . I have other sheep that do not belong to this fold. I must bring them also. . . . So there will be one flock, one shepherd." (John 10:11,16) ". . . that he might create in himself one new humanity in place of the two . . ." (Eph 2:15)

Ezekiel begins his message of hope for the future with condemnation of a whole succession of Israel's rulers, past and present, described as "shepherds" who have totally failed to carry out their responsibility to care for the sheep in their care (34:1–10). He goes on to predict that God will raise up a king like David who will be a faithful shepherd-king ruling over his people. He also foresees the coming together of Israel and Judah, the northern and southern kingdoms, into "one nation in the land," and an increase in the number of people in the nation.

Luke's account of the annunciation to Mary shows clearly that Jesus is seen as the fulfillment of Old Testament promises about the messianic descendant of David: "The Lord God will give him the throne of his father David, and he will reign over the house of Jacob for ever; his kingdom will never end" (Luke 1:32–33, containing clear echoes of 2 Sam 7:13–16).

The Gospel of John develops Ezekiel's theme of Yahweh as the shepherd of Israel and the increase in the numbers of his flock in a remarkably creative way. When Jesus claims "I am the good shepherd" (John 10:11, 16), he is claiming to represent Yahweh, who has promised that he himself will act as the shepherd who seeks for his sheep and brings them into their own land. Jesus also says that he has "other sheep that do not belong to this fold"—presumably gentiles—whom he must bring into this fold, so that there will be "one flock, one shepherd" (John 10:16).

Similarly, Paul writes of the way Jesus by his death on the cross has broken down the wall of hostility dividing Jews from gentiles in order "to create one new man out of two" (Eph 2:15, NIV), or "one new humanity in place of the two" (NRSV). His emphasis on the unity of the church as the body of Christ underlines the fact that Jewish and gentile believers are "all one in Christ Jesus": "You are all sons of God through faith in Christ Jesus. . . . If you belong to Christ, then you are Abraham's seed, and heirs according to the promise" (Gal 4:26–29); "through the gospel the gentiles are heirs together with Israel, members together of one body, and sharers in the promise in Christ Jesus" (Eph 3:6).

Ezekiel's vision of "one flock and one shepherd" seems therefore to be developed by New Testament writers into the idea of Jewish and gentile followers of Jesus the Messiah who together make up the church. The church for them is not a completely new creation replacing something that existed before, but an extension of Israel—and for this reason a further fulfillment of Ezekiel's prophecy. We therefore have every justification for repudiating the idea that the church has replaced or taken the place of ethnic Israel, the belief that is known as replacement theology or supersessionism (See further Part 1, chapter 8).

2. The sanctification of the name of God, and Israel and the nations knowing that he is God

"It is not for your sake, O house of Israel, that I am doing these things, but for the sake of my holy name. . . . I will show the holiness of my great name. . . . Then the nations will know that I am the LORD, . . . when I show myself holy before your eyes." (36:22–23; cf. 36:36; 37:28)	"Hallowed be your name. Your kingdom come." (Matt 6:9–10) "Father, glorify your name!" (John 12:28) "Father . . . glorify your Son, that your Son may glorify you . . . so that the world may believe." (John 17:1, 21)
"Then you, my people, will know that I am the LORD." (37:13).	"Go and make disciples of all nations." (Matt 28:19)

This theme emphasizes the connection between the sanctification of the name of God and the nations coming to recognize his sovereignty. God declares that he is going to demonstrate the holiness of his name in such a way that Israel and all the nations will ultimately recognize his authority; and he will begin to do this by restoring the nation to the land from which they have been exiled. The restoration of Israel is therefore to be seen in the broader context of the vindication of God's name and his ultimate purpose to bless all the nations of the world.

The four chapters in which the promise of restoration is introduced are followed by two chapters speaking about God's judgement on "Gog, of the land of Magog" (chapters 38 and 39). Woven into the message of judgment is this theme of the need for God to vindicate his name and for both Israel and the nations to recognize that he is God (e.g., 38:16, 23; 39:7, 21–23, 25–28). The formula "Then you shall know that I am Yahweh" is repeated more than seventy times in the whole book and has been described as "virtually the signature of Ezekiel."[1]

How is this theme taken up in the New Testament? The Lord's Prayer expresses the longing for the sanctification of the name of God: "Hallowed be your name," and this is followed by "your kingdom come" (Matt 6:9). The idea of sanctifying the name of God must therefore be very closely linked to the idea of God establishing his kingly rule in the world. In the words of David Crump, "Ultimately, God's name is sanctified when his kingdom definitively arrives on earth, an arrival that means that God judges this wicked world with righteousness and that he completes the salvation of his chosen people."[2]

Mark summarizes the main thrust of Jesus' message in terms of the coming of the kingdom of God: "The time is fulfilled, and the kingdom of God has come near; repent and believe in the good news" (Mark 1:15). The Gospel of John sees the life, death, and resurrection of Jesus as the clearest possible vindication of the name and honor of God. When Jesus prays, "Father, glorify your name!" (John 12:28), and in the high priestly prayer says "Father, glorify . . . your Son, that your Son may glorify you . . ." (John 17:1), he sees his coming death and all that follows from it as the supreme way by which God is going to glorify his name—or, in the language of Ezekiel, show the holiness of his great name.

Ezekiel constantly looks forward to the time when "the nations . . . will know that I am the LORD" (Ezek 36:23). The Gospel of Matthew ends with the Great Commission, "Go and make disciples of all nations . . ." (Matt 28:19). And the book of Acts begins with the commissioning of the disciples: ". . . and you will be my witnesses in Jerusalem, and in all Judea and Samaria, and to the ends of the earth" (Acts 1:8). For New Testament writers, therefore, it is through the proclamation of the good news of Jesus that the nations come to know that Yahweh is God and therefore to sanctify the name of God.

1. Christopher Wright, *The Message of Ezekiel*, 35.

2. Crump, *Knocking on Heaven's Door*, 121.

3. Return to the land, living and enjoying prosperity in the land

"I will take you out of the nations . . . and bring you back into your own land; . . . they will live there forever." (36:24; 37:25)	"And he will send his angels and gather his elect from the four winds, from the ends of the earth to the ends of the heavens." (Mark 13:27)
"You will live in the land I gave to your forefathers. . . . I will resettle your towns." (36:28, 33)	"We who have believed enter that rest." (Heb 4:3)
"I will call for the corn and make it plentiful, . . . the desolate land will be cultivated" (36:29, 34).	". . . new birth into a living hope . . . and into an inheritance that can never perish, spoil, or fade—kept in heaven for you." (1 Pet 1:3-4)

The vision of the valley of dry bones (37:1-10) is included in the four chapters in which all these seven themes are introduced (34-37), and the meaning of the vision is spelled out clearly in the following verses: ". . . these bones are the whole house of Israel, . . . I am going to open your graves and bring you up from them; I will bring you back to the land of Israel" (37:11-12). This return will amount to a resurrection of the nation; and when they return, they will be completely secure and enjoy the prosperity provided by the land. Towards the end of the book, we are given further details about the boundaries of the land and how it is to be divided equally between the twelve tribes (47:13—48:29).

The promise to bring exiles back to the land looks at first sight as if it has no echoes in the New Testament. But scholars like N. T. Wright have argued that Jesus' use of Old Testament texts concerning the return from the Babylonian exile—taken mostly from Isaiah—suggest that Jesus saw his people as still in a state of exile, and announced that he was going to lead them out of exile.[3] The clearest examples come in his address in the synagogue in Nazareth ("The Spirit of the Lord is on me . . . ," Luke 4:18-19, quoting Isa 61:1-2), and his response to the disciples of John the Baptist, in which he describes his healing miracles in the poetic language used by Isaiah to describes the exiles returning to the land ("The blind receive sight, the lame walk . . . ," Luke 7:22, quoting Isa 35:5-6).[4] Jesus is therefore using language associated with the return of exiles to the land from Babylon to describe what he is doing in his public ministry. Could it be also that when Jesus calls his first disciples with the words "Follow me, and I will make you

3. For example, in N. T. Wright, *The New Testament and the People of God* and *Jesus and the Victory of God*.

4. See Chapman, *Whose Promised Land?* 223-25.

fish for people" (Mark 1:17; "fishers of men," NIV), there is an echo of the words of Jeremiah, where God says: "I will bring them back to their own land . . . I am now sending for many fishermen . . . and they shall catch them . . ." (Jer 16:15–16)?

It may seem strange to include the words of Jesus about the Son of Man sending his angels to "gather his elect" (Mark 13:27) in this context. But since the word *angelos* can be translated as either "angel" or "messenger," it is perfectly possible that Jesus could be speaking about the proclamation of the gospel as a way of gathering the elect into the kingdom of God. The people referred to as "his elect" could hardly refer only to Jewish exiles being gathered from the nations to return to the land.

In discussing the theme of the land (in Part 1, chapter 7), we noted that the only clear and explicit reference to "the land" in the Gospels is the saying "Blessed are the meek, for they shall inherit the earth (i.e., the land)" (Matt 5:5), which is a straight quotation from Psalm 37:11.[5] We noted that some argue that Jesus has little to say about the land because he could assume that all the promises and prophecies about the land in the Old Testament would one day be fulfilled at some time in the future, and there was therefore no need for him to say anything further about the land. It was suggested, however, that the more convincing explanation is that Jesus was claiming that Old Testament promises and prophecies—*including* those about the nation and the land—were about to be fulfilled in the kingdom of God, which was coming through him.[6]

It was also pointed out that New Testament writers use Old Testament terminology about the land (in particular the word "inheritance," *kleronomia*) to speak about what all believers possess in Christ. Thus, Paul in his farewell address to the Ephesian elders, echoing Joshua's farewell address (Josh 23:1–16), speaks about "the word of his [God's] grace, which . . . can give you an inheritance among all those who are sanctified" (Acts 20:32). Peter speaks of how all believers experience "new birth into a living hope . . . and into an inheritance that can never perish, spoil or fade—kept in heaven for you . . ." (1 Pet 1:3–4). The letter to the Hebrews was addressed primarily to Jewish followers of Jesus, who might have been expected to hold onto the hope that promises and prophecies about the land would one day be fulfilled in a very literal way. But the writer gives no hint of any expectation of a literal fulfilment, and instead develops the theme of the land in a completely new direction. He speaks of the land as "that rest," saying that "we who have believed enter that rest" (Heb 4:3). And traditional

---

5. See Davies, *The Gospel and the Land*, 359–62.
6. See Chapman, *Whose Promised Land?* 221–23.

Jewish hopes about Jerusalem for the writer are no longer centered on the actual city of Jerusalem: "But you have come to Mount Zion, to the heavenly Jerusalem, the city of the living God. . . . But you have come to the church of the firstborn, . . . to God, . . . to Jesus the mediator of a new covenant" (Heb 12:22–24) (See further Part 1, chapter 7).

4. Cleansing from sin

"I will sprinkle clean water on you, and . . . you will be clean from all your impurities." (36:25)	". . . the blood of Jesus . . . purifies us from all sin." (1 John 1:7) ". . . let us draw near . . . having our hearts sprinkled to cleanse us." (Heb 10:22)

There can hardly be any doubt that New Testament writers consistently think of the death of Jesus as the one sacrifice that deals with human sinfulness, enabling believers to receive divine forgiveness and experience cleansing from sin. In the words of John, for example, "the blood of Jesus . . . purifies us from all sin" (1 John 1:7). And in the words of Hebrews, we are able to draw near to God with confidence "having our hearts sprinkled to cleanse us from a guilty conscience" (Heb 10:20). Christians of all kinds should have no difficulty in affirming that Ezekiel's vision concerning cleansing from sin has been fulfilled uniquely and once for all through the death of Jesus.

5. The gift of a new heart and God's Spirit leading to obedience

"I will give you a new heart and put a new spirit in you. . . . I will . . . give you a heart of flesh. . . . I will put my Spirit in you and move you to follow my decrees and be careful to keep my laws." (36:26–27)	"Receive the Holy Spirit . . . ." (John 20:22) ". . . in order that the righteous requirements of the law might be fulfilled in us, who . . . live according to the Spirit." (Rom 8:4)

This promise of "a new heart and . . . a new spirit" is linked in Ezekiel with promises about a return to the land and spiritual cleansing (36:24–25). When the risen Jesus breathes on the disciples and says, "Receive the Holy Spirit" (John 20:22), there is a clear echo of God's promise to the nation in Ezekiel: "I will put my Spirit in you" (Ezek 36:26). The end result of the gift of the new heart and the Spirit of God is that God's people are now better able to live up to the standards that God has set. Thus, in the words of Paul, "the righteous requirements of the law" can be fulfilled "in us, who live according to the Spirit" (Rom 8:4). It is only the gift of the Holy Spirit which creates "a new heart and . . . a new spirit" and which enables believers to fulfil "the righteous requirements of the law."

If Christian Zionists accept that this is how Ezekiel's prophecy about everything that is associated with a return to the land has been fulfilled in the coming of Christ, it is strange to see how these same verses are related by some also to the return of Jews to the land in recent history. Juster, for example, writes:

> In this passage on the New Covenant—parallel to Jeremiah 31—we have an amazing promise to the ethnic/national people that has not yet been fulfilled. The meaning is plain. The promise of being born again is connected to the return to the land, and there is a spiritual conversion.[7]

There is no recognition here that, for New Testament writers, it is through Jesus as Messiah that believers receive a new heart and a new spirit and experience a new birth. It is hard to believe that the same vision of all that is promised in the new covenant can be related *both* to what is offered to all who believe in Jesus *and* to the creation of the Jewish state in the twentieth century.

6. A covenant of peace, an everlasting covenant

| "I will make a covenant of peace with them . . . an everlasting covenant." (37:26) | "This is the new covenant in my blood." (Luke 22:20) |
| | "Jesus the mediator of a new covenant." (Heb 12:24) |

The promise in Ezekiel of "a covenant of peace . . . an everlasting covenant" is no doubt to be understood as a further affirmation and development of the covenants that God had already made with his people. The words of Jesus at the Last Supper emphasize the *newness* of what he is about to achieve, but at the same time imply a real *continuity* with all the previous covenants. A whole chapter in Hebrews develops the idea of Jesus as the high priest of the new covenant, and includes a long quotation from a chapter in Jeremiah that describes the new covenant in terms of return to the land, the law being written in the heart, the renewal of the covenant relationship between God

---

7. Juster, "A Messianic Jew Looks at the Land Promises," 75.

and his people, knowing God and enjoying forgiveness of sins (Heb 8:1–12, quoting Jer 31:31–34).

7. God's sanctuary among his people forever

"I will put my sanctuary among them for ever. My dwelling place will be with them. . . . This is where I will live among the Israelites forever." (37:26–27; 43:7)	"The Word was made flesh and dwelt among us . . . ." (John 1:14) "'Destroy this temple . . .' . . . the temple he had spoken of was his body." (John 2:19–21) "Do you not know that you are God's temple and that God's Spirit dwells in you? . . . God's temple is holy and you are that temple." (1 Cor 3:16–17) "Now the dwelling of God is with men, and he will live with them. They will be his people, and God himself will be with them and be their God." (Rev 21:3)

Ezekiel's final major theme in several of these chapters is the promise "I will put my sanctuary among them forever. My dwelling place will be with them" (Ezek 37:26–27). Since Ezekiel had for several years been in training for the priesthood in Jerusalem before he went into exile, he must have had intimate knowledge of the architecture of the temple and all its sacrificial rituals. During the exile, Ezekiel the priest is called to be a prophet, and when writing about the fall of Jerusalem, he is appalled to see the glory of God departing from the temple, since this action emphasizes that Israel's idolatry has led to God abandoning his sanctuary (10:1–22). In the second half of the book, however, he uses all his knowledge and experience of the temple to describe a new temple that God is going to bring into being after the return from exile. Having said that God is going to put his sanctuary among his people for ever (37:26–27), in later visions he describes in great detail his vision of this new temple and the area surrounding it (40:1—47:12). The climax of this description comes when he sees the glory of God returning to this temple, and hears that this is where God is going to "live among the Israelites forever" (43:1–9). From under the threshold of this same temple he sees life-giving water flowing down to the Dead Sea (47:1–12).

Did Ezekiel think he was drawing an architect's plan for a rebuilt temple in Jerusalem? The fact that he introduces the vision with the sentence "In visions of God he took me to the land of Israel and set me on a very high mountain . . ." (40:2) hardly suggests that he is describing a plan of this kind. Moreover, it doesn't look as if later generations understood Ezekiel's visions in this way, since, when the temple was later restored and rebuilt, there was no attempt to follow the details described by Ezekiel.

Are Christians today justified in believing it is God's plan that the temple should be rebuilt in Jerusalem—even to the point of taking Ezekiel's measurements literally and locating the exact place near the present Jerusalem where this temple will be rebuilt?[8] Is McDermott justified in claiming that "the New Testament authors believed the land continued to be God's holy abode"?[9] Or is Ezekiel using his knowledge of the temple and its rituals and his understanding of what the temple stood for to describe something that was much greater and more wonderful than any restored city or building could be?

His vision of a new temple and all the sacrificial rituals performed in it must surely be connected in some way with the central conviction that, through this new temple, the Lord was going to dwell among his people forever. This powerful image of a sanctuary through which God demonstrates his presence with his people forever is a major theme in the last chapters of the book, and the very last verse sums up the meaning of the city: "The name of the city from that time will be: The LORD is there" (48:35).

Christians should have no difficulty with the idea that all the writers of the New Testament see Jesus as the person through whom Almighty God had come to dwell among his people forever. Matthew connects Jesus with the name "Immanuel" in Isaiah's prophecy and explains its meaning with the simple words "God with us" (Matt 1:23, quoting Isa 7:14). And the same gospel ends with the promise of Jesus "And surely I am with you always, to the very end of the age" (Matt 28:20). If Christians see Jesus as the fulfillment of all that the temple had meant, is it reasonable for them to believe that Ezekiel's temple must one day be built in Jerusalem? After the incarnation, what would be the purpose and function of such a temple, and what further symbol of the presence of God among his people could be needed? When Jesus has "offered for all time one sacrifice for sins" (Heb 10:12), there is no longer any need for expiatory sacrifices in the temple.

The idea of Jesus as the fulfillment of all that the temple stood for is very prominent in the Gospel of John. In the first chapter, the word that is used to describe the eternal Word coming to dwell among his people (John 1:14) is *eskenenosen*, which is derived from *skene*, "tent," the word that was used for the tabernacle in the wilderness. It therefore means literally

8. See for example Glashouwer, *Why Israel?* 148.

9. McDermott, ed., *The New Christian Zionism*, 322.

"tabernacled." The tabernacle and the later temple built by Solomon in Jerusalem were seen as signs of God dwelling among his people ("Then I will dwell among the Israelites and be their God," Exod 29:45; cf. 25:8; 29:46; and "I will live among the Israelites . . .," 1 Kgs 6:13; cf. 8:12). And the glory of God had rested both on the tabernacle and on the temple (Exod 40:34–35; 1 Kgs 8:11). Ezekiel had seen the glory of God *departing* from the existing temple in Jerusalem; but in later visions sees the glory of God *returning* to the new temple, and life-giving water flowing out from under the temple down to the Dead Sea. It must have been this image that Jesus was referring to when he said, "Whoever believes in me, as the scripture has said, streams of living water will flow from within him . . ." (John 7:38). There is nothing else in the Old Testament except this vision of Ezekiel (which is described in slightly different forms in two other prophets: Zech 14:8–9 and Joel 3:18, 20) to which Jesus could be referring.

So when John speaks of the Word being made flesh and adds the words "and we have seen his glory" he seems to be saying: "We have seen the glory of God resting not on the tabernacle, nor on the Jerusalem temple, but on the face of Jesus of Nazareth. Jesus fulfils all that the tabernacle and the temple were meant to represent." He therefore sees Jesus as the fulfillment of Ezekiel's whole vision of the new temple. His account of the discussion between Jesus and the Jewish leaders after the cleansing of the temple underlines this same message: "Then the Jews demanded of him, 'What miraculous sign can you show us to prove your authority to do all this?' Jesus answered them, 'Destroy this temple, and I will raise it again in three days.' The Jews replied, 'It has taken forty-six years to build this temple, and you are going to raise it in three days?' But the temple he had spoken of was his body" (John 2:18–21). Burge sums up the idea of Jesus as the fulfillment of the temple in this way: "*Divine space is now no longer located in a place but in a person. . . .* In Christ the Temple had been eclipsed. In Christ, the holiest of all Judaism's places had found their fulfillment."[10]

One further development of the idea of the temple in the New Testament is the way Paul speaks of every Christian believer as a temple in which the Spirit of God lives: "Do you not know that you are God's temple and that God's Spirit dwells in you?" (1 Cor 3:16). N. T. Wright points out how surprising and significant this idea must have sounded to Paul's readers: "when Paul uses such an image within twenty-five years of the crucifixion (with the actual temple still standing), it is a striking index of the immense change that has taken place in his thought."[11]

10. Burge, *Jesus and the Land*, 52.

11. N. T. Wright, "Jerusalem in the New Testament," 70.

The book of Revelation reminds us that God's plan of salvation for the world has not yet reached its consummation: "I saw the Holy City, the new Jerusalem, coming down out of heaven from God. . . . And I heard a loud voice from the throne saying, 'Now the dwelling of God is with men, and he will live with them. They will be his people, and God himself will be with them and be their God'" (Rev 21:3). We shall see later (Part 3, chapter 4) that John's vision of the holy city coming down from heaven may be describing not only the final consummation of God's purposes for the world, but a present reality—that because of the incarnation and the gift of the Holy Spirit, Almighty God is even now living among his people.

There is ample evidence, therefore, that New Testament writers believed that Ezekiel's prophecy about God putting his sanctuary among his people and dwelling with them forever had been fulfilled in the coming of Jesus.

8. Conclusion

Christians generally have no difficulty in seeing most of these themes of Ezekiel's prophecy—about the Davidic shepherd-king, the sanctification of the name of God, the nations knowing that he is God, cleansing from sin, the gift of a new heart and of God's Spirit, the covenant of peace and God's sanctuary being among his people for ever—as being fulfilled in the coming of Christ. We have argued that the themes concerning the nation and the land are *also* related by New Testament writers to Jesus and to all that is offered through him.

It therefore becomes much harder for Christians to believe that the prophecies about the people and the land are in a special category, separate from all the other themes of Ezekiel's prophecy, and that they demand a literal fulfilment. If New Testament writers see the incarnation and the death and resurrection of Jesus as the further fulfilment of Ezekiel's prophecy about the restoration of Israel, how can we also use this same language to interpret the events of the last 140 years in the Middle East?

3

Can Ezekiel's prophecy be related to contemporary history?

If most Christians agree that New Testament writers see Jesus as a further stage (after the return from exile) in the fulfillment of Ezekiel's prophecy, does this rule out the possibility that *some* of the themes (especially those concerning the nation and the land) must be understood very literally, and *can* and *should* be related to the return of Jewish people to the land in recent history? Can we not accept the idea of "a double fulfilment or application—one for the church in the present and one for national Israel in the future"?[1]

There are three reasons for challenging this idea, which is a basic assumption of restorationism.

1. There are significant differences between the return of exiled Jews to the land after the Babylonian captivity and the return of Jews to the land since the 1880s

The return from exile between 538 and 445 BCE was a relatively peaceful return. While there was some friction with the local inhabitants, the exiles were returning to homes and land that had belonged to their families when they were taken into exile (Ezra 2:1). Jewish immigrants coming to the land since the 1880s have certainly come peacefully. But their return in increasing numbers over many decades and their determination to create not only "a Jewish homeland" but also "a Jewish state" in which they would be the majority and hold political power inevitably provoked hostility from Palestinian Arabs. The recent return of Jews to the land, the creation of the

---

1. Vlach, *Has the Church Replaced Israel?* 117.

State of Israel and the ongoing conflict between Israel and the Palestinians, therefore, have more in common with Joshua's conquest of the land than the relatively peaceful return to the land after the Babylonian exile.

2. The return in the nineteenth and twentieth centuries has not been preceded by repentance, and therefore does not fulfil the conditions laid down in Deuteronomy 30:1–10

The book of Deuteronomy spells out very clearly that if the people break the terms of their covenant with Yahweh, he will send them into exile. Moses is explicit about the consequences of disobedience: "I call heaven and earth to witness against you today that you will soon utterly perish from the land. . . . The LORD will scatter you among the peoples; only a few of you will be left among the nations" (Deut 4:26–27). Later, however, he assures them that if they repent in their exile, he will bring them back to the land:

> When all these blessings and curses I have set before you come upon you and you take them to heart wherever the LORD your God disperses you among the nations, and when you and your children return to the LORD your God and obey him with all your heart and with all your soul according to everything I command you today, then the LORD your God will restore your fortunes and have compassion on you and gather you again from all the nations where he scattered you."
>
> (Deut 30:1–3)

Zechariah in his first message to his people reminds them that the exile was God's judgment on the nation, but goes on to say: "So they repented and said, 'The LORD of hosts has dealt with us according to our ways and deeds, just as he planned to do'" (Zech 1:6). The prayers offered during the exile as recorded in Nehemiah and Daniel are clear expressions of repentance (Neh 1:4–11; Dan 9:1–19). These prayers suggest that because there was some genuine repentance—at least on the part of some of the leaders of the community—God was able to bring them back to the land in accordance with the terms that had already been laid down through Moses. Can those who see the recent return as being very similar to the return from Babylon point to any kind of repentance within Jewish communities comparable to the repentance expressed by the exiles returning from Babylon? Since the Zionist movement in its early years was a largely secular movement, where were the signs of the kind of repentance described in Deuteronomy?

Christian Zionists who recognize this problem point to several verses in Ezekiel and other prophets which speak about repentance which will *follow* the return (e.g., Ezek 36:25–26, 31). They argue that, while repentance for the exiles from Babylon came *before* and *after* their return, Jews returning in recent history have returned "in unbelief," but that *after* their return many are coming to accept Jesus as Messiah. Juster, for example, lists eleven passages which "indicate that a return to the land before transformation and righteousness is envisioned." Commenting on these verses and on the vision of the valley of dry bones, he writes:

> In this passage on the New Covenant . . . we have an amazing promise to the ethnic/national people *that has not yet been fulfilled.* The meaning is plain. The promise of being born again is connected to the return to the land, and there is a national conversion. . . . Ezekiel 37 is the famous "dry bones" passage that repeats the promise of Ezekiel 36 of the people coming back to the land and receiving the Spirit. They will be one nation under one King. *This is happening and will continue to happen.*[2]

Juster makes no reference here to ways in which New Testament writers relate Ezekiel's prophecy about new birth and the gift of the Spirit to Jesus. He simply by-passes the New Testament in order to make connections with recent history. But if Christian Zionists want to appeal to Ezekiel's prophecy about return to the land, they are still faced with the problem that, according to Deuteronomy 30, there must be repentance *before* God can bring exiled Israel back to their land.

3. It's hard to separate the prophecies about a return to the land from all the other prophecies that speak about the spiritual renewal of the nation of Israel

Ezekiel's prophecies about a return to the land are closely linked—often in the same sentence—to prophecies about the spiritual renewal of the nation. In 34:11–24, for example, return to the land is intimately bound up with the prophecy of the Lord as the shepherd-king who will look after his people by placing over them "one shepherd, my servant David." In 36:33 resettlement in the land is linked with cleansing. In 37:12–14 and 39:28–29 gathering into the land is linked to the pouring out of the Spirit. And in 37:21–23 the return is linked with the reuniting of the nation under one king, cleansing, and the renewal of the covenant relationship with God.

---

2. Juster, "A Messianic Jew Looks at the Land Promises," 74–75 (author's italics).

If New Testament writers consistently relate the Lord as the shepherd-king, cleansing from sin, and the giving of the Spirit to the work of Jesus, it is hard to see how promises about a return to the land can be extracted from all these other blessings that are described in these chapters and related to the recent return of the Jews to the land. It requires an impossible kind of surgery to separate the promise of return from all the other language—about cleansing from sin, the new heart, the gift of the Spirit, the uniting of the nation under one king and the establishing of God's sanctuary in the land—and claim that the recent return must be seen as a further, literal fulfillment of Ezekiel's vision of national and spiritual rebirth.

Conclusion to Part 2

Ezekiel's prophecy concerning the restoration of Israel was fulfilled initially in the return to the land after the exile. But for several centuries there were few signs of the national and spiritual renewal that was supposed to accompany the return. Our study of all the themes related to the restoration of Israel in Ezekiel's prophecy suggests that *all* of them—*including those related to the nation and the land*—were linked in one way or another by New Testament writers to Jesus and to his church. And there is nothing to suggest that they continued to look forward to the restoration of national sovereignty in the land as an important part of God's plan for Israel or for the world.

The way New Testament writers interpreted the visions of Ezekiel in the light of Christ suggests that there was something much more creative going on in their minds than simply seeing predictions being fulfilled. Ezekiel's visions of the restoration of Israel led to a glorious climax in the temple in which God was going to "live among the Israelites for ever" (Ezek 43:7) and in the city whose name would always be "The LORD is there" (Ezek 48:35). If we believe, therefore, that it was uniquely in Jesus that God has come to live among us, we shouldn't be looking to see the fulfillment of Ezekiel's visions *either* in the twentieth century return of Jews to the land *or* the establishment of the State of Israel *or* the present city of Jerusalem *or* in a future millennial reign of Jesus in Jerusalem.

Perhaps Ezekiel, the priest-turned-prophet, was using the only language and imagery that were available to him at the time (related to the land, the nation, the city, the temple, and the monarchy) to hint at something much more glorious than a return to the land, the revival of the nation, the restoration of a building, and the appointment of a godly king. Perhaps God was using him to prepare his people and to open their minds for what it would mean when, five centuries later, "the Word was made flesh and dwelt among us" (John 1:14) and "God was in Christ reconciling the world to himself'" (2 Cor 5:19). And the book of Revelation tells us that the best is yet to come—not in the land or in Jerusalem, but in "a new heaven and a new earth" and "the new Jerusalem, coming down out of heaven from God" (Rev 21:1–4).

PART 3

The Visions of Zechariah

Trailers of the end times or hints of the incarnation?

Introduction

Every year since 1980 many thousands of Christians from all over the world have converged on Jerusalem in the month of September or October to celebrate Sukkoth, the Feast of Tabernacles. The biblical prophecy on which this celebration is based is found in the book of Zechariah: "Then all who survive of the nations that have come against Jerusalem shall go up year after year to worship the King, the Lord of hosts, and to keep the festival of booths" (Zech 14:16).

These gatherings have been sponsored by the International Christian Embassy in Jerusalem, and have been described as "a celebration of a Jewish holiday bringing together Christians and Jews with a common purpose: to uphold the significance of Israel as both a nation-state and as a symbol of the truth of biblical prophecy."[1] In the words of David Parsons, vice-president of the International Christian Embassy in Jerusalem, "They're following the invitation of Zechariah 14 where it says that one day all the nations will come up to celebrate this biblical feast in Jerusalem, to worship the Lord and keep the Feast of Tabernacles and we're showing up now as a statement of faith that that day is coming when the Messiah will rule here."[2]

---

1. https://censamm.org/resources/profiles/christian-zionism [Accessed January 2019].

2. David Parsons, https://censamm.org/resources/profiles/christian-zionism [Accessed January 2019].

Here are Christians who interpret passages of Zechariah very literally—as straightforward descriptions of what is to happen in the end times. Many of them therefore interpret Zechariah chapter 14 as a description of a great battle at the climax of history, when the armies of many nations of the world will attack the city of Jerusalem but be defeated through divine intervention.

Zechariah is admittedly a difficult book to interpret—considerably harder than Ezekiel. But is this the only way to interpret it? An alternative approach offered here starts with two assumptions. The first is that there are significant differences between prophecy in general and the particular kind of prophetic writing found in this book, which is called "apocalyptic." Old Testament prophets, from the eighth century onwards, were attempting to interpret the past and present, addressing the particular historical contexts in which they were living, and looking forward to the future. Apocalyptic, however, developed some centuries later, mostly in times of national decline or disaster, and offered encouragement by interpreting a dire situation in the context of a great supernatural conflict. It often consisted of dreams and visions that were full of symbolic language. Zechariah, writing in the sixth century BCE, is much closer to apocalyptic than straightforward prophecy, and is often described as "proto-apocalyptic." Since symbols in these visions need to be interpreted to show their real meaning, they can hardly be interpreted literally.

The second assumption is that Christians need to read the Old Testament through the eyes of the writers of the New Testament. A genuinely *Christian* interpretation of every book in the Old Testament, therefore, needs to begin by asking the question "How did Jesus and the writers of the New Testament interpret this part of the Old Testament?" This will mean that, before attempting to make immediate connections between Zechariah's visions and contemporary history, we need to ask how the writers of the New Testament interpret these visions. Reading Zechariah in the light of the coming of Jesus should provide Christians with the lens through which they interpret his visions today.

If we follow this approach, we need to look first at the message that the prophet was conveying to his own people in their immediate context. What was God promising to do for his people, and what was he asking them to do in response? We will find that their immediate task was to continue with the work of rebuilding the temple, which had begun earlier through the encouragement of the prophet Haggai. In order to motivate his people, Zechariah was looking further ahead and presenting a vision that centered round Jerusalem and the temple—but was very much more wonderful than simply a restored temple. This vision was that, through what was going to happen in Jerusalem, God would one day establish his kingly rule not just in their land, but throughout the world. Christians believe that this kingdom of God came into being through the life, death, and resurrection of Jesus. Could it be, therefore, that Zechariah was using the imagery of battles, plagues, and earthquakes—which people could easily imagine—in order to describe something that would have been almost impossible for them to imagine?

We begin therefore by looking at recent examples of literal interpretation of the book of Zechariah, which focus on events that have been unfolding in the Middle East in recent history. This is the way that many millions of Christians all over the world interpret the book today, and it provides a biblical foundation for their Christian Zionism. Then, using the approach we have adopted with the book of Ezekiel, we focus on the message of the book of Zechariah as a whole and consider what the visions would have meant for his original hearers. This is followed by a study of how the writers of the Gospels and Epistles relate Zechariah's prophecy both to the coming of Jesus and to the end times, and how the writer of the book of Revelation seems to have interpreted Zechariah in developing his own unique kind of apocalyptic.

1

Zechariah interpreted as a literal description of the end times

In the writings of those who see literal fulfillments of Zechariah's prophecy in recent history and in the future, there are at least four major themes. All the following examples are taken from contemporary writers, most of whom interpret the book within a dispensationalist framework.

1. Zechariah linked to contemporary events

a) The city of Jerusalem will play a central role in the final battle at the end times

> Jerusalem's importance in history is infinitely beyond its size and economic significance. From ages past, Jerusalem has been the most important city on this planet. . . . More prophecies have been made concerning Jerusalem than any other place on earth.[1]
>
> —Hal Lindsey

> [Writing in 1994 about a future siege of Jerusalem by the Soviet army] There couldn't be a more perfect modern-day description of what was predicted hundreds of years ago in Zechariah 12–14. There it tells us that the last war of the world will be started by a dispute over Jerusalem. We've got that dispute right

1. Lindsey, *Israel and the Last Days*, 20, quoted in Sizer, *Zion's Christian Soldiers*, 103.

now. As a matter of fact, the West helped guarantee the world a dispute over Jerusalem by forcing the Israelis into a pact with the Palestinians.[2]

—Hal Lindsey

Let me present this brief summation. In the eternal counsel of Almighty God, He has determined to make Jerusalem the decisive issue by which He will deal with the nations of the earth. Those nations who align themselves with God's purposes for Jerusalem will receive His blessing. But those who follow a policy of opposition to God's purposes will receive the swift and severe judgment of God without limitation.[3]

—John Hagee

[Referring to Zech 14:9 and Jerusalem as the spiritual center of the world:] Jerusalem will be the capital city from which Jesus Christ will reign over the entire earth.[4]

—John Hagee

b) Many of Zechariah's predictions are related primarily, if not exclusively, to the Jewish people, ethnic Israel, and their future repentance after a return to the land

The order of events listed in Zechariah 13:7–9 describes the history of the Jewish people in a nutshell. First, the Shepherd Jesus is killed. Then the people of Israel are scattered. Then two thirds perish, even the little ones—1.5 million children were murdered in Auschwitz. Then the remaining one third in the land will be purified so that in the end: *"They will call on My Name and I will answer them; I will say, 'They are My people,' and they will say, 'The LORD is our God'"* (Zech. 13:9b).[5]

—Willem J. J. Glashouwer

Ezekiel 37 is the famous "dry bones" passage that repeats the promise of Ezekiel 36 of the people coming back to the land and receiving the Spirit. They will be one nation under one King. This is happening and will continue to happen. . . . [T]he

2. Lindsey, *Planet Earth 2000AD*, 247, quoted in Sizer, *Zion's Christian Soldiers*, 103.
3. Hagee, *Jerusalem Countdown*, 54.
4. Hagee, *Beginning of the End*, 183.
5. Glashouwer, *Why Israel?* 75.

idea that there is a return to the land as part of the process of bringing Israel to repentance and to her ultimate destiny is well established by these passages. In Zech 12:10 Israel looks on the One they pierced after the last days' war. Then all will repent.[6]

—Dan Juster

c) The modern State of Israel is associated with biblical Israel

There is a phrase in the sixth chapter of this book that Willem [Glashouwer] has used . . . which I believe goes to the root of the matter: "For Israel is a designated sign of God in the world." Her resurrection, her re-creation as a state, her survival through the sixty years of her modern history with its eight wars, are evidence of something God has constituted.[7]

—Lance Lambert

d) Descriptions of catastrophes like plagues, earthquakes, and topographical changes in and around Jerusalem are understood literally

The land of Israel and the surrounding area will certainly be targeted for nuclear attack. Iran and all the Muslim nations around Israel have already been targeted with Israeli nukes. . . . All of Europe, the seat of power of the Antichrist, would surely be a nuclear battlefield, as would the United States. . . . Zechariah gives an unusual, detailed account of how hundreds of thousands of soldiers in the Israel battle zone will die. Their flesh will be consumed from their bones, their eyes from their sockets, and their tongues from their mouths while they stand on their feet (Zechariah 14:12). This is exactly the sort of thing that happens from the intense radiation of a neutron type bomb.[8]

—Hal Lindsey

The lifeless Dead Sea will live for the first time since Creation, connecting through Jerusalem to the Mediterranean.[9]

—John Hagee

6. Juster, "A Messianic Jew Looks at the Land Promises," 75–76.

7. Lance Lambert in the Foreword to Glashouwer, *Why Israel?* 11.

8. Lindsey, *The Final Battle*, 184, quoted in Sizer, *Zion's Christian Soldiers*, 141.

9. Hagee, *The Beginning of the End*, 183.

The environs of Jerusalem will be transformed into a broad, low valley like the Arabah. This will both make Jerusalem stand out and make the surrounding areas more fertile.[10]

—John Hagee

The temple of Ezekiel, which will be the final temple, seems to be located in a different place—not on the Temple Mount in Jerusalem, but far outside the actual city. Zechariah says that Jerusalem will continue to be in its own place (see Zech. 12:6); the area to the south will become a plain (see Zech. 14:10), while the mountain of the house of the Lord will be established as the chief of the mountains and will be raised above the hills (see Isa. 2:2).

These details mean that the geography in and around Jerusalem will probably change. The Mount of Olives will split in two (see Zech. 14:4). Jerusalem will be hit by an earthquake (see Rev. 11:13), but in the end it will be an open place (see Zech. 2:4–5). No protective walls of any sort will be needed because there will be peace. The Prince of Peace will be there. No matter how dark history might yet become for the world and for the Middle East, Israel is on the way to her rest. He will come to give her rest. And the Lord will have His resting-place there forever (see Ps. 132:14).[11]

—Willem J. J. Glashouwer

Living waters are those which spring from the ground and last; rain water finds its way to the sea. . . . The water will flow through all the promised land bound on the east by the Dead Sea and on the west by the Mediterranean. These streams will be full not only in winter, when bodies of water are full everywhere in Palestine, but in summer also, when natural streams are dry in the holy land. The refreshing, abundant waters that God will give will flow perpetually.[12]

—Charles L. Feinberg

10. Hagee, *The Beginning of the End*, 183.

11. Glashouwer, *Why Israel?* 148.

12. Charles Feinberg, *God Remembers*, 199.

2. Some observations

a) No distinction is made between prophecy and apocalyptic

Biblical prophets claimed that they were speaking "the word of the LORD" into their different situations, conveying a divine perspective on the past, present, and future of their people. They did this by interpreting past and present events and by predicting the future, sometimes using straightforward statement of what God was going to do: e.g., "I will bring them out from the peoples and gather them from the countries, and I will bring them into their own land" (Ezek 34:13). At other times they describe this same return to the land in the language of poetry: e.g., "The wilderness and the dry land shall be glad; the desert shall rejoice and blossom. . . . And the ransomed of the LORD shall return, and come to Zion with singing" (Isa 35:1, 10).

But when Daniel describes a dream in which he says, "four great beasts came up out of the sea, different from one another" (Dan 7:3), he is not using the language of prophecy or poetry, but of *apocalyptic*, in which the fours beasts represent four different empires. Similarly, most scholars would argue that Ezekiel's vision of Gog and Magog, nations from the north that will attack the land but be defeated by a divine judgement through "pestilence and bloodshed, . . . torrential rains and hailstones, fire and sulfur" (Ezek 38–39), represents a kind of "proto-apocalyptic." In the following centuries, this kind of writing about the future developed into the clearly defined literary genre of apocalyptic, which was intended to assure people of the ultimate victory of God over all the powers of evil. Visions of this kind would not have been understood as a kind of video of the future, representing in exact detail what was about to happen. All the symbols and numbers and all the cataclysmic phenomena in the natural world that they described needed to be de-coded in order to convey their inner meaning.

If Zechariah's visions are full of apocalyptic language, it is inappropriate to read them as if they are intended to be understood as detailed descriptions of what is to happen in the future. One basic guideline, therefore, for understanding apocalyptic, in the words of Andrew Hill, is this: "be prepared to use your imagination to picture a world that transcends earthly reality."[13]

---

13. Hill, *Haggai, Zechariah and Malachi*, 114, summarizing L. Ryken, in *How to Read the Bible as Literature* (Grand Rapids: Zondervan, 1984).

b) While there is much emphasis in these writings on prophecies of Zechariah that are being fulfilled in contemporary history or are still to be fulfilled in the future, there is seldom any reference to how New Testament writers understood his prophecies being fulfilled in the first coming of Jesus

Willem Glashouwer, for example, sees Zechariah 13:7–9 as a summary of the future history of the Jewish people, and doesn't take into account that in Matthew's Gospel Jesus relates this prophecy very specifically to his arrest and the scattering of his disciples.

Zechariah 12:10 ("they look on the one whom they have pierced") is linked by Glashouwer and Juster with Revelation 1:7 (" every eye will see him, even those who pierced him; and on his account all the tribes of the earth will wail"). These verses are then related specifically to Jews turning in repentance to Jesus as Messiah, following the interpretation in Revelation. There is no recognition, however, that John's Gospel relates Zechariah's prophecy to the piercing of the side of Jesus in the crucifixion (John 19:37), while Matthew relates it to the destruction of the temple (Matt 24:30; see Part 3, chapter 3).

So what if, instead of reading Zechariah's visions as detailed descriptions of how history will unfold in the future, we take the book *as a whole* and work out first of all what it would have meant to Zechariah's contemporaries *in their context*? And what if, before trying to make a direct connection between Zechariah's prophecy and contemporary history in the Middle East, we take seriously how the writers of the New Testament interpret Zechariah and relate his prophecy to Jesus—both to his first and second comings?

2

Zechariah's message in his own context

After seventy years of exile in Babylon and the edict of Cyrus, the first group of exiles returned to Jerusalem in 538 BCE under Zerubbabel (Ezra 3:8; 5:16). Zechariah, who was born in exile in a priestly family (since his grandfather was a priest), could well have returned with them. The economic situation of the community in Jerusalem was dire, and the people would inevitably have felt discouraged—and perhaps even cynical—since they could see so little evidence of the national and spiritual revival that prophets like Isaiah, Jeremiah, and Ezekiel had predicted.

In 520, just seventeen years after the return, the prophet Haggai exercised his prophetic ministry over a period of only four months, calling his people to set to work to rebuild the temple (Hag 1:12–15). Zechariah began his ministry just two months after Haggai, and continued until 518. The visions and oracles described in chapters 1–8 probably come from this period. As a result of the encouragement from these prophets, the rebuilding of the temple was completed in 515. This was celebrated with a dedication (described in Ezra 6:13–18), and later that same year with a celebration of the Passover (Ezra 6:19–22). The oracles and visions described in Zechariah chapters 9 to 14 probably come from a later period of his life, and some scholars believe that these chapters were not the work of Zechariah.

Zechariah's immediate task was to encourage the people to complete the rebuilding of the temple, and he did so by assuring them that God had not given up on his promises to his people and wanted to see a restored theocracy under a godly leader with a functioning temple in Jerusalem. While calling his people to repentance and to immediate action in Jerusalem, he also looked further ahead to a more distant future ("on that day,

. . . ," a phrase that is repeated twenty times) when God would establish his kingly rule, not only within Israel, but also throughout the world (2:13; 6:1–8; 14:16–21). The basic message of Zechariah, therefore, is summed up by Barry Webb in the words "'Your kingdom come!' . . . It is about the future coming of the kingdom of God, and the need to live now in the light of it."[1]

1. The main message of the three main sections of the book

In the *Introduction* (1:1–6), Zechariah describes his call to be a prophet and sums up his basic message: "Thus says the LORD of Hosts: Return to me . . . and I will return to you" (1:3). In the light of what God is going to do among them, he is calling his people to repentance.

a) Zechariah's visions (1:7—6:15)

Each of the eight visions contains a particular message:

- the horsemen patrolling the earth represent God's sovereignty over all the nations, including those that have oppressed Israel (1:7–17).
- the four horns represent the nations that have scattered Israel and Judah and God's judgement on these nations (1:18–21).
- the man with the measuring line conveys the message that Jerusalem will be rebuilt and protected; it will also experience God's presence as "the glory within it" (2:1–5). God will continue to bring his people back from exile in Babylon, and as he dwells among his people in Jerusalem, "many nations shall join themselves to the LORD" (2:6–13).
- Joshua the high priest is confronted by Satan, but he and the people he represents will be cleansed from their sin (3:1–10).
- the lampstand and the olive trees symbolize the vital roles of Joshua the high priest and Zerubbabel the governor in the rebuilding of the temple (4:1–14).
- the flying scroll represents the judgement of God on all wrongdoing, reminding the people that they are under an obligation to be faithful to the covenant (5:1–4).
- the woman in a basket symbolizes the wickedness of the land, which needs to be removed (5:5–11).

---

1. Webb, *The Message of Zechariah*, 32.

- the four chariots patrolling the whole earth symbolize God's sovereignty over the nations and their history (6:1–8).

In these eight visions there are at least four main themes:
God is still passionately committed to his people and to the city of Jerusalem, and wants to see the temple restored and rebuilt as a sign that he is living among his people.

> Proclaim this message: Thus says the LORD of hosts: I am very jealous for Jerusalem and for Zion. . . . Therefore, thus says the LORD, I have returned to Jerusalem with compassion; my house shall be rebuilt in it; . . . the LORD will again comfort Zion and again choose Jerusalem.
>
> (1:14–17)

> Jerusalem shall be inhabited like villages without walls . . . and I will be a wall of fire around it . . . and I will be the glory within it. . . . I will come and dwell in your midst, says the LORD. . . . The LORD . . . will again choose Jerusalem.
>
> (2:4–5, 10–12)

The two key players are Joshua the high priest and Zerubbabel the governor, who has the task of rebuilding the temple.

> [Addressing Joshua:] See, I have taken your guilt away from you, and I will clothe you with festal apparel.
>
> (3:4)

> The hands of Zerubbabel have laid the foundation of this house; his hands shall also complete it.
>
> (4:9)

What God is doing for his people and Jerusalem in the immediate future will be "an omen of things to come" (3:8)—i.e., a foretaste of what God will do for all the nations in the more distant future, a time (referred to as "that day") in which the messianic figure, the Branch, will play a key role.

> Sing and rejoice, O daughter of Zion! For lo, I will come and dwell in your midst. . . . Many nations shall join themselves to the LORD on that day, and shall be my people; and I will dwell in your midst.
>
> (2:10–11)

> I am going to bring my servant the Branch . . . and I will remove the guilt of this land in a single day. On that day, says the LORD

of hosts, you shall invite each other to come under your vine
and fig tree.

(3:8–10)

Here is a man whose name is Branch; for he shall branch out in
his place, and he shall build the temple of the LORD.

(6:12; cf. 6:15)

*While God has a particular concern for Israel as his people, he is sovereign
over the nations and is at work in judging them.*

Thus says the LORD of hosts: I am very jealous for Jerusalem
and for Zion. And I am extremely angry with the nations that
are at ease; for while I was only a little angry, they made the
disaster worse.

(1:14–15)

These are the horns that scattered Judah . . . but these [the black-
smiths] have come to terrify them, to strike down the horns of
the nations that lifted up their horns against the land of Judah
to scatter its people.

(1:21)

b) Zechariah's messages (7–8)

This middle section of the book contains various prophetic messages, in
which some of the earlier themes are reinforced.
*God is calling his people to repentance and obedience to the ethical teaching
of the law. The earlier prophets had explained to people that their dispersion
and exile from the land came about because of their disobedience to the law.*

The word of the LORD came to Zechariah, saying: Thus says
the LORD of hosts: Render true judgments, show kindness and
mercy to one another; do not oppress the widow, the orphan,
the alien, or the poor; and do not devise evil in your hearts
against one another. But they refused to listen . . . and I scattered
them with a whirlwind among the nations.

(7:8–14)

*God is "jealous for Zion" and will "return to Zion"; a rebuilt and functioning
temple will demonstrate that God really is dwelling among his people.*

Therefore, thus says the LORD. I have returned to Jerusalem with compassion; my house shall be built in it, says the LORD of hosts.

(1:16)

The word of the LORD of hosts came to me, saying: Thus says the LORD of hosts: I am jealous for Zion with great jealousy, and I am jealous for her with great wrath. Thus says the LORD: I will return to Zion, and will dwell in the midst of Jerusalem: Jerusalem shall be called the faithful city, and the mountain of the LORD of hosts will be called the holy mountain.

(8:1–3)

While God has been at work among the nations in judgment, he has gracious purposes for them, and people of many different nations will one day come to seek God in Jerusalem.

Thus says the LORD of hosts: Peoples shall yet come, the inhabitants of many cities. . . . Many peoples and strong nations shall come to seek the LORD of hosts in Jerusalem, and to entreat the favor of the LORD. Thus says the LORD of hosts: In those days ten men from nations of every language shall take hold of a Jew, grasping his garment and saying, "Let us go with you, for we have heard that God is with you."
(8:20–23)

c) Zechariah's oracles (9–14)

These can be summarized under the headings (here in italics) of the NRSV.

i. Oracle 1. (9–11)

Judgment on Israel's enemies

God is going to judge many of the peoples and nations surrounding Judah, including Aram, Hamath, Tyre, Sidon, Ashkelon, Gaza, and Philistia. This judgment will mean that "no oppressor shall again overrun them [the people of Judah]."

The coming ruler of God's people

The promise of judgment on their enemies is followed immediately by the verses about the great king who will one day come to Jerusalem. These are the best-known verses in the book because of the way they are quoted in the Gospels. It is important to appreciate, however, that in its original context, this is a promise that, as the people commit themselves to rebuild the temple and live in accordance with the law, God is coming to dwell among his people once again. Since for several centuries there was no evidence of any kingly figure ruling the nations and bringing peace, it's very natural that Christians see the ultimate fulfilment of this promise in the coming of Jesus.

> Rejoice greatly, O daughter of Zion!
> Shout aloud, O daughter Jerusalem!'
> Lo, your king comes to you . . .
> He will cut off the chariot from Ephraim . . .
> and he shall command peace to the nations:
> his dominion shall be from sea to sea,
> and from the River to the ends of the earth. . . .
> On that day the LORD their God will save them
> for they are the flock of his people.
>
> (9:9–10, 16)

France comments that "The picture is of a humble and gentle king, who, like the Servant of Yahweh, is victorious only because God has vindicated and delivered him. And he comes to bring not war, but peace and prosperity."[2]

Restoration of Judah and Israel

In a situation where "the people wander like sheep" and "suffer for lack of a shepherd" (10:2), God is angry with the political and religious rulers, who are described as "shepherds" (10:3). But because "the LORD of hosts cares for his flock, the house of Judah" (10:3), he promises to restore them: "I will strengthen the house of Judah, and I will save the house of Joseph" (10:6). He will bring back more exiles who have been scattered among the nations and "bring them home from the land of Egypt, and . . . from Assyria" (10:10). "I will make them strong in the LORD, and they shall walk in his name" (10:12).

---

2. France, *Jesus and the Old Testament*, 105–6.

Two kinds of shepherds

In the first of two symbolic actions, Zechariah is asked by God to play the role of a good shepherd, i.e., a good leader, in order to demonstrate how God works out his covenant relationship with his people Israel. However, he has to watch the flock being destroyed because of their sinfulness. In the second symbolic act, Zechariah has to play the part of a "worthless shepherd"—probably representing all the leaders who have failed their people.

ii. Oracle 2. (12–14)

These chapters contain "visions of both judgment and salvation for Israel and the nations."[3]

Jerusalem's victory

The vision in 12:1–9 is of Jerusalem being attacked by "all the nations of the earth," but defended by God himself. As a result, all the nations that come against Jerusalem will be destroyed, and Jerusalem and its temple become "the cosmic centre of God's universal kingdom."[4] Emphasizing the significance of this battle, Webb writes, "This is not just 'another' battle; it is the last one—the battle of *that day* which will usher in the kingdom of God."[5] For Joyce Baldwin, the capture of Jerusalem "is the signal for the Lord's intervention to establish His kingdom over all the earth."[6]

Mourning for the pierced one

These verses describe the repentance of "the house of David and the inhabitants of Jerusalem." Their repentance and their mourning will take place "when they look on the one whom they have pierced"—or, as the Hebrew text says, "when they look *on me* [i.e., God] whom they have pierced." This repentance comes alongside the opening of a fountain that brings complete cleansing "from sin and impurity."

3. Hill, *Haggai, Zechariah and Malachi*, 257.
4. Hill, *Haggai, Zechariah and Malachi*, 270.
5. Webb, *The Message of Zechariah*, 158.
6. Baldwin, *Haggai, Zechariah and Malachi*, 60.

Idolatry cut off

All idols will be destroyed, and there will no longer be prophets who are able to deceive the people.

The shepherd struck; the flock scattered

"Strike the shepherd, that the sheep may be scattered." These enigmatic words suggest that the ruler, the shepherd who works with God to shepherd his people, will have to suffer and his people will suffer with him. But as a result of this testing experience, a remnant will be refined and Yahweh's covenant with his people will be renewed.

Future warfare and final victory

Chapter 14, the final section, begins with the words "See, a day is coming for the LORD . . . ," and the phrase "on that day" is repeated eight times. What follows is a whole series of pictures of what will happen on that day: the nations which attack Jerusalem are defeated and "then the LORD my God will come"; the natural order is transformed so that there will no longer be any night but only continual daytime; "living waters shall flow out from Jerusalem"; "the LORD will become king over all the earth"; Jerusalem "shall remain aloft on its site" and "shall abide in security": a plague "will strike all the peoples that wage war against Jerusalem," while those from the nations who refuse to join in the attack on Jerusalem instead "shall go up year after year to worship the King, the LORD of Hosts, and to keep the festival of booths"; finally Jerusalem will be a holy city in which every aspect of life will be holy.

2. Some observations

a) Because there is so much apocalyptic imagery in Zechariah, it can hardly be read as a straightforward prediction of history

The main features of apocalyptic, which are evident in Zechariah, are summed up by Hill as "divine revelation cast in the form of visions, the presence of angelic messengers who both deliver and interpret the visions, the use of symbolism, and the themes of judgment for the nations and the deliverance of Israel."[7] For this reason, as Ben Ollenburger explains, apocalyptic literature should not be read in the same way as prophecy and translated into a straightforward prediction of future historical events:

> In interpreting this vision in the contemporary setting, it is of the utmost importance to remember that this text is an expression of Zechariah's prophetic *vision* and not an objective reading of international history. The interpreter needs to struggle with this vision to discover what Zechariah is saying about God and God's people and not read it as a flat prophecy about international conflagration and the ultimate salvation of a chosen people.[8]

b) Jerusalem is important because of the temple; and the rebuilding of the temple needs to be accompanied by a rebuilding of the moral and spiritual life of the nation. The temple also points forward to an even greater way in which God is going to live among his people, thus fulfilling all that the temple stands for

"The book of Zechariah," writes Webb, "is about Jerusalem from beginning to end."[9] The first vision includes God's promise, "I have returned to Jerusalem with compassion, and my house shall be built in it" (1:16). In chapter 12, Jerusalem is mentioned twelve times, and the last paragraph of the book looks forward to the time when everything in the temple and every aspect of life in Jerusalem will be "holy to the LORD" (14:20–21). Zechariah's message, therefore, in the words of Hill, "extends beyond the material reconstruction of the Jerusalem temple to the moral and spiritual rebuilding of the Hebrew people, so that they might be holy unto the LORD and offer appropriate worship in the Second Temple."[10]

As we have already seen in Ezekiel, the tabernacle and the temple had been signs in Israel's history of God dwelling among his people. So when God says "I will come and dwell in your midst" (2:10), he is affirming that his presence will be there in the new rebuilt temple. There is, however, a suggestion that God is ultimately going to do something new, since his dwelling among his people is linked with the promise that "Many nations shall join themselves to the LORD on that day and shall be my people" (2:11).

7. Hill, *Haggai, Zechariah and Malachi*, 113.
8. Ollenburger, "The Book of Malachi," 829.
9. Webb, *The Message of Zechariah*, 33.
10. Hill, *Haggai, Zechariah and Malachi*, 116.

Elsewhere we're told that the person described as "the Branch" will build "the temple of the LORD" (6:13), and that "those who are far off [presumably gentiles] shall come to help to build the temple of the LORD" (6:15). Later we hear that "Many peoples and strong nations shall come to seek the LORD of hosts in Jerusalem" (8:23)—which would mean seeking him in the temple. Thus, in the words of Hill, "The restoration of the divine presence in Israel promised by the prophet has both an immediate and an eschatological fulfilment,"[11] and Yahweh's temple in Jerusalem will one day be seen as "the cosmic centre of God's universal kingdom."[12]

c) There are several figures which are generally understood as messianic

i. The Branch

The vision of Joshua the high priest is associated with a figure described as "Branch" or "the Branch": "I am going to bring my servant the Branch . . . and I will remove the guilt of this land in a single day" (Zech 3:8–9). Zechariah here is taking up the prophecy of Jeremiah, which identifies this person as a descendant of David: "The days are surely coming, says the LORD, when I will raise up for David a righteous Branch, and he shall reign as king and deal wisely, and shall execute justice and righteousness in the land. In his days Judah will be saved and Israel will live in safety. And this is the name by which he will be called: 'The LORD is our righteousness'" (Jer 23:5–6; cf. 33:15–16 and Isa 11:1).

Later we are told that this person will play a key role in the building of the temple: "Here is a man whose name is Branch; for he shall branch out in his place, and he shall build the temple of the LORD. It is he that shall build the temple of the LORD; he shall bear royal honor, and shall sit and rule on his throne" (6:12–13). This person somehow combines the roles of priest and king, as France explains:

> In Zechariah 6:11–13 the High Priest Joshua is symbolically crowned, and hailed as "the Branch" (Hebrew *tsmch*, a Messianic title derived from Jer 23:5 = 33:15; cf. Is 4:2), and it is predicted that he will rebuild the Temple and bear royal office, supported by a priestly figure. Joshua is thus set up as a type of the coming Messiah, and the prediction of building the Temple

11. Hill, *Haggai, Zechariah and Malachi*, 117.
12. Hill, *Haggai, Zechariah and Malachi*, 279.

is a symbol, probably of the Messiah's creation of a true worship-ing community.[13]

ii. The king

The king who comes to Jerusalem is described as "triumphant and victori-ous . . . , humble and riding on a donkey." Isaiah, Jeremiah, and Ezekiel had all looked forward to the future Davidic king (Isa 9:6–7; 11:1; Jer 33:15; Ezek 34:23–24; 37:24). This king would be like the king in Psalm 2, who "shall command peace to the nations; his dominion shall be from sea to sea, and from the river to the ends of the earth" (9:9–10; cf. Ps 72:8).

iii. The shepherd

Zechariah is told by God to play the part of "a shepherd of the flock doomed to slaughter," but is rejected by the sheep he is caring for (11:4–14). Later we read of God's shepherd being struck and his sheep scattered: "'Awake, O sword, against my shepherd, against the man who is my associate,' says the LORD of hosts. 'Strike the shepherd, that the sheep may be scattered.'" (13:7–8). The remnant who survive this refining process will be included among God's covenant people: "They will call on my name, and I will an-swer them. I will say, 'They are my people'; and they will say, 'The LORD is our God'" (13:9).

France notes the connection between the figures of the king and the shepherd:

> This section [chapters 9–13] introduces four figures which may be taken as Messianic: the king riding on an ass (9:9–10), the good shepherd (11:4–14), the one "whom they have pierced" (12:10), and the smitten shepherd (13:7). . . . Thus the four passages are seen as four aspects of a single Messianic concep-tion, "the Shepherd-King," presenting successive phases of his coming and the reaction of the people. It is a conception built up through reflection on the figure of the Servant of Yahweh in Isaiah, and therefore concentrating on the problem of the rejec-tion, suffering and death of the Messiah.[14]

---

13. France, *Jesus and the Old Testament*, 100.
14. France, *Jesus and the Old Testament*, 104.

3. Conclusion

We can conclude that Zechariah's immediate task was to encourage the people of Jerusalem to continue the work of rebuilding the temple, which had begun as a result of Haggai's ministry. They needed to hear that Jerusalem and the temple still had an important place in God's purposes for his people. But Zechariah had a message not only for his immediate situation but also for the more distant future, since, in the words of Hill, "The lines between the present reality and the future hope blur in apocalyptic literature."[15] Zechariah therefore wanted to motivate them by presenting a vision of a more glorious future in which the rule of God would be established "over all the earth." The messianic figure of the Branch, the Davidic king, and the shepherd would play an important role in the coming of the kingdom of God.

If this was Zechariah's message in his own context, how was this vision understood by the writers of the New Testament? Did they believe that the kingdom of God was still to come in the future? Or did they believe that it had begun to come in and through Jesus of Nazareth? Did they think in terms of a great battle that would take place in Jerusalem? How, in short, did they relate Zechariah's visions to the life, death, and resurrection of Jesus and to the end of time?

---

15. Hill, *Haggai, Zechariah and Malachi*, 249.

3

Zechariah as interpreted in the Gospels and Epistles

We will be looking here, firstly, for places where Jesus himself is recorded as quoting verses from Zechariah, and passages where a Gospel writer makes a clear connection with Zechariah, pointing out how Jesus has in some way fulfilled his prophecy. Secondly, we will be looking for any passages where significant words, phrases, or themes in Zechariah are taken up in the Gospels and Epistles and related in some way to Jesus.

When we speak of fulfillment, however, we're not simply thinking of Old Testament predictions of future events being fulfilled in the life of Jesus. Luke tells us that when the risen Jesus met the two disciples on the road to Emmaus, "beginning with Moses and all the prophets, he interpreted to them the things about himself in all the scriptures" (Luke 24:27). And when he met with the disciples in the upper room, he said: "These are my words that I spoke to you while I was still with you—that everything written about me in the Law of Moses, the Prophets, and the Psalms must be fulfilled" (Luke 24:44). This would suggest that Jesus was not only referring to predictions, but to all the major themes of the Old Testament—the promise to Abraham, the land, the children of Israel as the people of God, the Davidic monarchy, and the temple.

If the whole of the Old Testament, therefore, is pointing forward to Jesus in different ways, what we can expect to find in the New Testament is much more than a recognition of particular predictions that have been fulfilled in particular events in the life of Jesus. We can also expect to find many Old Testament themes being related to Jesus. What we are dealing with here is the difference between prophecy and typology. This is how the basic idea of typology is explained by Christopher Wright:

When somebody we know does something that we recognize as the way they always act, something very characteristic of them, we smile and say, "just typical!" or, "Typical John!" They are act-ing "true to type." It's what we've come to expect from that per-son. Once you get to know somebody well, you can see patterns and similarities in the way they behave. . . . God certainly acts in typical ways, so that those who knew him well in Bible times began to recognize God's ways. They saw the patterns and simi-larities between how God acted at one time and then another. . . . Now those who encountered Jesus in the New Testament . . . point out significant correspondences between things in the Old Testament and what God had now done in and through Jesus Christ. And they used those Old Testament things in order to explain many aspects of the meaning of Christ's birth, life, death, resurrection and ascension.[1]

France explains how typology differs from predictive prophecy:

A prediction looks forward to, and demands, an event which is to be its fulfilment; typology, however, consists essentially in looking back and discerning previous examples of a pattern now reaching its culmination. . . . [T]ypology is essentially the recognition of a correspondence between New Testament and Old Testament events, based on a conviction of the unchanging character of the principles of God's working, and a consequent understanding and description of the New Testament event in terms of the Old Testament model. The idea of fulfilment inher-ent in New Testament typology derives not from a belief that the events so understood were explicitly predicted, but from the conviction that in the coming and work of Jesus the principles of God's working, already imperfectly embodied in the Old Testa-ment, were more perfectly re-embodied, and thus brought to completion. In that sense, the Old Testament history pointed forward to Jesus. For the Old Testament prophets the antitypes were future; for the New Testament writers they have already come.[2]

Here then are eleven themes in Zechariah that are taken up and echoed in one way or another in the Gospels and Epistles. Some of them are very similar to themes that we have already noted in Ezekiel (Part 2). Words

1. Christopher Wright, *How to Preach and Teach the Old Testament for All Its Worth*, 69.

2. France, *Jesus and the Old Testament*, 40.

from Zechariah are in the column on the left and the verses in the Gospels, Epistles, and Revelation on the right.

1. Passages where Jesus himself quotes Zechariah or where a Gospel writer sees the action of Jesus as a fulfillment of Zechariah

a) The king coming to Jerusalem

"Rejoice greatly, O daughter of Zion! Shout aloud, O daughter Jerusalem! Lo, your king comes to you; triumphant and victorious is he, humble and riding on a donkey, on a colt, the foal of a donkey. . . . [H]e shall command peace to the nations; his dominion shall be from sea to sea, and from the River to the ends of the earth." (9:9–10)	"This took place to fulfil what had been spoken through the prophet, saying, 'Tell the daughter of Zion, Look, your king is coming to you, humble and mounted on a donkey, and on a colt, the foal of a donkey.'" (Matt 21:4–5; John 12:14–15; cf. Mark 11:1–6; Luke 19:28–34)

After listing cities and nations surrounding Judah that have been enemies in the past, Zechariah gives God's assurance that he will protect his people, so that "no oppressor shall again overrun them" (9:8). In order to fulfil this promise to give them security among the nations, God is going to send a king. But, instead of a warrior king riding on a horse, he will be a humble and gentle king riding on a donkey. This promise about Zion's coming king contains a clear echo of the promises in the Psalms about the anointed king whose rule will extend to the nations:

> I will tell of the decree of the LORD:
> He said to me, "You are my son;
>   today I have begotten you.
> Ask of me, and I will make the nations your heritage,
>   and the ends of the earth your possession.
> You shall break them with a rod of iron,
>   and dash them in pieces like a potter's vessel."
>
> (Ps 2:7–9)

> May he have dominion from sea to sea,
>   and from the River to the ends of the earth.
>
> (Ps 72:8)

Zechariah's picture of the promised king needs also to be related to the earlier promises of the ruler whom God is going to raise up: "I am going to bring my servant the Branch" (3:8), and "Here is a man whose name is Branch . . . and he shall build the temple of the LORD" (6:12). Through Zion's coming king, therefore, God is going to build a lasting temple, defeat his enemies, bring "peace to the nations," and establish his kingly rule throughout the world.

Matthew introduces the quotation from Zechariah with the formula about fulfillment used with variations twelve times in his gospel: "This took place to fulfil what had been spoken through the prophet." When John quotes the verses, he adds, "His disciples did not understand these things at first; but when Jesus was glorified, then they remembered that these things had been written of him and had been done to him" (John 12:16). Two of the Gospel writers therefore clearly see the way Jesus entered Jerusalem on a donkey as a direct fulfillment of this prophecy of Zechariah. Jesus for them is the human agent through whom God has begun to bring in his kingdom, bringing peace and security, not only to Israel, Judah, and Jerusalem, but to the whole human race.

b) The rejection of the good shepherd

"I became the shepherd of the flock doomed to slaughter. I took two staffs . . . and they also detested me. So I said, 'I will not be our shepherd. . . .' I took the staff Favor and broke it, annulling the covenant I had made. . . . I then said to them, 'If it seems right to you, give me my wages; but if not, keep them.' So they weighed out as my wages thirty shekels of silver. Then the LORD said to me, 'Throw it into the treasury'—this lordly price at which I was valued by them. So I took the thirty shekels of silver and threw them into the treasury in the house of the LORD." (11:4–13)	"Judas . . . brought back the thirty pieces of silver to the chief priests and elders. . . . But . . . they used them to buy the potter's field. . . . Then was fulfilled what had been spoken through the prophet Jeremiah, 'And they took the thirty pieces of silver, the price of the one on whom a price had been set . . . and they gave them for the potters' field.'" (Matt 27:3–10)

These difficult verses about the thirty shekels of silver being thrown into the treasury can only be understood in the context of the whole passage about two kinds of shepherds (11:4–17). Zechariah has declared God's anger against Judah's leaders, its "shepherds," whose failure has led to the people being scattered in exile. Yet he has also promised that God will gather them again and bring them back to the land (10:6–12).

In the following chapter (11), Zechariah is asked to perform two symbolic acts, a kind of enacted prophecy, that sum up the history of Israel—a history in which they have consistently broken the covenant that God had made with them. In the first, he is given the role of a good shepherd who cares for God's people, and takes two staffs. However, he is rejected by the very people he seeks to serve, and he breaks the first staff to demonstrate that God's covenant with his people has been annulled. He then asks the people to show their response—either by paying him or refusing to pay. They respond by giving thirty pieces of silver—probably related to the amount required in the Mosaic law as compensation for the death of a slave, and therefore "an indication of the high value placed on human life rather than of the paltry nature of the sum itself."[3] Zechariah is then told to throw the money he has been given into the treasury of the temple—no doubt because it was in the abuse of the temple that the nation's leaders had demonstrated their rejection of Yahweh, and thereby called down his judgment on the nation. After this, he breaks the second staff, signifying the break-up of the kingdom and the separation of Israel from Judah.

In the second symbolic act, Zechariah plays the role of a "worthless shepherd" (11:17), probably representing the bad shepherds/rulers of Israel who have been raised up by God as punishment for the rejection of the good shepherd. These rulers are going to be judged because of the way they have failed their people.

These two symbolic acts, taken together, are a reflection of the whole history of Israel. Their kings were intended to rule on behalf of God, but have completely failed in this role. It is in response to this situation that the prophet has earlier announced that God is going to send a different kind of king, "humble and riding on a donkey . . . and he shall command peace to the nations" (9:9–10).

Matthew's reference to the thirty pieces of silver paid to Judas for betraying Jesus can't be suggesting the fulfillment of a prophetic prediction. He seems rather to be making a connection between the rejection of the good shepherd by his sheep and the rejection of Jesus by his own people. And as the thirty shekels of silver are given to the shepherd as his severance pay and then thrown into the temple, so the Jewish leaders give Judas thirty pieces of silver for betraying Jesus, and the money is then returned to the leaders. In the words of Barry Webb, "In Zechariah it is God whom Israel values at 'thirty pieces of silver'; in the New Testament it is Jesus. The same

3. Webb, *The Message of Zechariah*, 151.

is true of the identity of the 'pierced one.' In Zechariah it is God who pours out his Spirit to bring about true repentance; in the New Testament it is the risen and ascended Christ. This (at first sight) puzzling use of Zechariah in the New Testament makes perfect sense in the light of the incarnation of God in Christ."[4]

In explaining the connection made by the Gospel writer, D. A. Carson points out that Matthew conflates passages from both Zechariah and Jeremiah while referring only to Jeremiah:

> The central parallel is stunning: in both instances Yahweh's shepherd is rejected by the people of Israel and valued at the price of a slave. And in both instances the money is flung into the temple and ends up purchasing something that pollutes. . . . Matthew sees in Jeremiah 19 and Zechariah 11 not merely a number of verbal parallels to Judas' betrayal but a pattern of apostasy and rejection that must find its ultimate fulfilment in the rejection of Jesus, who was cheaply valued, rejected by the Jews, and whose betrayal money was put to a purpose that pointed to the destruction of the nation.[5]

c) Looking on the pierced one

"And I will pour out a spirit of compassion and supplication on the house of David and the inhabitants of Jerusalem, so that, when they look on the one whom they have pierced, they shall mourn for him . . ." (12:10)	"But when they came to Jesus and saw that he was already dead, they did not break his legs. Instead, one of the soldiers pierced his side with a spear, and at once blood and water came out. . . . These things occurred so that the scripture might be fulfilled, 'None of his bones shall be broken.' And again another passage of scripture says, 'they will look on the one whom they have pierced.'" (John 19:33–37)
	"Then the sign of the Son of Man will appear in heaven, and then all the tribes of the earth will mourn, and they will see 'the Son of Man coming on the clouds of heaven' with power and great glory." (Matt 24:30)

4. Webb, *The Message of Zechariah*, 173.
5. Carson, *The Expositor's Bible Commentary: Matthew 13–28*, 563, 566.

The second of Zechariah's two oracles in chapters 12–14 focuses on the climax of the coming of the kingdom of God. It begins with a final conflict in which "all the nations of the earth" gather together to lay siege to Jerusalem, but are destroyed by God himself. Immediately after this assurance that God will protect his people and win the final victory of the nations, we have this surprising passage (12:10—13:1) in which it is not the defeated nations who are mourning, but "the house of David and the inhabitants of Jerusalem." This will happen "when they look on the one whom they have pierced"—or as the Hebrew text reads, "when they look *on me* [i.e., the LORD] whom they have pierced (*wahibbitu elai eth asher daqaru*)."

Webb writes of this passage, "Now indeed we are on holy ground, for we are approaching the most mysterious and profound part of Zechariah's message, and it has to do with the necessary place of suffering and weeping in the coming of the kingdom of God."[6] He goes on to explain the significance of the mourning:

> The picture that unfolds here is of a victorious army suddenly plunged into grief by the realization that its supreme commander has been slain in the battle and (worst of all) that his own followers have been responsible for his death. . . . The "pierced one" is none other than God himself, for it is he who expressly says: *they will look on me, the one they have pierced*. There is the essence of the matter. The victory that will usher in the kingdom will not be won without suffering, and none will suffer more keenly than the King himself. . . . The deepest pain is caused by the knowledge of who has done it. It is not the enemy that pierces God in this battle, but his own people, just as the son of 13:3 is stabbed by his own parents.[7]

In John's account of the crucifixion of Jesus, we are told that, instead of breaking his legs, a soldier pierced his side with a spear. John connects this action firstly with the Passover instruction that no bones of the lamb should be broken (Exod 12:46), and secondly with Zechariah's prophecy about the house of David and the inhabitants of Jerusalem looking on "the one whom they have pierced."

Matthew's echo of Zechariah's prophecy about the mourning of those who look on the one they have pierced comes in the eschatological discourse in which Jesus speaks about the coming of the Son of Man. For this reason, "This eschatological mourning of repentance," writes France, "will occur,

---

6. Webb, *The Message of Zechariah*, 159.

7. France, *Jesus and the Old Testament*, 160.

according to Jesus, when they see his triumphant judgment on Jerusalem."[8]
He explains further:

> The explicit allusion is to the mourning of Israel, which Jesus
> says will occur in AD 70, when the Jews see his act of judge-
> ment on their capital and nation. Such an allusion, however,
> could hardly be made without reference to what in Zechariah
> 11 is the cause of their mourning: "they shall look on me whom
> they have pierced." . . . The cause of the Jewish mourning at the
> destruction of Jerusalem is, then, the realization that the one
> whom they have rejected and killed has been given the domin-
> ion of the Son of Man, and is now their judge. . . . It is only after
> they have murdered him that the memory of his martyrdom will
> cause their repentance, and thus, after thorough purification,
> their final salvation. It seems, then, that in this martyrdom with
> its issue in the salvation of God's people Jesus saw a prediction
> of his own fate.[9]

It must also be significant that when Matthew echoes Zechariah's words
about the mourning, it's not only the Jewish people who will be mourning,
but "all the tribes of the earth" (Matt 24:30). France draws attention to the
fact that, while the rabbis at the time of Jesus believed that Zechariah was
naming the people of Israel as those who would be mourning, Jesus wid-
ened this out to include "all the tribes of the earth":

> The Rabbis, in accordance with the original meaning, saw the
> mourning as leading to the salvation of the mourners, Israel, by
> giving them the opportunity of restoration to fellowship with
> God. Jesus, however, sees the salvation as coming to God's elect
> in all parts of the world, not to the mourning Jews. Thus his
> idea of the Christian community as the true Israel leads to an
> unprecedented application of Zechariah 12:10ff. In this case, the
> rabbinic application, as far as it can be ascertained, is closer to
> the original sense.[10]

Perhaps it should not surprise us to find that two Gospel writers interpret Zechariah's words about mourning in different ways. John relates them
to the crucifixion, while Matthew relates them to the whole sequence of
events leading up to the destruction of Jerusalem. We shall see later that the
writer of Revelation relates these words neither to the crucifixion of Jesus

---

8. France, *Jesus and the Old Testament*, 90.

9. France, *Jesus and the Old Testament*, 106–7.

10. France, *Jesus and the Old Testament*, 198.

nor the destruction of Jerusalem, but to the second coming of Jesus (Part 3, chapter 4).

d) The suffering of the shepherd ruler

"'Awake, O sword, against my shepherd against the man who is my associate,' says the LORD of hosts. 'Strike the shepherd, that the sheep may be scattered.'" (13:7)	"Then Jesus said to them, 'You will all become deserters because of me this night; for it is written, "I will strike the shepherd, and the sheep of the flock will be scattered."' (Matt 26:31)

In Zechariah it is "the LORD of hosts" himself who calls for the sword to strike "my shepherd," the shepherd who, in the words of Hill, "partners with God in leading his people."[11] And the striking of the shepherd leads to the scattering of the sheep. Two thirds of them will perish, while one third will survive. They will go through a process of refining and out of this will come a remnant whom God will claim as his own people, embracing them within the familiar covenant promise, "They are my people."

In Matthew's account it is Jesus himself who makes the connection with Zechariah's prophecy. In doing so, he sees that God is at work in his arrest and the scattering of the disciples. He also identifies himself as Yahweh's shepherd, and sees his disciples as the flock of Israel which is being scattered.

2. Other passages in the Gospels and Epistles where significant themes in Zechariah are related in some way to Jesus

a) Comforting Zion

"I have returned to Jerusalem with compassion; my house shall be built in it; . . . the LORD will again comfort Zion and again choose Jerusalem." (1:16–17)	"Now there was a man in Jerusalem whose name was Simeon; this man was righteous and devout, looking forward to the consolation of Israel." (Luke 2:25)
	"There was also a prophet, Anna. . . . At that moment she came, and began to praise God and to speak about the child to all who were looking for the redemption of Jerusalem." (Luke 2:36–38)

---

11. Hill, *Haggai, Zechariah and Malachi*, 255.

Isaiah's message about the return from exile in Babylon had been a message of comfort to his people: "Comfort, O comfort my people, says your God. Speak tenderly to Jerusalem . . ." (Isa 40:1–2); "Break forth together into singing, you ruins of Jerusalem; for the LORD has comforted his people, he has redeemed Jerusalem" (Isa 52:9). Taking up this same theme, Zechariah sees the rebuilding of the temple after the return from exile as a demonstration of God's compassion for Jerusalem, since the city still has an important place in God's plan.

The expressions "the consolation of Israel" and "the redemption of Jerusalem" must have been understood at the time of Jesus to sum up these hopes, which had built up over many centuries. According to Luke, Simeon and Anna were both convinced that the hopes about God visiting his people were going to be fulfilled in Jesus.

b) The coming of the kingdom of God

"... the LORD will become king over all the earth." (14:9)	"The time is fulfilled, and the kingdom of God has come near; repent and believe in the good news." (Mark 1:15)
	"But if it is by the finger of God that I cast out the demons, then the kingdom of God has come to you." (Luke 11:20)
	"And he said to them, 'Truly I tell you, there are some standing here who will not taste death until they see that the kingdom of God has come with power.'" (Mark 9:1)

The basic message of the whole book, as we have already seen, can be summed up in the words "'Your kingdom come!' It is about the future coming of the kingdom of God."[12] Zechariah is looking beyond his immediate situation in Jerusalem in 520 BCE to the time when God's kingly rule will be established in the whole world. Chapter 14 contains a whole succession of vivid pictures pointing to what the coming of this kingdom will mean for Israel and for the world.

The gospel message of Jesus is summarized by Mark at the beginning of his gospel with the words, "The time is fulfilled (*peplerotai ho kairos*), and the kingdom of God has come near (*engiken he basileia tou theou*)." This must mean that Jesus was claiming that "the day," "the day of the LORD," to which Zechariah and all the prophets had looked forward, had at last

---

12. Webb, *The Message of Zechariah*, 32.

come; that the predictions of the prophets were about to be fulfilled; and that the kingly rule of God was about to be established on earth. The Greek word translated "has come near (*engiken*)" is the same word that is used in the same gospel to speak about the arrival of Judas in the Garden of Gethsemane: "my betrayer is at hand (*engiken*)" (14:42). So just as in the Gethsemane incident Judas was in sight, so now in Jesus the coming of the kingdom of God is in sight.

In Luke 11:20 Jesus points to his healing miracles as evidence that the kingdom of God has already come. In Mark 9:1 Jesus claims that the kingdom of God will come "with power" during the lifetime of some of his hearers—"some standing here." Since he taught his disciples to pray "your kingdom come" (Matt 6:10), he evidently believed that the kingly rule of God had not yet fully arrived. Yet he clearly claimed that the whole process by which God was going to establish his kingdom had already begun to unfold through his life.

c) God dwelling in the midst of his people

"I will return to Zion, and will dwell in the midst of Jerusalem." (8:3)	". . . the Word was made flesh and lived among us (*eskenosen*, literally, tabernacled)." (John 1:14)
	"'Destroy this temple, and in three days I will raise it up.' . . . But he was speaking of the temple of his body." (2:19, 21)

Zechariah was encouraging his people to continue and complete the rebuilding of the temple by assuring them that God had not given up on his promises to his people, and that the rebuilding of the temple would be a sign of God dwelling among his people.

As we have already seen in our study of Ezekiel (Part 2), knowing that the tabernacle and the temple were signs of God dwelling among his people (Exod 25:8; 29:45–46; Num 5:3; 1 Kgs 8:27–30; 9:2–3), John speaks of Jesus as the fulfillment of both the tabernacle and the temple. When he declares "we have seen his glory" (John 1:14), he is saying that they have now seen the glory of God resting not on the tabernacle in the wilderness or on the temple in Jerusalem but on Jesus of Nazareth. When Jesus says to his disciples, "Where two or three are gathered in my name, I am there among them" (Matt 18:20) and (in the very last words of this gospel) "I am with you always, to end of the age" (Matt 28:20), this is nothing less than a claim to be the fulfillment of God's promise to live among his people—and perhaps an echo of the last verse of Ezekiel: "the LORD is there" (Ezek 48:35). It is for this reason that Webb can suggest that "Zerubbabel's temple has given way to the reality it symbolized: God the King in the midst of his saved people—forever."[13]

d) God the Shepherd saving his flock

"On that day the LORD their God will save them for they are the flock of his people." (9:16)	"I am the good shepherd. The good shepherd lays down his life for the sheep." (John 10:11)

When the Psalmist says "For he is our God, and we are the people of his pasture, and the sheep of his hand" (Ps 95:7), it is because Yahweh is thought of as the Shepherd of Israel. Before Zechariah, Ezekiel had described all Israel's rulers—both political and religious—as "shepherds," and condemned them because they had not taken care of their flock and so allowed them to be scattered over the whole earth (Ezek 34:1–10). It is because of the failure of these shepherds that God promises that he himself is going to step in to rescue his people: "I myself will search for my sheep, and will seek them out. As shepherds seek out their flocks when they are among their scattered sheep, so I will seek out my sheep. I will rescue from all the places to which they have been scattered . . . and will bring them into their own land" (Ezek 34:11–13). Zechariah takes up from Ezekiel this same theme of God as the Shepherd of Israel coming to save his flock.

So when Jesus says "I am the good shepherd," he is clearly identifying himself with Yahweh, the God who had promised to come in person to look after his sheep. He is therefore claiming to be the one through whom God is fulfilling promises made through the prophets to save his people.

13. Webb, *The Message of Zechariah*, 183.

e) Cleansing from sin

". . . and I will remove the guilt of this land in a single day." (3:9) "On that day a fountain shall be opened for the house of David and the inhabitants of Jerusalem, to cleanse them from sin and impurity." (13:1)	"If we walk in the light as he himself is in the light . . . the blood of Jesus his Son cleanses us from all sin." (1 John 1:7) "When he had made purification for sins, he sat down at the right hand of the majesty on high." (Heb 1:3) ". . . he has appeared once for all at the end of the age to remove sin by the sacrifice of himself. . . . Christ, having been offered once to bear the sins of many, will appear a second time . . . ." (Heb 9:26–28)

The promise of the removal of guilt from the land in a single day comes in the context of words addressed to Joshua the high priest. In a symbolic act, his filthy clothes, which symbolize his guilt and the guilt of his people, are taken away. Because of what the person described as "the Branch" will do, in the promise that follows, it is not only the guilt of Joshua that is taken away in a single day, but the guilt *of the whole land*: "Now listen, Joshua, high priest, you and your colleagues who sit before you! For they are an omen of things to come: I am going to bring my servant the Branch. For on the stone that I have set before Joshua . . . I will engrave its inscription, says the LORD of hosts, and I will remove the guilt of this land in a single day" (3:8–9).

The promise to Joshua the high priest that the guilt of the land will be removed "in a single day" (3:9) is reaffirmed later in the promise that "on that day" a fountain will be opened that brings cleansing from sin and impurity (13:1). This promise comes immediately after the picture of the people mourning for the sin of piercing God himself (12:10).

For the writers of 1 John and Hebrews, cleansing and purification of sin can come only through the death of Jesus on the cross. We may well wonder whether the emphasis that Jesus has achieved this "once and for all" (Greek *hapax*) is an echo of the promise to Joshua the high priest that guilt would be removed "in a single day."

f) Water flowing from Jerusalem

"...that day living waters shall flow out from Jerusalem, half of them to the eastern sea and half of them to the western sea; it shall continue in summer as in winter." (Zech 14:8)	"On the last day of the festival, the great day, while Jesus was standing there, he cried out, 'Let anyone who is thirsty come to me, and let the one who believes in me drink. As the scripture has said, "Out of the believer's heart shall flow rivers of living water."' Now he said this about the Spirit . . . ." (John 7:37–39)

Zechariah's vision of water flowing from Jerusalem is also found, with some variations, in Ezekiel (47:1–12) and Joel (3:18). Zechariah is no doubt drawing from Ezekiel's fuller picture, in which the life-giving water flows from the temple in Jerusalem down towards the Dead Sea in the east and the Mediterranean to the west.

These prophecies seem to be the only ones in the Old Testament to which Jesus can be referring when he says, "As the scripture has said . . ." (John 7:37-39). Jesus is therefore claiming to be the fulfillment of all that the temple stood for. It is through him that life-giving water, representing the Holy Spirit, will flow for all who believe in him. This is a very clear example of non-literal interpretation of Zechariah's prophecy.

g) The holiness of Jerusalem and the temple

"On that day there shall be inscribed on the bells of the horses, 'Holy to the LORD.' And the cooking pots in the house of the LORD shall be as holy as the bowls in front of the altar; and every cooking pot in Jerusalem and Judah shall be sacred to the LORD of hosts, so that all who sacrifice may come and use them to boil the flesh of the sacrifice. And there shall no longer be traders [literally, Canaanites] in the house of the LORD of hosts on that day." (14:21)	"... as he who has called you is holy, be holy yourselves in all your conduct; for it is written, 'You shall be holy, for I am holy.'" (1 Pet 1:16–17) "Pursue peace with everyone, and the holiness without which no one will see the LORD." (Heb 12:14)

In this final paragraph of Zechariah's prophecy, he is looking forward to the time when everything in Jerusalem will be holy and therefore set apart for the service of God, breaking down any distinction between the religious and the secular. In the Exodus account of the tabernacle in the wilderness, the words "holy to the LORD" had been written on the turban of the high priest

(Exod 28:36). In Zechariah's vision of the new Jerusalem, however, these words will even be written "on the bells of the horses." Every ordinary cooking pot in Jerusalem will be as sacred as the pots used in the temple worship. The temple courts will no longer be a place for traders making money. Since Zechariah's immediate concern in the whole book is for the rebuilding and the full functioning of the temple, it is fitting that these last verses of the book are about the temple. They point forward to the time when the temple will fulfil its true function as "the house of the LORD of hosts." Webb points out how this takes up the same theme that has been dealt with earlier in the book and in the prophecy of Isaiah:

> So the presence of holiness and the absence of the "Canaanite" are two sides of the same reality—perfect purity. Here at last is the complete fulfilment of the promise of chapter 3 that the sin of the land will be removed "in a single day" (3:9). The double reference to the Lord's *house* (20–21) completes the picture of the elevated Jerusalem of verses 11–12. Free at last of all impurity, and filled with the redeemed of all nations, Jerusalem has at last become "the mountain of the Lord's house," in perfect agreement with the vision of Isaiah, whose powerful words had inspired so much of Zechariah's preaching. Zerubbabel's temple has given way to the reality it symbolized: God the King in the midst of his saved people—forever.[14]

It is perhaps surprising that none of the Gospel writers connects Jesus' action of cleansing of the temple with these last words of Zechariah's prophecy. France, however, doesn't hesitate to make this connection:

> Jesus' action in clearing the Temple of various kinds of traders is probably a conscious fulfilment of the prediction of Zechariah 14:21 that, in the eschatological purity of Jerusalem, "there shall no longer be a trader in the house of the LORD of hosts on that day." Thus by a literal fulfilment of the prediction Jesus claims that the eschatological age described in Zechariah 14, with its purification of worship, has arrived.[15]

There is a similar question about whether Luke, in writing about the ascension of Jesus and his second coming, had this prophecy of Zechariah in mind: "See a day is coming for the LORD. . . . For I will gather all the nations against Jerusalem to battle. . . . Then the LORD will go forth and fight against those nations as when he fights on a day of battle. On that day

---

14. Webb, *The Message of Zechariah*, 182–83.

15. France, *Jesus and the Old Testament*, 92–93.

his feet shall stand on the Mount of Olives, which lies before Jerusalem on the east; and the Mount of Olives shall be split in two from east to west . . ." (Zech 14:1–4). Many—and especially Christian Zionists—believe that Luke must have had these words in mind when he wrote about Jesus' entry to Jerusalem from the Mount of Olives on Palm Sunday and the ascension of Jesus from the Mount of Olives (Acts 1:9–12). They also believe that the words of the angel to the disciples "This Jesus . . . will come in the same way as you saw him go into heaven" are a clear indication that Jesus' appearance at his second coming will take place on the Mount of Olives.

3. Some observations and conclusions

a) Out of twenty uses of the phrase "on that day" in Zechariah, six are related to Jesus by writers of the Gospels, and it is hard to see how these can be isolated from all the other descriptions of what will happen "on that day"

When Zechariah is not addressing his immediate context, he is looking forward to a time in the more distant future when God will do something even more significant and wonderful than the restoration of the people to their land and the restoration of the temple—which is what he is witnessing in his own time. He describes this time as "that day," and on twenty occasions describes something that will happen "on that day" (*bayom ha-hu*). In the eleven themes we have studied, six of these pictures include the phrase "on that day" and are explicitly related by New Testament writers to Jesus:

- the guilt of the land will be removed (3:9–10)
- God will save the flock of his people (9:16)
- people will mourn when they see the one they have pierced (12:11)
- a fountain will be opened for purification from sin (13:1)
- living waters will flow from Jerusalem (14:8)
- the LORD will be king (14:9)

Seven of the other instances relate to the nations waging war on Jerusalem. But it is hard to see how these descriptions of the battle (in 12:1–9 and 14:1–5) can be separated from all the images that come before and after. So, for example, the passages about the people of Jerusalem mourning (12:10–14) and the opening of a fountain to cleans from sin (13:1) follow immediately after the description of the attack on Jerusalem (12:1–9). And the passage about the striking of the shepherd and the scattering of the sheep is followed immediately by the defeat of the nations that attack Jerusalem (14:1–5). Are we to allow that some of these can be related to Jesus, but that the attack on Jerusalem is in a different category and must be seen as a description of an attack that is still to take place in the future?

Similarly, verses 6 to 9 in chapter 14 contain three images of what it will be like in "that day": the image of "continuous day" in which there is neither cold nor frost (14:6), then of water flowing from Jerusalem (14:8) and the Lord being king over the whole earth (14:9). If the last two of these pictures are seen by the Gospel writers as being fulfilled in the first coming of Jesus, it requires a strange—if not impossible—kind of surgery to separate these images and to say that the first describes a transformation of the natural order in the future, while the second and third describe the new age that has already dawned in the first coming of Jesus. It makes more sense to take *all* the pictures of what will happen "on that day" closely together. Zechariah is painting one vivid picture after another in his attempt to describe the radically new situation that will come about when God establishes his kingly rule in the world.

b) By his action in entering Jerusalem on Palm Sunday and by quoting Zechariah's prophecy about the striking of the shepherd and the scattering of the sheep, Jesus is identifying himself with both the messianic Davidic king and the rejected and suffering shepherd

When Jesus was addressed as "the son" both at his baptism and at the transfiguration (Mark 1:11; 9:7), he would have understood the echo of the words addressed to king David in Psalm 2:7, "He [the LORD] said to me, 'You are my son; today I have begotten you.'" This would have confirmed his awareness of his role as the descendant of David, the messianic king. He must also have reflected on Zechariah's picture of the king coming to Jerusalem, who is "triumphant and victorious" and yet "humble and riding on a donkey." And he could hardly avoid reflecting on Zechariah's picture of the shepherd/ruler who rescues his people in spite of being rejected and suffering at the hand of his own people. The French scholar P. Lamarche has pointed out how these messianic prophecies in Zechariah must have helped to shape the way Jesus had come to think of his role. He suggests that these passages

> present a unified picture, of the lowly king, rejected and killed
> by the people to whom he comes, whose martyrdom is the cause

of their repentance and salvation. The correspondence of this figure with the actual mission of Jesus is striking, and it is clear that he expected it to be so. In alluding to these passages of Zechariah he made clear both to his disciples and to the crowds the sort of Messianic work he envisaged himself as accomplishing. It was not to be one of triumphant and majestic sovereignty, bringing political deliverance for the Jews, but one of lowliness, suffering and death. If he was their king, it was in the character of the lowly and rejected Shepherd-King. The many Old Testament passages which speak of the Messiah's glory and triumph are largely passed over, and his emphasis falls . . . almost exclusively on Zechariah 9–14, Isaiah 53 and Daniel 7.[16]

Webb comments on the way Zechariah identifies the Messiah with the stricken shepherd:

> Here is perhaps the profoundest and most precious aspect of the theology of this book: like the great prophet Isaiah before him, Zechariah understood that the Messiah would have to suffer if sin were to be atoned for and Israel's relationship with God were to be restored. Furthermore, this suffering would be expressly brought about by God. In Isaiah 53:10 it is God who "crushes his Servant" and "causes him to suffer"; here in Zechariah it is God who *strikes* the shepherd. He does not strike him because he deserves it, but because he has assumed responsibility for the wrongdoing of others.[17]

c) If these themes are directly related to Jesus by New Testament writers, this suggests that for them "the day" that Zechariah looked forward to had already dawned; Zechariah's visions of the distant future had already been fulfilled—or at least had begun to be fulfilled—in the life of Jesus

Jesus was for them the promised descendant of King David, but wasn't an ordinary kind of king because of the way he entered Jerusalem. Jesus was the good shepherd, who was acting on behalf of Yahweh, the Shepherd of Israel. He had been rejected by his own people; but they would mourn when they saw the suffering they have caused him. God had fulfilled his promise of coming to comfort Zion and to dwell among his people. The promise of the removal of sin had been fulfilled through Jesus' death on the cross,

16. Quoted in France, *Jesus and the Old Testament*, 109.
17. Webb, *The Message of Zechariah*, 169–70.

and the forgiveness of sins had created the possibility of a life of holiness. In short, the kingdom of God had already begun to arrive in and through Jesus.

If all these themes in the final chapters of Zechariah have, in the minds of the New Testament writers, *already* been fulfilled in the life of Jesus, could this also apply to the graphic pictures of a great battle in Jerusalem in chapters 12 and 14? As we have already seen, many would argue that they must be interpreted very literally as a straightforward description of events that have not yet taken place but are still to take place in the future. These passages are then linked with descriptions in the book of Revelation of great battles at Armageddon (Rev 15:16) and Jerusalem (Rev 20:7–9).

But what if, instead of looking forward to events at the end of the world, these passages are put alongside all the other passages in Zechariah that New Testament writers relate to Jesus and the incarnation? What if this vision—with all its apocalyptic language—is describing the great battle between God and the forces of evil that would be involved in the coming of the kingly rule of God on earth? This is the interpretation followed by Webb when he writes: "The first stage of the climactic battle to usher in the kingdom of God has already been fought in Jerusalem, in the death, resurrection and ascension of Jesus Christ."[18] He goes on to explain the significance of the great battle described by Zechariah:

> The distinct contribution of the closing chapter of Zechariah is to remind us that this mission involves a battle. The decisive, opening campaign of that battle was fought when Jew and Gentile conspired together to nail the Son of God to the cross, only to have the futility of their rebellion exposed three days later by his resurrection from the dead. The battle continued in the months and years that followed as the Jewish and Gentile authorities combined again to try to destroy the church and silence its gospel witness. It continues today whenever a hostile world is confronted with the truth that God reigns, and it will be ended only when Jesus returns in glory. It is a titanic battle, and there is a cost to being involved in it. But it is no futile struggle; indeed, it is a battle that has already been won. Continued resistance is futile, for God is King, and his kingdom will come. There will be a great harvest! That is the note on which Zechariah's message concludes.[19]

18. Webb, *The Message of Zechariah*, 174.
19. Webb, *The Message of Zechariah*, 185.

d) This way of seeing Jesus as the fulfillment of all the hopes of the Old Testament must go back to Jesus himself

Luke describes how, in his meeting with the disciples on the road to Emmaus, "beginning with Moses and all the prophets, he interpreted to them the things about himself in all the scriptures" (Luke 24:27). France explains how Jesus consistently revealed his identity in terms drawn from the Old Testament:

> The essence of his new application was that he saw the fulfilment of the predictions and foreshadowings of the Old Testament in himself and his work. . . . From this same source too sprang his insistence that in his coming "the time is fulfilled," that there was no need any longer to look to the future for the fulfilment of the hopes of the Old Testament, but that in his coming the day of salvation had come, the last days had arrived, and God had come to bless his people; from this point men would live in the eschatological age, and in the community of his followers the blessings promised to Israel would be realized, until he should come again to bring this age to an end. This "inaugurated eschatology," which saw the last days as begun, but yet to be completed in the future, is Jesus' unique approach to the soteriological predictions and types of the Old Testament. To his coming the whole of the Old Testament had looked forward; not only the actual predictions in the prophets and the psalms, but the very pattern of God's working recorded in the Old Testament was preparing for the final and perfect work of God, which his coming had begun. In him we move from shadows to reality; in him God's purposes are fulfilled at last, and all that now remains is the working out of this fulfilment to its final consummation. Thus Jesus' use of the Old Testament falls into a single coherent scheme, with himself as the focus.[20]

e) All of the four passages from Zechariah that are expressly quoted by Jesus or the Gospel writers are related to the death of Jesus and the events leading up to it

What is so significant about this is that *none* of these themes (or the other seven that are echoed elsewhere in the New Testament) are related to the end of the world. It is also significant that Jesus seems to have had very little

20. France, *Jesus and the Old Testament*, 223–24.

to say about events leading up to the end. Each of the three Synoptic Gospels contains a version of what is known as the "eschatological discourse" of Jesus (Mark 13:1–37; Matt 24:1–44; Luke 21:5–38). In Mark's account, Jesus tells his disciples that the temple is going to be destroyed, and the disciples respond immediately by asking: "Tell us, when will this be, and what will be the sign that all these things are about to be accomplished?" (Mark 13:4).

Readers have often been puzzled by the way that, in Jesus' response, warnings about the destruction of Jerusalem ("when you see the desolating sacrifice set up where it ought not to be . . .") are followed immediately by verses that seem to be describing the second coming ("in those days . . . the sun will be darkened, and the moon will not give its light. . . . Then they will see 'the Son of Man coming in clouds' . . ." (Mark 13:14–26). How can this prediction of the destruction of Jerusalem be placed alongside what seems to be a prediction about the end of the world?

This problem can be resolved, firstly, by understanding that the language about the darkening of the sun is taken from Isaiah's prediction of the fall of Babylon, which took place in 539 BCE: "For the stars of the heavens and their constellations will not give their light; the sun will be dark at its rising, and the moon will not shed its light" (Isa 13:10). Jesus' audience would have been very shocked if they understood that Jesus here was using Isaiah's words associated with God's judgement on the pagan city of Babylon to describe the judgement that was about to fall on the holy city of Jerusalem. When Jesus, therefore, quotes apocalyptic imagery about cosmic disturbances, he is not using it to describe natural phenomena that will occur at the end of the world, but to describe God's judgement on Jerusalem that will come very soon.

The second clue to resolving the problem is to recognize that the words about the coming of the Son of Man are a clear echo of Daniel's vision in Daniel 7:13ff. Jesus' words about people seeing the Son of Man coming in clouds have traditionally been understood as describing the second coming, and there is no reason to question this interpretation. It is widely recognized now, however, that they need to be related *primarily* to what was to happen in Jerusalem some forty years after Jesus' discourse. This is because what Daniel is describing in his vision is not a coming of the Son of Man *to earth*, but his coming *into the presence of God* to receive "dominion and glory and kingship, that all peoples, nations, and languages should serve him" (Dan 7:14). Jesus refers to the Son of Man coming in clouds in the context of his prediction that Jerusalem is to be destroyed. He is therefore saying that the destruction of Jerusalem will be culmination of a series of events following on from his death and resurrection—events that, taken together, will demonstrate that he has been vindicated and entered into the dominion and kingship that God has given him as the Son of Man.

The third clue is that the major part of the eschatological discourses in Matthew, Mark, and Luke concerns the period leading up to the destruction of Jerusalem, and it is only the last shorter section—which speaks of "that day and hour" (Matthew), "that day or hour" (Mark), or "that day" (Luke)—that seems to refer to the end of the world. Luke makes this point by adding "For it will come upon all who live on the face of the whole earth" (Luke 21:35).

If Jesus himself said so little about the end of the world, this might explain why the Gospel writers don't seem to relate anything in the visions of Zechariah to the end of history. When Jesus speaks of seeing "Jerusalem surrounded by armies" (Luke 21:20), he could be echoing Zechariah's vision of all the nations of the earth coming together to lay siege to Jerusalem (Zech 12:3). But if so, he is speaking here about what was going to happen in 70 CE, and not about a battle that would take place in Jerusalem at the end of time. France points out why it is so significant that descriptions of the eschatological battle that are found in the prophets and in Jewish apocalyptic at the time of Jesus seem to find no place at all in the teaching of Jesus:

> Jesus is not interested in the Jewish preoccupation with earthly empires and their overthrow. The construction (using *e.g.* Dn 7 and Zc 14) of detailed pictures of the eschatological battle, with the vindication of Israel and the discomfiture of her enemies, finds hardly an echo in his teaching. Thus he applies Daniel 7 not to earthly conquest, but to a dominion which can coexist with the earthly empire of Rome, because it refers to a different sphere, and which can even involve the judgment rather than the vindication of the Jewish nation. . . . While the Jews all looked forward to a Messiah for whose coming they hoped and prayed, Jesus proclaims that this Messiah has already come; he is the Messiah. In himself and his work the eschatological, Messianic age has arrived, and these passages are applied generally not to the future but to the present. His application of Daniel 7:13–14 and Zechariah 12:10–14 to future events is not to a new era to come, but to the inevitable outworking of the eschatological work he has already begun. Already the era of salvation is present, and his disciples are the purified, blessed Israel of the Messianic age.[21]

---

21. France, *Jesus and the Old Testament*, 200–201.

Does this hold true also for the book of Revelation? Isn't this book mostly about "the last things," "the end"? Since Revelation was written thirty or forty years after the Gospels and Epistles, is there any evidence that further reflection on the incarnation introduces anything new? And if Zechariah and Revelation are both prophecy and apocalyptic and therefore of the same literary genre, how do John's visions compare with Zechariah's visions?

4

Zechariah's prophecy as understood in Revelation

It is estimated that the book of Revelation contains around four hundred references to the Old Testament, and around thirty of these are to Zechariah. Joyce Baldwin goes so far as to say that "Zechariah has influenced the author of Revelation more than any other Old Testament writer."[1] How then does John read the visions of Zechariah about the coming of the kingdom of God? Does he believe that it has already arrived as a result of the life, death, and resurrection of Jesus? If it hasn't been established fully, how is it finally going to come? In speaking about the end of the world, does John take up and develop the pictures in Zechariah of armies laying siege to Jerusalem, and the Mount of Olives being split in two?

1. John's context and message

If it's important to understand the book of Zechariah in its historical con-text, it's equally important to understand the book of Revelation in the con-text—and especially the political context—in which it was written. Whether he was the disciple John or another John, he was probably writing in Asia Minor around 95 CE. The Roman Empire was becoming more and more totalitarian, and the emperor Domitian was claiming divine status and ex-pecting to be worshiped. John was in prison "because of the word of God and the testimony of Jesus" (1:9) and could see that the church was about to face fierce persecution from the Roman state. In the first three chapters, he is writing a pastoral letter to struggling Christian churches in Asia Minor, encouraging them to stand firm in their Christian witness, and preparing

1. Baldwin, Haggai, *Zechariah and Malachi*, 59.

them to face martyrdom. He reminds them that, since the crucified, risen, and ascended Jesus has all authority in heaven and earth, God will ultimately judge the emperor for his blasphemous claims and will bring down the whole Roman system.

Both Zechariah and John are therefore speaking about the coming of the kingdom of God. Zechariah is looking forward to it as a series of future events, while John understands that God's kingly rule has already begun through the work of Jesus. As Richard Bauckham explains, John uses the language of holy war to explain the secret of *how* the kingdom of God has come in and through Jesus and his followers:

> The distinctive feature of Revelation seems to be, not its repudiation of apocalyptic militarism, but its lavish use of militaristic *language* in a non-militaristic *sense*. . . . [I]nstead of simply repudiating apocalyptic militancy, he *re-interprets* it in a Christian sense, taking up its reading of Old Testament prophecy into a specifically Christian reading of the Old Testament. He aims to show that the decisive battle in God's eschatological holy war against all evil, including the power of Rome, has already been won—by the faithful witness and sacrificial death of Jesus. Christians are called to participate in his war and his victory—but by the same means as he employed: bearing witness to Jesus to the point of martyrdom, . . . active engagement in the Lamb's war.[2]

2. While the book describes itself as "prophecy," it is full of apocalyptic language

If John describes what he is writing as "prophecy" (*propheteia*) (1:3), what kind of prophecy is it? "The function of the prophet," writes G. B. Caird, "is to declare to God's people, and through them to the world, the whole counsel of God. John's book is a prophecy because it reveals the true nature of the conflict between the monster and the Lamb, between Babylon the great and the new Jerusalem, and summons men to the one victory that can overcome the world."[3]

It hardly needs to be said, however, that the style of the whole book—apart from the letters to the churches in the first three chapters—has more in common with the proto-apocalyptic passages in Zechariah and Daniel than

---

2. Bauckham, *The Climax of Prophecy*, 233–34.

3. Caird, *The Revelation of St John the Divine*, 283.

prophetic books like Isaiah and Jeremiah. In the centuries after the return from exile, in situations where the Jewish people were facing persecution or oppression under foreign rulers, Jewish apocalyptic had developed into a unique genre which would have been well known to John and his readers.

One of the most obvious features of apocalyptic is that it is full of symbols; and symbols, by definition, need to be interpreted. Just as, for example, the four beasts in Daniel represent four kingdoms—Babylonia, Media, Persia, and Greece—the Beast in Revelation stands for Rome. Certain numbers have particular meanings: three represents completeness; seven also signifies completeness and wholeness. A throne is a symbol of divine sovereignty, while a horn represents strength. An eye is a symbol for wisdom, and white robes represent victory and purity.

If numbers are symbolic, the period of one thousand years, the millennium (20:2–6) is also likely to be symbolic and can hardly mean a literal period of a thousand years. Similarly, the name "Armageddon" (16:16), the site of "the battle of the great day of God Almighty," is probably also symbolic and is not to be imagined as taking place at Megiddo on the plain of Esdraelon—although Megiddo would have been the origin of the symbol.

The reference to the battle of Armageddon comes in the context of the vision of the seven bowls of God's wrath being poured out on the earth to cause disturbances on the earth and in the sea, rivers, and sky. The sixth angel pours his bowl on the river Euphrates, causing the water to dry up "to prepare the way for the kings from the East." Then out of the beast (representing Rome) come the spirits of demons who "go abroad to the kings of the whole world to assemble them for battle on the great day of God the Almighty. . . . And they assembled them at the place that in Hebrew is called Harmagedon" (16:12, 14, 16). The account continues with the pouring out of the seventh bowl, which leads to Babylon the Great being given "the wine-cup of the fury of his [God's] wrath" (16:19). This brief reference to the battle is hardly enough to suggest that for John the battle of Armageddon is one great battle of the end times that is to be fought out on the Esdraelon Valley. The climax of the pouring of the seven bowls of God's wrath comes with the fall of Rome, and therefore has nothing to do with a final battle at the end of history. Caird is quite sure that "like John's other names, it [Armageddon] is a symbol. He was not expecting a battle in northern Palestine, but at Rome."[4]

4. Caird, *The Revelation of St John the Divine*, 207.

3. John feels free to adapt and modify details drawn from Zechariah

If John had interpreted Zechariah's prophecy very literally, he might have developed Zechariah's vision of nations sending their armies to surround Jerusalem. He might have speculated what it would mean for God to "go forth and fight against those nations," with his feet standing on the Mount of Olives (14:3–4). But he doesn't interpret Zechariah's visions as descriptions of literal events, and his focus is on Rome rather than Jerusalem.

These, for example, are some of the ways in which John takes up—and often adapts—details from the visions of Zechariah:

- Zechariah sees "a man riding on a red horse, and . . . red, sorrel, and white horses," which are sent out to patrol the peaceful earth (Zech 1:8); John sees four horses that represent four different kinds of disaster (Rev 6:4–5).

- Zechariah sees four horns (1:18–21); John sees the woman on the beast who has ten horns (17:3).

- Zechariah sees the "filthy clothes" of Joshua the high priest taken away and replaced by "festal apparel" (3:4); John sees the saints in heaven in robes that have been washed in the blood of the lamb (7:14).

- Zechariah sees Satan as the accuser of the high priest (3:1–10); John sees Satan as the deceiver who accuses (12:10).

- Zechariah sees "a single stone with seven facets [literally, eyes]" (3:9); John sees "seven horns and seven eyes" (5:6).

- Zechariah's single "lampstand all of gold" (4:2) becomes for John seven "golden lampstands" (1:12).

- Just as Zechariah has to ask for an explanation of the meaning of what he has seen (4:13), John has to ask for an explanation (7:14). Both Zechariah and John ask the question "How long?" (Zech 1:12; Rev 6:10).

- While Zechariah sees "white horses" (6:2–3), John sees "a white horse" (6:2).

- Zechariah sees a crown on the head of Joshua the high priest (3:5); John sees the rider on the white horse who is given a crown (6:2).

- For Zechariah, the sounding of a trumpet signals the arrival of the king (9:14); John hears the sounding of the trumpet to signal the fact that God's kingly rule has been established through Jesus the Messiah (8:2).

- Zechariah hears God's promise: "I will come and dwell in your midst" (2:10); John writes "he is coming with the clouds" (1:7), and hears that in the new Jerusalem, "the home of God is among mortals. He will dwell with them as their God" (21:3).

- Zechariah sees that "on that day" there will be no difference between day and night (14:7); for John, in the new Jerusalem, there will be no night, no sun, and no moon (21:23, 25; 22:5).

- Zechariah sees water flowing out of Jerusalem (14:8); John sees "a river of the water of life . . . flowing from the throne of God and of the Lamb" (22:1–3).

- Zechariah sees that the curse of destruction will be removed (14:11); John says that in the new Jerusalem "Nothing accursed will be found there . . ." (22:3).

Because of the way John interprets Zechariah, Caird describes him as "an artist handling his material with creative originality . . . with complete freedom from any literalness or pedantry. . . . The symbolism is drawn from the Old Testament, but modified to carry a radically new meaning. . . . He bursts the bounds of language in an attempt to hint at what is essentially beyond imagination."[5]

4. John gives a new interpretation to Zechariah's prophecy about mourning

"And I will pour out a spirit of compassion and supplication on the house of David and the inhabitants of Jerusalem, so that, when they look on the one whom they have pierced [literally, me whom they have pierced], they shall mourn for him . . . ." (Zech 12:10)	"Look! He is coming with the clouds; every eye will see him, even those who pierced him; and on his account all the tribes of the earth will wail." (Rev 1:7)

We have already seen how the Gospel of John relates Zechariah's words about "looking on the one whom they have pierced" to the crucifixion (John 19:36–37), while the Gospel of Matthew relates them to the fall of Jerusalem and the coming of the Son of Man (Matt 24:30). In the book of Revelation, however, these words are conflated with Daniel 7:13 ("I saw one like a

5. Caird, *The Revelation of St John the Divine*, 7, 234, 79, 272.

human being [one like a son of man] coming with the clouds of heaven"), and related neither to the crucifixion nor the coming of the Son of Man, but to the second coming of Jesus (1:7). France spells out the significance of this new interpretation of Zechariah's prophecy:

> We may note a discrepancy between Matthew 24:30 and Revelation 1:7, in that the first applies the mourning to the time of the fall of Jerusalem, the second to the Parousia, and therefore probably to "all the nations of the earth" rather than to "all the tribes of the land" (as in Mt. 24:30).[6]

> It is in the book of Revelation that the one striking departure from Jesus' application occurs, the shift of Daniel 7:13 and Zechariah 12:10ff from the fall of Jerusalem to the Parousia. . . . This is perhaps the clearest example of the tendency of this book [Revelation] to work independently of Jesus' use of the Old Testament passage, and to initiate a new application which then becomes a dominant influence on patristic use of the passage concerned. The way it takes is that of Jewish apocalyptic thought. Thus while Jesus and the rest of the New Testament show no interest in the apocalyptic imagery of Daniel 7 and Zechariah 14, Revelation is captivated by it. While Jesus' use of Daniel 7 ignores Jewish discussion of the political identity of the four kingdoms and the time of their final overthrow, and concentrates on the overthrow of spiritual opposition to the purposes of God, Revelation expounds Daniel 7 in terms of the empire of Rome and its imminent downfall. While Jesus claims that in his death and resurrection he has entered into the triumph and exaltation of the Son of Man, and received all power in heaven and earth, Revelation sees the opposing kingdom as still rampant, and the triumph of Jesus as future.[7]

This is a reminder, therefore, that although most of the references to Zechariah in the New Testament relate to what God has already done in the incarnation, we still await the final consummation, the final completion of God's plan of salvation.

---

6. France, *Jesus and the Old Testament*, 207.

7. France, *Jesus and the Old Testament*, 220–21.

5. John has little or no interest in Jerusalem or a final battle in Jerusalem

We have already seen that Jerusalem and its temple are a major theme throughout the book of Zechariah, and his visions of "that day" in the future contain pictures of armies from the nations laying siege to Jerusalem. In Revelation, however, it is hard to see how the few oblique references to Jerusalem and the temple apply to the actual city of Jerusalem.

a) The temple of God and the trampling on the holy city (11:2)

Ezekiel in his vision had seen an angel who was measuring the temple, while Zechariah had seen an angel measuring Jerusalem. In both cases the measuring is part of the preparation for the restoration of the destroyed temple. John, however, would have known that the temple had been destroyed in 70 CE, as Jesus had predicted, and therefore no longer existed. He therefore develops the vision of measuring the temple in a completely different direction. This is Caird's explanation of the reference in Revelation 11 to Jerusalem and the temple:

> Indeed, it is hardly too much to say that, in a book in which all things are expressed in symbols, the very last thing the temple and the holy city could mean would be the physical temple and the earthly Jerusalem. If John had wanted to speak about them, he would have found some imagery to convey his meaning without lapsing into the inconsistency of literalism. . . . The temple, the outer court, and the holy city are symbols. The temple stands for the church, the house of God not made with hands, but built of living stones; . . . the trampling of the holy city is equivalent to the great martyrdom.[8]

b) The Lamb standing on Mount Zion (14:1)

"Then I looked," says John, "and there was the Lamb, standing on Mount Zion, and with him one hundred forty-four thousand who had his name and his Father's name written on their foreheads." If some Christian Zionist insist that a picture of this kind requires no de-coding or interpretation, the same principle needs to be applied to every single image of this kind in the book of Revelation.

8. Caird, *The Revelation of St John the Divine*, 131–32.

c) "The camp of the saints and the beloved city" (20:9–10)

Some interpreters believe that there is a reference to the city of Jerusalem in the verses immediately following the passage about the millennium (20:1–16). We read here of "the nations at the four corners of the earth, Gog and Magog" gathering for battle. "They marched over the breadth of the earth and surrounded the camp of the saints and the beloved city. And fire came down from heaven and consumed them" (20:8–9). Many writers have interpreted this verse as John developing Zechariah's picture of the siege of Jerusalem. However, as we shall see, "the beloved city" is much more likely to be identified with "the holy city, the new Jerusalem coming down out of heaven from God" than the city of Jerusalem (21:10).

6. Some observations and conclusions

a) John's message is especially relevant to his readers in their context

John uses his understanding of the message of Zechariah to declare a prophetic word that is appropriate for his readers, preparing them for "what must soon take place" (1:1; cf. 22:6–7, 10), "the great ordeal" (7:14). In order to encourage them as they face increased persecution and even martyrdom, his pastoral letter doesn't give detailed descriptions of the end of the world, but looks forward, in the words of Caird, to "the obliteration of the grandeur that was Rome."[9] He speaks enigmatically towards the end about the time when the universe as we know it comes to an end: "The earth and the heaven fled from his presence, and no place was found for them" (20:11). And he holds out the hope of "a new heaven and a new earth" (21:1). But in his immediate context what his readers need to understand is the judgment that is coming to Rome. This is why a substantial part of the book—chapters 13 to 19—is concerned with the fall of the Beast/Babylon/Rome. God's final answer to Babylon the Great is the holy city, the new Jerusalem, that comes down from heaven. Caird explains further:

> The utmost limit of his prophetic vision was the end of Rome's world, which he believed to be inherent in her forthcoming persecution of the church. In her attack on the church Rome would let loose into the world powers which would compass her own downfall. To describe this conviction he uses eschatological language, and in this limited use of eschatological language he was true to his calling as a prophet. . . . Amos had a vision of the

9. Caird, *The Revelation of St John the Divine*, 227.

End, but it was the end of Israel's world: "the end has come upon my people Israel" (Amos 8:2). Daniel had visions of the End, but for him the only end that mattered was "when the power of the persecutor of the holy people comes to an end" (Dan 12:7). . . . It may well be that the prophets believed in a literal beginning and end to history. But, just as the language of myth was regularly used to denote that which was not the Beginning, so the language of eschatology was regularly used to denote that which was not the end. Broadly speaking, it is true to say that no prophet ever used eschatological language except to give theological depth and urgency to the historical crisis which he and his people were facing at the moment.[10]

b) John interprets Zechariah in the light of the teaching of Jesus and of all that he achieved through his life and death

We have seen how indebted the writer of Revelation is to the book of Zechariah. He must also have been familiar with the Synoptic Gospels and understood how Jesus had spoken in some detail about the immediate future leading up to the destruction of Jerusalem in 70 CE (e.g., Mark 13:1–31) and in more general terms about "that day" in the more distant future (Mark 13:32–37). But in thinking about the future, he doesn't simply repeat what Zechariah and Jesus had said. He uses his understanding of the message of Zechariah and of Jesus to communicate a message for his own time.

Seeing Jesus as Israel's Messiah and the incarnation as God dwelling among his people becomes for John the lens through which he interprets Zechariah. This, for example, shapes his description of "the new Jerusalem." He assures his fellow Christians that the Roman state, which is going to persecute them fiercely, is ultimately going to fall under the judgment of God. And God's alternative to Babylon is the new Jerusalem. The voice that John hears from the throne concerning the new Jerusalem is speaking about "a new heaven and a new earth" (21:1). But it is speaking at the same time about something that has *already happened* through the incarnation: "See the home of God is among mortals. He will dwell with them as their God; they will be his peoples, and God himself will be with them . . ." (21:3). Since in the incarnation God has come to dwell among his people, as Zechariah had prophesied, these words cannot simply be about something that will happen at the end of time. They must at the same time describe a new reality

---

10. Caird, *The Revelation of St John the Divine*, 209–10.

that has come into being through the Word made flesh and the people who form the body of Christ. This is why Caird suggests that

> the descent from heaven is not a single nor even a double event, but a permanent characteristic of the city. . . . The descent of the city is not a single far-off divine event but a permanent spiritual fact. Just as the monster is a rising-from-the abyss kind of monster, so the beloved city is a descending-from-heaven kind of city. In whatever place and at whatever time God's people are gathered together, there is the city of God (cf 3:12; 11:2); . . . this is a future which interpenetrates and informs the present. . . . [T]he descent of the new Jerusalem is not only a single event, but one of which Christians have had a foretaste throughout the history of the church. . . . At all times past and future are embraced in his eternal present.[11]

He explains further:

> The city of God is described as the new Jerusalem which comes down out of heaven from my God. John uses this same description twice more in his account of his vision of the new heaven and earth (21:2,10). We might therefore conclude that he regarded the descent of the city as a wholly future event, destined to happen only at the end of time. In that case we must take the present participle in the context before us as a futuristic present. But this is by no means the most obvious or natural way of taking it. The natural way is to treat it as an interactive present, denoting a permanent attribute of the new Jerusalem. Wherever a man lives by faith in Christ and bears witness to that faith without counting the cost, there is the holy city coming down out of heaven from God.[12]

This emphasis on what has already been achieved through the work of Jesus and the new reality that has come into being through him does not mean that there is nothing new that is still to come. John looks forward to the final consummation of God's plan since he speaks of "a new heaven and a new earth" (Rev 21:1), and the book ends with the prayer "Come, Lord Jesus!" (Rev 22:20).

---

11. Caird, *The Revelation of St John the Divine*, 271, 257, 263.

12. Caird, *The Revelation of St John the Divine*, 55.

c) While John is thoroughly familiar with the prophecy of Zechariah, there is no hint that he imagines a literal fulfilment of Zechariah's vision of armies laying siege to Jerusalem and being defeated by God. For him, the decisive battle has already been fought in Jerusalem, and won through the death and resurrection of Jesus

John's understanding of the death and resurrection of Jesus transforms his picture of the final, great battle of history. Zechariah had described this conflict as a battle that would be fought in the city of Jerusalem. But for John the final great conflict has *already taken place* in Jerusalem, and it happened when Jesus died on the cross and rose from death. John is therefore encouraging his fellow Christians to see the persecution that is coming to them in the context of the bigger conflict for sovereignty over the universe, and wants them to be assured that the victory has already been won through Jesus: "The kingdom of the world has become the kingdom of our Lord and of his Messiah, and he will reign forever and ever" (11:15). "Now have come the salvation and the power and the kingdom of our God, and the authority of his Messiah, for the accuser of our comrades has been thrown down, who accuses them day and night before our God. But they have conquered him by the blood of the Lamb and by the word of their testimony, for they did not cling to life even in the face of death" (12:10–11). His readers need to understand not only that Jesus has already won the victory, but also that martyrdom plays a vital part in God's ultimate plan to defeat evil.

Conclusion to Part 3

1. Zechariah motivates his people to address their immediate situation by holding out the hope of a more glorious future in the coming of the kingdom of God.

Zechariah's wanted to encourage his people to continue the work of rebuilding the temple. He assured them that God would be faithful to all his promises about the nation, the royal line, and the temple. He also encouraged them by saying that in the more distant future God was going to work through his people to establish his kingdom in the world and to bless all nations. Jerusalem and its temple would play a highly significant role in what God was going to do.

2. Since there is a clear difference between prophecy and apocalyptic, the symbolic language of Zechariah's visions cannot be interpreted literally and has to be decoded.

Like the visions of Ezekiel and Daniel, Zechariah's visions would not have been heard as straightforward descriptions of actual events. When Jesus used apocalyptic imagery from the Old Testament about cosmic disturbances (Mark 13:24–25; Matt 24:29; Luke 21:25), he wasn't speaking about events at the end of the world but about the fall of Jerusalem. Zechariah's visions of a great battle around Jerusalem and the defeat of the nations which would attack the city can be interpreted as a graphic way of saying that the coming of the kingdom of God would involve an intense conflict between God and the forces of evil—and that this conflict would be fought and won in Jerusalem.

3. Zechariah speaks of several figures which have been interpreted as messianic, and must have played an important role in enabling Jesus to understand his identity and his mission.

The figure of "my servant the Branch" recalls Jeremiah's prophecy that God would raise up "for David a righteous Branch" (Jer 23:5–6). For Zechariah, however, this figure is modelled on Joshua the high priest, and it is through

him that the guilt of the land will be removed "in a single day" (3:9). Another significant detail about this priestly figure is that he "shall build the
temple of the LORD, . . . he shall bear royal honor, and shall sit and rule on
his throne" (6:13). This person, therefore, combines the roles of both priest
and king. But this king, who brings joy to Jerusalem, will not be a warlike
king riding on a horse but humble, riding on a donkey and bringing peace
to the nations (9:9–10). Later, this messianic figure is described as the shep-
herd-ruler who is rejected by his people. Jesus identified himself with *both*
the messianic king *and* suffering shepherd, and it must have been through
reflecting on Isaiah's Suffering Servant and the messianic figures described
in Zechariah that Jesus understood the necessity of his suffering and death.

*4. Zechariah's prophecy can hardly provide a basis for expectations or specula-
tion about developments in Israel-Palestine in the near or distant future. It
can, however, strengthen our confidence that God is at work in the unfolding
of history, since he is still at work, and will ultimately carry out all his loving
purposes for the nations and for the universe.*

Since Jerusalem was the site of the crucifixion and resurrection, it was the
site of the ultimate confrontation between God and the forces of evil that
took place at Calvary. The message of Jesus was then to be preached "in
Jerusalem, in all Judea and Samaria, and to the ends of the earth" (Acts 1:8).
Jerusalem therefore ceased to have any special theological or eschatological
significance, and we have no reason to look forward to a literal battle on the
ground in Israel—either at Megiddo or Jerusalem. There is no justification
for identifying biblical Israel with the State of Israel, as if prophecies about
Israel in the Old Testament can apply to the modern state. If the kingdom
of God did begin to come through the life of Jesus, we can be confident
that God will ultimately establish his kingly rule in the world in a way that
is recognized by every human being. Like the first readers of Revelation,
Christians living today under brutal, corrupt, authoritarian regimes can
take comfort from the assurance that these regimes will ultimately come
under divine judgment.

Epilogue

Christian Zionists of all kinds assume that the return of Jews to the land and the creation of the State of Israel can—and should—be interpreted in the light of what the Bible says about the restoration of Israel. While we have had to engage at certain stages with some of the more extreme examples of Christian Zionism, which are based on a very literal interpretation of the biblical text, our main concern has been this basic assumption of all Christian Zionists—that the whole Zionist project can be seen as part of the fulfillment of promises and prophecies in the Old Testament about the descendants of Abraham and their land.

How then can we summarize our answers to the ten basic questions about Christian Zionism? Does our interpretation of Ezekiel and Zechariah support these answers? Is Christian Zionism the only way to understand what the Bible says about the restoration of Israel? Does it really matter how we interpret what the Bible says about the end times and the restoration of Israel? And how does the earliest gospel sum up Jesus' teaching about preparing for the end?

1. Answers to the ten basic questions about Christian Zionism

- Christians are very divided in their responses to these issues partly because they have different understandings of the nature and history of the Israeli-Palestinian conflict, and partly because they have such different starting points in interpreting what the Bible says about the people of Israel and their land. So if there is to be any meeting of minds, there's no alternative to serious and prolonged discussion in both these areas. Even if we can't convince each other about our convictions, we can at the very least make sure that we have understood each other and developed some empathy for the other side (Part 1, chapter 1).

- Paul is certainly thinking about ethnic Israel in Romans 9–11. But he sees Jesus as the Jewish Messiah who has come to bring blessing to all nations of the world. He therefore believes that gentiles who believe in Jesus are incorporated into Israel, like wild olive shoots that are grafted into the original stock of an olive tree. When he speaks of "all Israel" being saved, therefore, he is thinking of what ethnic Israel has now become—the people of God renewed and restored in the Messiah. So "all Israel" includes both Jews and gentiles, who share together as members of the body of Christ (Part 1, chapter 2).

- The sayings of Jesus concerning Jerusalem speak consistently in terms of judgment rather than restoration. He speaks of the coming destruction of Jerusalem as a consequence of its refusal to recognize him as Messiah: "because you did not recognize the time of your visitation from God" (Luke 19:44). Immediately after speaking about the destruction of Jerusalem in the eschatological discourse, he does not speak about its restoration in the more distant future, but about "the coming of the Son of Man" in the lifetime of many of his hearers, using images drawn from Daniel 7. There is therefore no justification for linking the words of Jesus about "the times of the gentiles" being fulfilled to the restoration of Jewish sovereignty over Jerusalem in the Six Day War of June 1967 (Part 1, chapter 3).

- Jesus understood very well what was in the minds of his disciples who believed that a sovereign, independent Jewish state in the land must be an integral part of the coming of the kingdom of God. But instead of affirming this assumption, Jesus wanted them to understand that the kingdom of God was not tied to one particular people and their land, but would embrace people from every nation in the world. He commissioned them to go out and draw both Jews and gentiles into the people of God by communicating the good news about himself. Understanding what Jesus meant by the kingdom of God made them change their ideas about the kingdom of Israel (Part 1, chapter 4).

- While the Old Testament needs to be understood in its own terms, this does not mean that Christians today are bound to interpret it literally. It is important to appreciate how the message of each of the prophets would have been understood in its original context. But any genuinely *Christian* interpretation of the Old Testament must *also* ask how the writers of the New Testament interpreted the Old Testament. As they reflected, in the light of the coming of Jesus, on all the basic themes of the Old Testament—like the nation, the land, the temple, and the Davidic dynasty—and reflected on how these had found their fulfillment in Jesus, they couldn't continue to interpret them in a very literal way. Rather they *enlarged* their understanding of these great themes and prophecies, seeing that they had come to mean "more than their original authors and readers had in mind"[1] (Part 1, chapter 5).

- The themes of nation and land are inextricably linked together. While the disciples of Jesus must have started out with very traditional ideas about the nation of Israel, their experience of living with Jesus, their understanding of his death and resurrection, and their experience of seeing gentiles becoming disciples of Jesus forced them to enlarge their concept of the chosen people. They believed that these gentile believers shared *all* the privileges of the people of God, and that there must be complete equality between Jews and gentiles within the body of Christ (Part 1, chapter 6).

- Just as the disciples had to change their ideas about the nation, in the same way they had to change and enlarge their understanding of the land. The land of Israel now had to be understood in the context of the coming of the kingdom of God, because the people of God now embraced people from all nations and lands in the world. They universalized the idea of land, so that ideas about the land were now relevant to all the lands of the earth, and they now saw the land as a symbol of all the blessings and privileges inherited by believers of every race (Part 1, chapter 7).

- Gentiles who believe in Jesus the Messiah are incorporated into Israel, becoming full members of "the commonwealth of Israel." The worldwide church, as the body of Christ, therefore, is not something completely new that came into existence after Pentecost. It does not replace or supersede Israel, but is a *continuation* of Israel. If in Jesus ethnic Israel has broadened out to include gentiles, people of every nation and land, and if this is how the church is related to Israel, there is no justification for Christians to make a close connection between biblical Israel and the State of Israel today (Part 1, chapter 8).

- The idea of "the millennium" is based on one particular passage in the book of Revelation, a book that is full of symbols. If all the numbers and images in Revelation have to be interpreted, there is no reason to understand the period of a thousand years as a literal period of time. The picture of the millennium in Revelation 21 was particularly appropriate as an encouragement to Christians who were about to face persecution and even martyrdom, because it assured them that martyrs

---

1. Hays, "Response to Robert Wilken," 526.

were sharing in the victory that Christ had already won through his death. It is far more convincing, therefore, to see this picture of the millennium in Revelation as a way of describing a present reality than to see it as a literal period of a thousand years in which Jesus rules the world from Jerusalem (Part 1, chapter 9).

- There is nothing in the history of Zionism that is so exceptional that it cannot be understood or explained in the way that historians explain other historical movements. However surprising it may seem that a new, Jewish state was created in the middle of the twentieth century, there is no need to resort to explanations in terms of the miraculous. This doesn't mean that God has not been involved in the whole process. If we believe in the sovereignty of God in history, he must been involved in all that has happened and is happening, because he is always at work in human affairs—both in judgment and redemption. But if we can't see the whole history of Zionism as the fulfilment of biblical promises and prophecies, we need to find other ways of using the Bible to make judgment about these events (Part 1, chapter 10).

2. The message of Ezekiel about the restoration of Israel

Ezekiel the priest was called to be a prophet to his community of exiles in Babylon in the mid-sixth century BCE. As they mourned the loss of so much that was a vital part of their national life—the land, the temple, and the monarchy—he had to explain that God had sent them into exile because they had broken the covenant. He assured them, however, that God had not broken his side of the covenant, and that he would one day bring them back to the land, raise up a faithful shepherd-king, and restore a functioning temple. The best-known chapter in the book contains the vision of the valley of dry bones coming to life, which is interpreted as a picture of the nation coming back to life after it is restored to the land. This restoration would be accompanied by material prosperity and spiritual renewal, described, for example, in terms of cleansing from sin and the giving of a new heart.

In the five centuries after Ezekiel, however, there was little sign of the renewal of the spiritual life of the nation that he had predicted. What is so significant in the New Testament, therefore, is that writers use images from Ezekiel to describe what Jesus has achieved through his life, death, and resurrection. When Jesus claims to be "the good shepherd" (John 10:11), describes his body as the temple (John 2:13–22), and speaks of living water flowing from within him (John 7:38), he is claiming to be the fulfillment of the glorious future that Ezekiel had described. The final chapters of Ezekiel describe the glory of the Lord returning to a restored temple in Jerusalem, and the book ends with the sentence "And the name of the city from that time on will be: The LORD is there" (Ezek 48:35). If Matthew identifies Jesus with the word "Emmanuel," meaning "God is with us" (Matt 1:23), and if John says that "the Word became flesh and lived among us" (John 1:14), they must see Jesus as the fulfillment of Ezekiel's prophecy about God living among his people.

If New Testament writers, therefore, consistently speak of Jesus as the fulfillment of Ezekiel's prophecy, it is hard to see how the return of Jews to the land and the establishment of the State of Israel can be seen as a *further* fulfilment of the very same promises. It's perfectly understandable for Jews to see the creation of the Jewish state as the fulfilment of Ezekiel's vision of the valley of dry bones. But for Christians, if Jesus the Messiah really did represent Israel and if Ezekiel's vision of the valley of dry bones was fulfilled initially in the return to the land from exile and then in the resurrection of Jesus, it's hard to see how this prophecy could *also* be used to explain the significance of the recent return of Jews to the land.

3. The message of Zechariah about the restoration of Israel

While Ezekiel had exercised his prophetic ministry among the exiles in Babylon between 586 and 538 BCE, Zechariah began his ministry in Jerusalem in 520, just eighteen years after the return from exile. The people had already begun to rebuild the temple in response to the prophetic ministry of Haggai. Zechariah now encourages them to continue the work, assuring them that God is still "very jealous for Jerusalem" (Zech 1:14) and has "returned to Jerusalem with compassion" (Zech 1:16). Having a restored, functioning temple is extremely important because it symbolizes the way God wants to live among his people.

Zechariah also encourages his people by looking beyond their immediate situation to a more distant future, described as "that day." When this time comes, the sin of the whole land will be removed in a single day, Jerusalem will be a genuinely holy city, and foreign nations will benefit from all that God is doing. There are several pictures of a messianic figure who will be the special agent in the outworking of God's plan—"the Branch," the king entering Jerusalem on a colt, and the shepherd who ultimately suffers. In visions that are full of apocalyptic language about a battle in Jerusalem, disturbances in the natural world, water flowing from the temple, and gentiles coming to worship in Jerusalem, Zechariah is looking forward to the time when God will establish his kingly rule in the whole world: "And the LORD will become king over all the earth" (Zech 14:9).

According to all the Gospel writers, Jesus describes his mission in terms of the coming of the kingdom of God. Mark, for example, sums up the message of Jesus with the words: "The time is fulfilled, and the kingdom of God has come near; repent, and believe in the good news" (Mark 1:15). Jesus identifies himself with Zechariah's humble king who will bring peace to the nations, describes himself as the shepherd who suffers, and looks forward to gentiles coming from east and west to sit in the kingdom.

We have good reason, therefore, to question—if not completely reject—the view that Zechariah's prophecy must be read today as a literal description of the end times. Understanding his message in his own context, appreciating the difference between prophecy and apocalyptic, and reading it through the eyes of the New Testament points to a convincing alternative to literal interpretation. Although Zechariah didn't understand it at the time, what he was looking forward to was the incarnation and how that would lead eventually to the completion of God's purposes for the world. We need to take careful note of all Zechariah's prophecy that has *already* been fulfilled in the first coming of Christ before rushing on to construct scenarios of what will happen in the build-up to his second coming.

It's understandable that Martin Luther had problems with chapter 14 of Zechariah, admitting, "I am not sure what the Prophet is talking about." But if the kingdom of God really did begin to come in and through Jesus (Zech 14:9 and Mark 1:15), and if he spoke of "living waters" coming from himself, not from Jerusalem (Zech 14:8 and John 7:37–39), this difficult chapter can be seen not as a video of what will happen at the end of the world, but as hints about what was to come in the incarnation. In this case, the picture of the great victory over nations that gather against Jerusalem and are defeated by divine intervention (Zech 14:1–5) need not be seen as a picture of a literal battle that will take place in Jerusalem, but as a picture of the victory which Jesus was going to win over all the forces of evil through his death and resurrection in Jerusalem. This is the same conflict and the same victory that Peter describes when he says in a speech soon after Pentecost: "For in this city . . . both Herod and Pontius Pilate, with the gentiles and the people of Israel gathered together against your holy servant, Jesus, whom you anointed, to do whatever your hand and your plan had predestined to take place" (Acts 4:27).

Zechariah, therefore, played a significant role in this whole process by encouraging his fellow citizens to rebuild the temple. But he was using images and pictures that his contemporaries could visualize and imagine to describe something much more significant and wonderful than the rebuilding of the temple. The apostle Peter understood that Old Testament prophets believed they were writing about what would happen in the more distant future. They were trying to describe something that they couldn't fully understand or explain—the coming of the kingdom of God in the incarnation:

> Concerning this salvation, the prophets who prophesied of the grace that was to be yours made careful search and inquiry, inquiring about the person or time that the Spirit of Christ within them indicated when it testified in advance to the sufferings destined for Christ and the subsequent glory. It was revealed to them that they were serving not themselves but you, in regard to the things that have now been announced to you through those who brought you good news by the Holy Spirit sent from heaven—things into which angels long to look!
>
> (1 Peter 1:10–12)

When we read Ezekiel and Zechariah today, therefore, we should begin by putting ourselves into the shoes of those who first heard their prophecies. How would they have understood what these prophets were saying about God and his will for the world? What were they being challenged to do? We should then reflect on what they tell us about Jesus and his incarnation. If the risen Jesus interpreted to his disciples "the things about himself in all the scriptures" (Luke 24:27), he must have explained how Ezekiel and Zechariah pointed to him.

It had taken centuries of tumultuous history leading to the Babylonian exile for idolatry to be rooted out of Israel's system. They had eventually come to believe that "the LORD our God, the LORD is one" (Deut 6:10. NIV). But what kind of preparation was needed to enable them to believe that Almighty God, the creator of the universe, would one day come to live among them? How could they ever imagine that someone would be born who was fully human and fully divine and who would fulfil all the great covenant prophecies? The very idea might have seemed just as shocking to most Jews—and perhaps even as blasphemous—as it has seemed for centuries to Muslims, who are equally passionate about the oneness of God and cannot conceive of God taking on human flesh. What Ezekiel and Zechariah did was to work from everything that Israel knew—about the nation, the land, the temple, and monarchy—to point to a divine plan that was much bigger and more wonderful than what they already knew. "The fulfilment," says Philip Jenson, "goes well beyond the starting text in unexpected and surprising ways."[2]

2. Jenson, *The Servant Songs of Isaiah 40–55*, 21.

These prophets had far more to say about their immediate situation and about the coming of Jesus than about the end of the world. Those who challenge Christian Zionism find it hard to believe that Ezekiel and Zechariah could be looking forward to Jesus and the incarnation *and at the same time, in the very same words,* to the creation of a Jewish state in Palestine in the twentieth century.

4. Is Christian Zionism therefore the only way to understand what the Bible says about the restoration of Israel?

The two disciples on the road to Emmaus expressed their extreme disappointment that Jesus, by his death, had failed to achieve the redemption of Israel: "We had hoped that he was the one to redeem Israel" (Luke 24:21). They clearly assumed that the redemption of Israel—which must have meant the same thing as the restoration of Israel—was primarily about the Jewish people regaining sovereignty and independence in their own land. Jesus tried to explain in response that he *had* achieved the redemption of Israel—although not the kind of redemption that they had in mind. Jesus wanted them to understand that the redemption or restoration of Israel did not mean the expulsion of Roman rulers and the establishment of an independent Jewish state. It meant the fulfillment of the prophecies of Ezekiel, Zechariah, and the other prophets about the coming of the kingdom of God—a kingdom that would include people of all races (Luke 24:13–35).

We have seen in our study of Ezekiel and Zechariah that, in addition to the message of encouragement that they delivered to their contemporaries, they were looking forward to the time in the more distant future when the kingdom of God would come on the earth. We have also noted the many ways in which the writers of the New Testament expressed their conviction that the kingdom of God really had begun to come through the life, death and resurrection of Jesus. As they came to understand how the gospel was to be shared all over the world and how gentiles of all nations would be incorporated into Israel, they had to abandon their assumption that the coming of the kingdom of God would include—either in the own lifetime or in the end times—the establishment of a Jewish state in the Holy Land. They now believed that *the restoration of Israel had already been carried out through what Jesus had done.*

As they and succeeding generations of disciples spread this new understanding of the kingdom of God, what they had to look forward to was the second coming of Jesus. The clearest expression of this hope was given in the words of the two angels to the disciples at the time of Jesus' ascension:

"This Jesus, who has been taken up from you into heaven, will come in the same way as you saw him go into heaven" (Acts 1:11). Peter speaks about the return of Jesus, which will inaugurate "the time of universal restoration that God announced long ago through his holy prophets" (Acts 3:20–21). And the book of Revelation ends with the confident expectation of his second coming: "Come, Lord Jesus!" (Rev 22:20).

As the gospel spread among gentiles, Jews would continue to come to faith in their Messiah. And now that the dividing wall between Jews and gentiles had been broken down, Jews and gentiles in the body of Christ now formed "one new humanity" (Eph 2:15). If this is how New Testament writers understood the restoration of Israel, it's hard to see how Christians today can use this same terminology to speak about the Zionist movement and the creation of the State of Israel.

5. Does it really matter how we interpret prophecy about the restoration of Israel?

Is it a fruitless exercise to argue about these issues? Is it pure speculation about the future? Does it really matter one way or the other? Does it make any difference to the way we think about all that has been happening in Israel-Palestine and is happening today? Let's consider some reasons for suggesting that it really is important for Christians to wrestle with these questions.

a) It matters because it affects the way we relate the Old and New Testaments to each other

Should Christians read the Old Testament through the spectacles of the New Testament, or read the New Testament through the spectacles of the Old Testament? Christians Zionists insist that the coming of Jesus makes no substantial difference to the way we should interpret Old Testament teaching about the nation of Israel and the land. Their interpretation of the New Testament is therefore determined largely by the way they interpret the Old Testament. Those who challenge Christian Zionism insist that if the Old Testament really is looking forward to the coming of Jesus as the Word made flesh, he must be the lens through which Christians interpret the Old Testament. If we find that New Testament writers believed that the restoration of Israel really had begun to unfold through the life, death, and resurrection of Jesus, this should determine the way Christians read the Old Testament today.

If this is true, the most fundamental weakness of Christian Zionism is that, instead of reading the Old Testament through the spectacles of Jesus and the writers of the New Testament, it reads the New Testament through the spectacles of the Old Testament.

b) It matters because we're dealing with one of the most bitter and prolonged conflicts of the last 150 years

These issues are not purely theoretical, since there can't be another situation in the world where the way Christians interpret the Bible has such a direct effect on political choices that have far-reaching practical consequences. This is not an abstract theological controversy for detached observers. This is a conflict that has led, and continues to lead, to intense suffering for many millions. After enduring centuries of anti-semitism in Europe, Jewish settlers in Palestine from the 1880s could hardly avoid provoking resistance from the Palestinian Arabs living in the country. While Israeli Jews have suffered from Palestinian terrorism, Palestinians have experienced ethnic cleansing in the months before and after the creation of Israel, and have been living under Israeli occupation on the West Bank, in East Jerusalem, and Gaza since 1967. The Israeli-Palestinian conflict developed into the Israeli-Arab conflict, and in recent years has been caught up in the wider conflicts of the Middle East involving Iran. In spite of countless peace talks and frequent debates at the UN, there is no peaceful solution in sight, and at the present moment it looks as if Israel, as the most powerful party, with the support of the United States, is attempting to impose its own solution on the Palestinians. Christians should be longing to see a resolution to this conflict and an end to all the suffering.

c) It matters because Christian Zionism makes it harder for Christians to be peacemakers and at the same time to work for justice

Those who seek to live by the values of the kingdom of God are supposed to be peacemakers and to "hunger and thirst after righteousness" (Matt 5:9, 6). Most Christians probably think righteousness has to do with our relationship with God—having a right relationship with God, being right with God. But the Greek word *dikaiosyne* can also be translated "justice." Some English translations try to convey this broader meaning: "Blessed are those who hunger and thirst to see right prevail" (NEB); "Happy are those whose greatest desire is to do what God requires" (TEV).

In the context of Israel-Palestine, being a peacemaker means, at the very least, understanding the nature and history of the conflict, and being able to empathize with both sides in such a way as to bring them together. But this isn't easy for Christian Zionists who have such strong sympathy for Israel that they find it difficult to appreciate the experience of the Palestinians. They are often more concerned to see history unfolding in accordance with their understanding of the end times than with the personal well-being of all the people on both sides who are caught up in the conflict.

And what should it mean in this context to "hunger and thirst after righteousness/justice"? Several Messianic Jewish leaders—especially in Israel—have openly admitted that their communities often find it hard to address justice issues.[3] If Christian Zionists feel any tension between their understanding of the Bible and their understanding of justice and human rights issues, they generally believe that their theology must determine their approach to these questions. They are convinced that their interpretation of the Bible must trump purely human ideas of justice.[4]

When Christian Zionists believe that the Jewish people have a special right to the whole land, many of them see no problem in Israel's continuing occupation of the West Bank, East Jerusalem, and Gaza, in spite of the fact that most of the world believes that the occupation is a violation of international law. If there are as many as 50 million Christian Zionists of one kind or another in the US, they are bound to support government policies that are strongly pro-Israel, and they often provide moral and financial support for Jewish settlers on the West Bank. The combination of sympathizing for one side in the conflict and downplaying of the importance of justice issues inevitably makes it harder for Christians Zionists to be genuine peacemakers.

3. For example, Harvey, "Towards a Messianic Jewish Theology of Reconciliation in the Light of the Arab-Israeli Conflict.," 100.

4. Dan Juster, for example, writes: "Contrary to a humanistic understanding of justice, God has different destinies for different people. . . . Justice in regard to the land requires that there be submission to what God has declared about this land. . . . So if Palestinians do not acknowledge God's promises, they are foundationally unjust and are themselves resisted by God and lose their rights to this land." In "A Messianic Jew Looks at the Land Promises," 79.

d) It matters because Christian Zionism presents a major stumbling block for Muslims and for Arab Christians

When Muslims around the world learn about the situation of the Palestinians—most of whom are Muslims—they inevitably feel strong sympathy for them and share their sense of injustice over all that they have suffered. They too have a scriptural basis for their ideological attachment to the land. They therefore find it very difficult to understand why so many Christians support Israel without question and seem to have little concern for issues of justice. The Cambridge Muslim scholar Abdal-Hakim Murad sums up the perceptions of many Middle Eastern Muslims:

> The perception of the leading Western nation as profoundly driven by Christian dispensationalism has become widespread in the Middle East. The consequence has been far-reaching: whereas ten years ago Muslims tended to view America as a secular republic containing many religious Christians, the perception is now gaining ground that America is a specifically Christian entity, whose policies on Israel, and whose otherwise mystifying violence against Muslims, whether in occupied countries or in detention, can most helpfully be explained with reference to the Bible.[5]

Because of this perception some Muslims refuse to open their minds to the gospel.

Christian Zionism also often creates a real crisis of faith for Arab Christians living in the Middle East and the Muslim world.[6] They find it hard to understand how Christians and Messianic Jews all over the world make such an easy and simple connection between Israel in the Bible and the modern State of Israel. When they hear that the book of Joshua is studied in Israeli schools, they understand very well that Israeli children grow up identifying Palestinians with the Philistines and the Canaanites.[7] This therefore is the kind of message that they hear from many Christians: "You Palestinians simply have to accept what the Bible says about the chosen people and the promised land and recognize that the Jewish people have a special right to live in the land. It's bad luck for you if you're not willing to accept what God is doing in bringing the Jewish people back to the land in preparation for the second coming." It's hardly surprising, therefore, that many Christians in the Middle East find the Old Testament very difficult

5. Murad, "America as a Jihad State," quoted in Fink, "Fear Under Construction."

6. Deik, "Christian Zionism and Mission," 74–81.

7. See for example Peled-Elhanan, *Palestine in Israeli School Books*.

because of the way it is used by many Jews and Christians to justify Zionism and the policies of the State of Israel.

6. The teaching of Jesus about preparing for the end

Several times during this study we have looked at what Jesus says about the future. We have noted that in the version of his eschatological discourse recorded by Mark, the earliest of the four Gospels, most of the chapter (verses 1–31) deals with the period leading up to the destruction of Jerusalem. It is only the last verses (32–37) that speak about the end, which is referred to as "that day or hour." It must surely be significant that in this chapter the main thrust of what Jesus says is about the destruction of Jerusalem and the vindication of the Son of Man.

In the final verses (32–37), Jesus makes no attempt to describe a series of events leading up to the end. He has nothing to say about the people or the land of Israel. No less than three times he emphasizes that "about that day or hour no one knows." And to prepare his disciples in succeeding generations for the end at his second coming, his main concern is to encourage watchfulness:

> But about that day or hour no one knows, neither the angels in heaven, not the Son, but only the Father. Beware, keep alert; for you do not know when the time will come. It is like a man going on a journey, when he leaves home and puts his slaves in charge, each with his work, and commands the doorkeeper to be on the watch. Therefore, keep awake—for you do not know when the master of the house will come, in the evening, or at midnight, or at cockcrow, or at dawn, or else he may find you asleep when he comes suddenly. And what I say to you I say to all: Keep awake.
>
> (Mark 13:32–36; cf. Matt 24:36–51; Luke 21:34–36).

Bibliography

Ateek, Naim Stifan. *A Palestinian Christian Cry for Reconciliation*. New York: Orbis, 2009.

Bailey, Kenneth E. *Jesus Through Middle Eastern Eyes: Cultural Studies in the Gospels*. London: SPCK, 2008.

———. "St. Paul's Understanding of the Territorial Promise of God to Abraham: Romans 4:13 in Its Historical/Theological Context." *Near East School of Theology Review* (Beirut) 15.1 (1994) 59–69.

Baldwin, Joyce G. *Haggai, Zechariah and Malachi: An Introduction and Commentary*. Leicester, UK: IVP, 1972.

Bauckham, Richard. *The Climax of Prophecy: Studies in the Book of Revelation*. London: T. & T. Clark, 1998.

Benne, Robert. "Theology and Politics: Reinhold Niebuhr's Christian Zionism." In *The New Christian Zionism*, edited by Gerald McDermott, 221–48. Downers Grove, IL: IVP Academic, 2016.

Blaising, Craig. "Biblical Hermeneutics: How Are We to Interpret the Relation between the Tanak and the New Testament on This Question?" In *The New Christian Zionism*, edited by Gerald McDermott, 79–105. Downers Grove, IL: IVP Academic, 2016.

Bock, Darrell. "How Should the New Christian Zionism Proceed?" In *The New Christian Zionism*, edited by Gerald McDermott, 305–18. Downers Grove, IL: IVP Academic 2016.

Brickner, David. "Don't Pass Over Israel's Jubilee." Jews for Jesus Newsletter, April 1998.

Brown, Wesley H., and Penner, Peter F., eds. *Christian Perspectives on the Israeli-Palestinian Conflict*. Pasadena, CA: William Carey International University Press and Neufeld Verlag, 2008.

Brueggemann, W. *The Land: Place as Gift, Promise and Challenge in Biblical Faith*. Minneapolis: Fortress, 2002.

Bruno, Christopher R. "The Deliverer from Zion: The Source(s) and Function of Paul's Citation in Romans 11:26–27." *Tyndale Bulletin* 59.1 (2008) 119–34.

Burge, Gary. *Jesus and the Land: The New Testament Challenge to "Holy Land" Theology*. Grand Rapids: Baker Academic, 2010.

Caird, G.B. *The Revelation of St John the Divine*. London: Adam and Charles Black, 1966.

Calvin, John. *Commentary on the Acts of the Apostles*. Translated by W. J. D. MacDonald. Grand Rapids: Eerdmans, 1989.

Carson, D.A. *The Expositor's Bible Commentary Matthew 13–28*. Grand Rapids: Zondervan, 1995.

Chapman, Colin. *Whose Promised Land?* Rev. ed. Oxford: Lion Hudson, 2015. (First published in 1983.)

Clouse, Robert G. *The Meaning of the Millennium: Four Views*. Downers Grove, IL: IVP, 1997.

Crombie, Kelvin. "CMJ and the Restoration of Israel." *Shalom* 1 (1998).

Crump, David. *Knocking on Heaven's Door: A New Testament Theology of Petitionary Prayer*. Grand Rapids: Baker Academic, 2006.

Davies, W.D. *The Gospel and the Land: Early Christianity and Jewish Territorial Doctrine*. Berkeley: University of California Press, 1974.

Deik, Anton. "Christian Zionism and Mission: How Does Our Understanding of Christianity Impact Our Witness in the World?" In *The Religious Other: A Biblical Understanding of Islam, the Qur'an and Muhammad*, edited by Martin Accad and Jonathan Andrews, 74–81. London: Langham, 2020.

Feinberg, Charles L. *God Remembers: A Study of Zechariah*. Eugene, OR: Wipf & Stock, 2003.

Feinberg, Joseph S. "Dispensationalism and Support for the State of Israel." In *The Land Cries Out*, edited by Salim J. Munayer and Lisa Loden, 104–31. Eugene, OR: Cascade, 2012.

Fink, Steven. "Fear Under Construction: Islamophobia within American Christian Zionism." *Islamophobia Studies Journal* 2.1 (2014) 26–43.

France, R.T. "Old Testament Prophecy and the Future of Israel: A Study in the Teaching of Jesus." *Tyndale Bulletin* 26 (1975) 53–78.

———. *Jesus and the Old Testament: His Application of Old Testament Passages to Himself and His Mission*. London: Tyndale, 1971.

Glashouwer, Willem J. J. *Why Israel? Understanding Israel, the Church, and the Nations in the Last Days*. Pescara, Italy: Destiny Image Europe, 2007.

Glatzer, Nahum N. *Franz Rosenzweig: His Life and Thought*. New York: Schocken, 1971.

Goldingay, John. "The Jews, the Land, and the Kingdom." *Anvil* 4.1 (1987) 9–22.

Hagee, John. *The Beginning of the End*. Nashville: Thomas Nelson, 1996.

———. *Jerusalem Countdown*. Lake Mary, FL: Frontline, 2006.

Harvey, Richard. "Towards a Messianic Jewish Theology of Reconciliation in the Light of the Arab-Israeli Conflict: Neither Dispensationalist Nor Supersessionist?" In *The Land Cries Out*, edited by Salim J. Munayer and Lisa Loden, 82–103. Eugene, OR: Cascade, 2012.

Hays, Richard. "Response to Robert Wilken." In *In Dominico Eloquio, Communio* 25 (1998) 520–28.

Hill, Andrew E. *Haggai, Zechariah and Malachi*. Tyndale Old Testament Commentaries. Nottingham, UK: IVP, 2012.

Hoekema, Anthony A. "Amillennialism." In *The Meaning of the Millennium: Four Views*, edited by Robert G. Clouse, 155–208. Downers Grove, IL: IVP, 1997.

———. *The Bible and the Future*. Grand Rapids: Eerdmans, 1979.

Hornstra, Wilrens L. "Western Restorationism and Christian Zionism: Germany as a Case Study." In *Christian Perspectives on the Israeli-Palestinian Conflict*, edited by Wesley Brown and Peter Penner, 131–48. Pasadena, CA: William Carey International University Press and Neufeld Verlag, 2008.

Isaac, Munther. *From Land to Lands, from Eden to the Renewed Earth: A Christ-Centred Biblical Theology of the Promised Land*. Carlisle, UK: Langham Monographs, 2015.

Jenson, Philip. *The Servant Songs of Isaiah 40–55: Interpreting Old Testament Prophecy*. Cambridge: Grove, 2020.

Juster, Daniel C. "A Messianic Jew Looks at the Land Promises." In *The Land Cries Out*, edited by Salim J. Munayer and Lisa Loden, 63–81. Eugene, OR: Cascade, 2012.

———. *Passion for Israel: A Short History of the Evangelical Church's Commitment to the Jewish People and Israel*. Clarksville, MD: Lederer, 2012.

Kinzer, Mark S. *Jerusalem Crucified, Jerusalem Risen: The Resurrected Messiah, the Jewish People, and the Land of Promise*. Eugene, OR: Cascade, 2018.

———. "Zionism in Luke-Acts: Do the People of Israel and the Land of Israel Persist as Abiding Concerns in Luke's Two Volumes?" In *The New Christian Zionism*, edited by Gerald McDermott, 141–65. Downers Grove, IL: 2016.

Koestler, Arthur. *Promise and Fulfilment*. London: Macmillan, 1949.

Leibowitz, Yeshayahu. *Judaism, Human Values, and the Jewish State*. Harvard: Harvard University Press, 1992.

Lewis, Donald M. *A Short History of Christian Zionism: From the Reformation to Today*. Downers Grove, IL: IVP Academic, to be published 2021.

Lightfoot, J. B. *St Paul's Epistle to the Galatians: A Revised Text with Introduction, Notes, and Dissertation*. 8th ed. London: Macmillan, 1884.

Lindsey, Hal. *The Final Battle*. Palos Verdes, CA: Western Front, 1995.

———. *Planet Earth 2000AD: Will Mankind Survive?* Palos Verdes, CA: Western Front, 1994.

Loden, Lisa. "Messianic Jewish Views on Israel's Rebirth and Survival in the Light of Scripture." In *Christian Perspectives on the Israeli-Palestinian Conflict*, edited by Wesley Brown and Peter Penner, 43–55. Pasadena, CA: William Carey International University Press and Neufeld Verlag, 2008.

———. "Where Do We Begin? The Hermeneutical Questions and Their Effect on the Theology of the Land." In *The Land Cries Out*, edited by Salim J. Munayer and Lisa Loden, 40–59. Eugene, OR: Cascade, 2012.

Marcus, Amy Dockser. *Jerusalem 1913: The Origins of the Arab-Israeli Conflict*. New York: Penguin, 2007.

Martin, Frederic M. *American Evangelicals and Modern Israel: A Plea for Tough Love*. Sisters, OR: Deep River, 2016.

McDermott, Gerald R., ed. *The New Christian Zionism: Fresh Perspectives on Israel and the Land*. Downers Grove, IL: IVP Academic, 2016.

Moberly, R. W. L. "Christ in All the Scriptures? The Challenge of Reading the Old Testament as Christian Scripture." *Journal of Theological Interpretation* 1.1 (2007) 79–100.

Munayer, Salim J., and Lisa Loden, eds. *The Land Cries Out: Theology of the Land in the Israeli-Palestinian Context*. Eugene, OR: Cascade, 2012.

———. *Through My Enemy's Eyes: Envisioning Reconciliation in Israel-Palestine*. Milton Keynes, UK: Paternoster, 2013.

Murad, Abdal-Hakim. "America as a Jihad State: Middle Eastern Perceptions of Modern American Theopolitics." Faith and Public Policy Seminar, Kings College, London, 2009.

Nolland, John. *Luke 18:35—24:53*. Word Biblical Commentary. Dallas, TX: Word, 1993.

Ollenburger, Ben C. "The Book of Malachi." In *The New Interpreter's Bible*, Vol VII. Nashville: Abingdon, 2016.

Paas, Steven, ed. *Israelism and the Place of Christ: Christocentric Interpretation of Biblical prophecy*. Zurich: LIT Verlag, 2018.

Pappé, Ilan. *The Ethnic Cleansing of Palestine*. Oxford: One World, 2006.

Pawson, David. *Defending Christian Zionism*. Ashford, UK: Anchor Recordings, 2013.

Peled-Elhanan, Nurit. *Palestine in Israeli School Books: Ideology and Propaganda in Education*. London: I. B. Tauris, 2012.

Prince, Derek. *The Last Word on the Middle East*. Fort Lauderdale, FL: Derek Prince Ministries International, 1982.

Robertson, Owen Palmer. "The Israel of God in Romans 11." In *Israelism and the Place of Christ: Christocentric Interpretation of Biblical Prophecy*, edited by Steven Paas, 212–32. Zurich: LIT Verlag, 2018.

———. "A New Covenant Perspective on the Land." In *The Land of Promise: Biblical, Theological and Contemporary Perspectives*, edited by Philip Johnston and Peter Walker, 121–41. Leicester: IVP, 2000.

Scofield, C. I. *Scofield Bible Correspondence Course*. Chicago: Moody Bible Institute, n.d.

Sizer, Stephen. "Dispensational Approaches to the Land." In *The Land of Promise: Biblical, Theological and Contemporary Perspectives*, edited by Philip Johnston and Peter Walker, 142–71. Leicester: IVP, 2000.

———. *Zion's Christian Soldiers? The Bible, Israel and the Church*. Nottingham: IVP, 2007.

Stern, David. "The People of God, the Promises of God, and the Land of Israel." Paper presented in conference on Theology of the Land, Droushia, Cyprus, 1996.

Strengholt, Jos M., "Zechariah 14: 'Why not take it literally?' in *Israelism and the Place of Christ*, edited by Steven Paas. 246-261. Zurich: LIT Verlag, 2018.

Tooley, Mark. "Theology and the Churches." In *The New Christian Zionism: Fresh Perspectives on Israel and the Land*, edited by Gerald McDermott, 197–219. Downers Grove, IL: IVP Academic, 2016.

Vlach, Michael J. *Has the Church Replaced Israel? A Theological Evaluation*. Nashville: B&H Publishing Group, 2010.

Walker, Peter. *Jesus and the Holy City: New Testament Perspectives on Jerusalem*. Grand Rapids: Eerdmans, 1996.

———. "The Land in the New Testament: The Land in the Apostles' Writings." In *The Land of Promise: Biblical, Theological and Contemporary Perspectives*, edited by Philip Johnston and Peter Walker, 81–99. Leicester: IVP, 2000.

Webb, Barry. *The Message of Zechariah*. Nottingham: IVP, 2003.

Williams, Rowan. *Luminaries: Twenty Lives That Illuminate the Christian Way*. London: SPCK, 2019.

Willits, Joel. "Zionism in the Gospel of Matthew: Do the People of Israel and the Land of Israel Persist as Abiding Concerns for Matthew?" In *The New Christian Zionism: Fresh Perspectives on Israel and the Land*, edited by Gerald McDermott, 107–40. Downers Grove, IL: IVP Academic, 2016.

Wright, Christopher J. H. *How to Preach and Teach the Old Testament for All Its Worth*. Grand Rapids: Zondervan, 2016.

———. *The Message of Ezekiel*. Nottingham: IVP, 2011.

Wright, N.T. *The Climax of the Covenant: Christ and the Law in Pauline Theology.* London: T. & T. Clark, 1991.

———. "Jerusalem in the New Testament." In *Jerusalem Past and Present in the Purposes of God*, edited by Peter Walker, 53–77. Cambridge: Tyndale, 1992.

———. *Jesus and the Victory of God.* London: SPCK, 1996.

———. *The New Testament and the People of God.* London: SPCK, 1992.

Author Index

Ateek, Naim Stefan, 20

Bailey, Kenneth E., 56, 70
Baldwin, Joyce G., 4,142, 171
Bauckham, Richard, 172
Benne, Robert, 96
Blaising, Craig, 38, 54–55, 74, 76,
    94–95
Bock, Darell, 21, 51, 95–96, 102
Brickner, David, 94
Brown, Wesley H., 5
Brueggeman, W., 67
Bruno, Christopher R., 27–28
Burge, Gary, 63–64, 68, 74, 85, 118

Caird, G.B., 172–73, 175, 177–80
Calvin, John, 39
Carson, D.A., 153
Chapman, Colin, 112–13
Crombie, Kelvin, 103
Crump, David, 111

Davies, W.D., 43, 67–69, 113
Deik, Anton, 195

Feinberg, Charles L., 54, 133
Feinberg, Joseph, S., 78
Fink, Steven, 195
France, R.T., 58, 141, 145–46, 149,
    154–55, 162, 164–65, 167, 169,
    176
Friedman, David, 103

Glashouwer, Willem J.J., 117, 131, 133
Glatzer, Nahum N., 79–80

Goldingay, John, 53

Hagee, John, 2, 131–33
Harvey, Richard, 42–43, 194
Hays, Richard, 52, 186
Hill, Andrew, 134, 142–48, 156
Hoekema, Anthony A., 62, 92–93
Hornstra, Wilrens L., 1

Isaac, Munther, 75, 86–87

Jenson, Philip, 190
Juster, Daniel C., 51, 65–66, 103, 115,
    122, 131–32, 194

Kinzer, Mark S., 35, 38–39, 71–72, 96,
    100
Koestler, Arthur, 100

Leibowitz, Yeshayahu, 97
Lambert, Lance, 132
Lewis, Donald M., 1
Lightfoot, J.B., 64
Lindsey, Hal, 130–32
Loden, Lisa, 5, 21, 42, 66, 78

Marcus, Amy Docker, 100
Martin, Frederic M., 50
McDermott, Gerald R., 3, 5, 22, 37, 54,
    57, 60, 75, 90, 94–96, 101–2, 117
Munayer, Salim J., 5, 21
Murad, Abdal-Hakim, 195

Nolland, John, 32

Ollenburger, Ben C., 143–144

Parsons, David, 127
Pappé, Ilan, 100
Pawson, David, 3, 5, 53, 73, 79, 97
Peled-Elhanan, 195
Penner, Peter, 5
Prince, Derek, 53
Robertsn, Owen Palmer, 25–26, 70

Scofield, C.I., 42
Sizer, Stephen, 2, 79
Stern, David, 76
Strengholt, Jos M., 4

Tooley, Mark, 99

Vlach, Michael J., 5, 46, 48, 62, 64,
    77–78, 87, 96–97, 104, 120

Walker, Peter, 34, 39, 59
Webb, Barry, 137, 142, 144, 152–54,
    157, 159, 162, 165–66
Williams Rowan, 41
Willits, Joel, 34, 54, 56–57, 67
Wright, Christopher J.H., 105, 111,
    148–49
Wright, N.T., 24, 28, 58–59, 71, 83–84,
    86–87, 112, 118

Subject Index

Abraham, 7–8, 19, 23–24, 45, 49, 51,
    54–55, 57–58, 62–70, 73–76, 78,
    80, 83, 87, 184
America, see USA
amillennialism, 91
apartheid, 17, 101
anti-semitism, 12, 17–18, 97
apocalyptic, 91, 128–29, 134, 143, 147,
    166, 170, 172–73, 182
Arabs, 10–17, 21, 95–96, 99–101, 120,
    193, 195
Armageddon, 3, 166, 173

Babylon, Babylonians, 4, 19, 34–36,
    46, 48, 59, 82, 85, 102, 104, 106,
    112, 120–22, 136, 157, 168, 173,
    178–79, 187–88, 190
Balfour Declaration, 11, 98, 100, 104

Christ, see Jesus
Christian Zionism, Zionist, 1–5, 7–8,
    19, 21, 24, 30, 37, 48–49, 51, 60,
    65–66, 68, 87, 97–99, 104, 115,
    122, 129, 163, 177, 184, 191–95
church, 4–5, 8, 19, 24, 48, 54, 64–66,
    74–88, 109–10, 124, 186
covenant, 23, 27, 63, 66, 78–79, 107,
    114, 122, 152, 187
covenant theology, 19–20, 24

Darby, John Nelson, 1, 18
David, king, 10, 39, 43–50, 59, 80,
    106, 109, 119, 122, 142, 145–48,
    153–54, 160, 164–65, 175, 182,
    185

dispensationalism, 1–3, 18, 20, 79–80,
    130, 195

Egypt, Egyptians, 13, 27, 45, 80–83, 85
ethnic cleansing, 12–13, 100
Europe, 1, 10, 12, 17, 97
exile, Babylonian, 34–35, 43, 48, 59–60,
    102, 104–5, 112, 116, 120–21, 136,
    173, 187–88

filfillment, 1–5, 7, 18–20, 27, 30–31,
    41–48, 50–59, 61, 68, 70, 76, 96,
    102, 104, 108–24, 135, 141, 145,
    148–52, 157–59, 161–62, 165, 167,
    181, 185–91

Gaza, 13–14, 17, 101, 140, 193–94
gentiles, 7, 19, 24–29, 30–33, 46, 48,
    55, 58, 61–66, 70, 75, 77, 79–81,
    84–86, 109–10, 185–86, 191–92
Great Britain, 2, 11, 98
Greece, Greeks, 71, 173

Hamas, 15, 17
Herzl, Theodor, 1, 14, 98
Hizbullah, 15
Holocaust, 16, 98, 104

incarnation, 127–183, 189–91
Iran, 15–17, 98, 132, 193
Iraq, 13, 17
Islam, Muslims, 15, 17, 132, 190, 195
Israel in the Old Testament, 3, 4, 8,
    22, 32, 45, 47, 53–66, 72, 80–83,
    107–19, 132, 136–83

Israel in the New Testament, 3–4, 7–8, 19, 22–29, 31, 37–41, 43, 52, 55, 57, 58–59, 62–65, 72, 74–88, 96, 124, 157, 184–87
Israel, State of, 1–4, 7–8, 10–16, 18–19, 48, 59–60, 94–104, 121, 124, 132, 183–84, 186, 188, 191–92, 195–96
Israeli-Palestinian conflict, 7, 9, 15, 96–97, 184, 193–97

Jerome, 4
Jerusalem, 2, 4, 7–8, 10–11, 14–15, 18–19, 22, 27, 30–36, 37–41, 43–46, 48–50, 57–58, 60, 70–71, 73–75, 81–82, 90, 101, 104–6, 111, 114, 116–17, 119, 124, 127–31, 133, 136–47, 150–51, 154–57, 161–64, 166, 168–69, 174–85, 187–89, 193–94, 196
Jesus Christ, 2–5, 8, 19, 22, 27, 30–41, 43–45, 48, 50–52, 55, 58, 63, 66–68, 70, 73, 76–77, 79–80, 83–85, 89–93, 104, 108, 112–18, 124, 129, 135, 147–49, 152–58, 160–62, 164–67, 171–72, 176, 179–83, 188–92, 196
Jews, 1, 2, 3, 8–19, 21–29, 51, 55, 57, 59, 61, 63–70, 75, 77–79, 83–87, 95, 97–98, 115, 120, 122, 131, 135, 140, 155, 169, 185–88, 190, 192–94, 196
Jordan, 14, 17
justice, 20, 43, 96, 193

kingdom of God, 19, 29, 37- 41, 55–56, 65, 68–69, 74, 83, 111, 113, 121, 137, 142, 147, 154, 157–58, 164, 166, 172, 181–82, 185, 189–91, 193

land, 1, 3–5, 7–8, 10, 12, 18, 19, 26, 35, 39, 42–43, 47, 49, 53–66, 67–76, 78, 81, 90, 96–97, 101, 105–6, 112–14, 116, 120, 122, 124, 131–32, 137–39, 152, 160, 184–88, 190–192, 195–96

Luther, Martin, 4, 189

Messiah, 4, 8. 18, 22–29, 34, 39–41, 51, 59, 61, 64–66, 74–77, 80, 84–87, 90, 107, 110, 115, 122, 127, 129, 135, 146, 164–65, 168–69, 175, 179, 181, 183, 185–86, 188, 192
Messianic Jews, 21–22, 42, 62, 66, 78, 87, 195
millennium, 2, 4, 8, 18, 30, 44, 89–93, 186
Moses, 40, 45–47, 60, 79, 85, 121, 148, 152, 167

New Testament, 1, 7–8, 18–19, 42–53, 55, 65, 67–76, 78, 80, 86, 92, 96, 104, 108–19, 128–83, 185–86, 188, 191–93

Old Testament. 1, 3–4, 7–8, 18–20, 26, 32, 42–52, 53, 61, 65–76, 78, 80, 83, 85–86, 89, 96, 102, 104, 107–19, 128–83, 185, 190–93, 195

Palestine, Palestinian, 2–3, 9–17, 20, 67, 95–97, 99–100, 103, 121, 131, 133, 173, 191, 193, 195
postmillennialism, 90–91
premillennialism, 2, 91
prophets, 1, 18–19, 40–41, 61, 80, 128, 134, 157–58, 167, 190–91
prophecy, 1, 3–5, 13–14, 18–20, 27, 32, 48, 52, 58–59, 102, 104, 124, 133, 135, 149, 152, 161, 172–76, 181–82, 187
Protestant, 1, 99
Puritans, 18

rapture, 3
reconciliation, 5, 20–21
replacement theology, 19, 66, 77, 87, 110
restorationism, 1–3, 18, 20
redemption of Israel, 31–32, 43, 96, 187, 191–192
restoration of Israel, 1–2, 4, 34, 46–48, 103–25, 184, 191–96

Rome, Romans, 10, 33, 38, 54, 58–59,
    68, 71, 168, 171–74, 178–79, 191

Son of Man, 31, 36, 45, 58, 83, 113, 153,
    155, 168–69, 175–76, 185, 196
Six Day War (1967), 1, 10, 30, 185
supersessionism, 19–20, 77, 110

temple, 3, 34, 43, 50, 56, 66, 75, 81,
    116–19, 124, 128, 133, 135–36,
    144–48, 151–52, 158–59, 161–63,
    168, 177, 182, 187–88, 190
tribulation, the great, 3
typology, 148–49

United Nations, UN, 10, 12, 14–15, 17,
    101, 193
USA, 2, 10, 17, 91, 98–99, 101, 104,
    132, 193–95

West Bank, 10, 14, 17, 101, 193–94
World War I, 11, 16, 79, 91
World War II, 2, 98

Zion, 21, 26–27, 32, 43, 74, 82, 99, 114,
    168, 134, 138–40, 150–51, 158,
    156, 165, 177
Zionism, 1–14, 16, 96–100, 104, 121,
    184, 187, 192, 196

Scripture Index

Genesis

2;7	60
12–23	8, 63, 69
17:4–8	7, 49, 54, 63, 69
23:	73
41:45	80

Exodus

2:15–22	80
12:14–17	49
12:46	154
19:6	61
25:8	118, 158
28:36	162
29:45–46	118, 158
31:17	49
40:34–35	118

Leviticus

16:29	49
23:41	49
25:8	158
29:7–9	49
29:45–46	158

Numbers

5:3	158

Deuteronomy

4:26–27	121
6:10	190
18	51
18:15–20	45, 60
30:1–10	121

Joshua

1:11	70
6:25	80
7	71
11:23	71
14:15	71
21:44	71
23:1–19	71, 113

Ruth

4:18–22	80

2 Samuel

7:12–16	44, 49, 109

1 Kings

6:13	118
8:11–12	118
8:27–30	158

1 Kings (continued)

9:2–3	158
9:5	49

2 Kings

21:7	50

1 Chronicles

28:7	49

2 Chronicles

13:5	49
33:4	50
36:22–23	106

Ezra

1:1–3	106
2:1	106, 120
3:8	136
5:16	136
6:13–22	136

Nehemiah

1:3	106
1:4–11	121

Psalms

2:7–9	150, 164
10:16	49
23:1	61
37:3–34	68
37:11	68, 113
45:6	49
48:8	50
72:8	146, 150
68:16	50
72:8	146, 150
72:54–55	72
78:52–55	72
80:8–19	83
87:1–7	82–83
89:4	49
95:7	159
95:11	72
102:12	49
105:7–11	54, 67
106:1	49
107:1	49
118:1	49
132:13–14	50, 133
136:1	49
146:10	49

Isaiah

2:1–4	26–27
4:2	145
5:1–7	56
7:14	117
9:6–7	146
10:12–14	32
11:1	145–146
13:9–15	31, 45
13:10	168
19:1–25	80–81
27	27
27:6	27
27:9	26
27:12–13	27
33	32
35:1–10	112, 134
40:1–2	157
42 – 53	45
47	32
49:6	47
52:1–9	32, 157
53	165
53:10	165
56:6–8	81
59:20–21	26–27
61:1–2	112

Jeremiah

16:15–16	113
17:25	50
23:5–6	145, 182
31:31–34	25,115–116
31:35–36	54
33:15–16	145–146
50:51	32

Ezekiel

10:1–22	34, 116
33 – 48	4, 105, 108, 112
33:21–33	105
34:1–10	109, 159
34:11–31	61, 109, 122, 134, 146, 159
36	103
36:22–25	110–112, 114
36:26–34	112, 114, 122
36:36	110
36:37	109
37	103, 131
37:1–14	60, 104, 112, 122
37:11–13	59, 110, 112
37:21–25	109, 112, 122, 146
37:26–28	109–110, 115–116
38 – 39	32, 110, 134
38:16–23	111
39:7, 21–29	111,122
40:1–47:12	116–117
43:1–9	50, 116, 124
47:13–48;29	112
47:1–12	116, 161
47:21–23	81
48:35	117, 124, 158, 188

Daniel

7	165, 169, 176, 185
7;3	134
7:13–27	36, 45, 168–169, 175–176
9:1–19	121
9:26–27	32
12:7	179

Hosea

1:10	63
2:23	63
6:1–2	58
11:1	45

Joel

2:30–31	46
3:18–20	118, 161

Amos

8:2	179
9:11–15	47–48, 102

Habakkuk

1:11–2:3	32

Haggai

1:12–15	136

Zechariah

1 – 8	136, 174
1:1–6	121, 137, 144
1:7 – 6:15	137, 175
1:7–17	137–139, 174–175, 188
1:15–21	33, 137–140, 156, 188
2:1–13	82, 133, 137–138, 144, 175
3:1–10	137–139, 145, 151, 160, 162–163, 174, 183
3:20–21	162
4:1–14	137–138, 174
5:1–11	137
6:1–8	137–138, 174
6:12–15	82. 139, 145, 151, 183
7:8–14	139, 174
8:1–3	140, 158
8:20–23	82, 140, 144
9 – 14	136, 140, 146, 165

Zechariah (continued)

9:8–10	82, 141, 146, 150, 152, 183
9:14–16	141, 159, 163, 174
12 – 14	130, 142, 166
12:1–11	133, 142, 163–164, 169
12:10–14	45, 132, 135, 146, 153–154, 160, 163, 169, 175–176
13:1	160, 163
13:7–9	45, 83, 131, 135, 146, 156
14	4, 127–128, 133, 143, 157, 162, 166, 169, 176
14:1–5	133, 163–164
14:6–9	118, 131, 157, 161, 163–164, 175, 189
14:10	133
14:11–12	162, 175
14:16–21	82, 127, 137. 144, 161–162

Matthew

1:2–5	80
1:23	117, 188
2:1–12	55
2:15	45
3:9–10	55
5:5	68, 113
5:6–9	193
6:9–10	110–111, 158
8:11–12	55, 57, 83
15:24	55
18:20	158
19:28	57, 83
19:29	69
21:4–5	150
21:33–46	55–56
23:37–39	34
24:1–44	168
24:26–51	182, 196
24:29–30	45, 135, 153, 155, 175–176, 182
24:36–51	196
25:34	69
26:31	45, 83, 156
27:3–10	151–152
28:19	55, 110–111
28:20	117, 158

Mark

1:11	164
1:15	111, 157, 189
1:17	113
8:31	58
9:1	157–158
9:7	164
10:45	45
11:1–6	150
13:1–37	33, 45, 112–123, 168, 179, 182, 196
14:42	158

Luke

1:30–33	44, 57, 109
1:67–79	57
1:68	32
2:18	43
2:25	31, 43, 107, 156
2:36–38	31, 107, 156
3:7–9	55
4:18–19	112
7:18	107
7:22	112
13:31–35	33–35
11:20	157
18:31–33	58
19:28–34	150
19:41–44	35, 185
20:9–18	56
20:30	57, 83
21:5–38	31–32, 35, 168–169
21:24	3, 7, 30, 33
21:25–26	36, 182
21:27	36
21:28	31, 32
21:32	33
21:34–36	169, 196
22:20	115
24:13–35	40, 107, 191
24:21	31, 43, 191
24:25–27	40, 45, 148, 167, 190
24:44	45, 148

John

1:14	75, 116–117, 124, 158, 188
2:13–32	75, 116, 118, 158, 187
4:21–23	75
7:37–39	46, 118, 161, 187, 189
10:11–16	61, 109, 159, 187
11:49–52	61
12:14–16	150–151
12:28	110–111
15:1–11	83
17:1–21	84, 110–111
19:33–37	45, 135, 153, 175
20:22	59, 114

Acts

1:1–8	3, 7, 26, 37–40, 70, 72, 111, 183
1:9–12	72, 163, 192
2:19–20	46
2:30–31	39
2:36	37
2:47	71
3:20–21	192
3:22–24	60
4:27	45, 189
5:1–11	71
6:7	71
9:31	71
12:24	71
13:49	71
15:1–21	46–47
19:20	71
20:32	71, 113
23:6	43
24:15	43
24:44	148
26:6	43
28:20	43
28:17–30	59

Romans

2:25	23
2:28–29	23

8:4	114–115
9 – 11	22, 28–29, 66, 77, 84, 185
9:4–6	23
9:6–7	23
9:14	28
9:25–27	63
9:27	23
9:31	23
10:1–21	23
11:1–25	23–26
11:25–27	3, 7, 22–27, 64, 85
11:28–29	23
11:30–32	28

1 Corinthians

3:16–17	75, 116, 118
6:9–10	69
10:18	64
15:50	69

2 Corinthians

1:19:	70
5:19	124

Galatians

3:26–29	19, 62, 70
4:24–29	63, 110
5:21	69
6:16	64

Ephesians

1:11–14	70
2:11–22	62, 75, 84, 87, 109, 192
3:6	110

Philippians

2:9–11	35
3:3	85
3:26–29	19, 62, 70

Philippians *(continued)*

4:24–26	63
5:21	69

Hebrews

1:3	160
4:1–13	19, 72, 112–113
9:26–28	160
10:12	117
10:20	114
11:1	73
11:8–40	73
11:16	74
12:14	161
12:18–24	19, 74, 114–115

James

1:1	85

1 Peter

1:1	85
1:3–5	19, 72, 112–113
1:10–12	190
1:16–17	161
2:9–10	19, 61, 85, 87

1 John

1:7	114, 160

Revelation

1:1	178
1:7	135, 175
1:12	174–176
3:12	180
5:6	174
6:2–5	174
6:10	174
7:4–8	65
7:9–17	65, 86, 174, 178
8:2	175
11:2	177, 180
11:13	133
11:15	181
12:10–11	174, 181
13 – 19	178
14:1	177
16:12	19, 160, 173
17:3	174
20:1–16	89, 93, 125, 173, 178
20:7–11	166, 178
21:1–12	86, 116, 119, 125, 178–180
21:23–25	175
22:1–10	175, 178
22:20	180, 192

9 781725 297333